Heartland Utopias

Heartland Utopias

ROBERT P. SUTTON

NORTHERN

ILLINOIS .

UNIVERSITY

PRESS

DeKalb

Library of Congress Cataloging-in-Publication Data

Sutton, Robert P.

Heartland utopias / Robert P. Sutton.

  p.   cm.

Includes bibliographical references and index.

ISBN 978-0-87580-401-9 (clothbound : alk. paper)

1. Utopias—Middle West—History—19th century. 2. Communal living—Middle West—History—19th century. 3. Collective settlements—Middle West—History—19th century. 4. Frontier and pioneer life—Middle West. 5. Middle West—History—19th century. I. Title.

HX655.M53S87 2009

307.770977—dc22

2009009087

Contents

Heartland Utopias

Introduction

The history of the Heartland during the nineteenth and early twentieth centuries is unrivaled for the number and importance of utopian communities found here. Initially, the term "Heartland" meant the Old Northwest Territories: Ohio, Indiana, Illinois, Michigan, and Wisconsin. Except for southern counties of Indiana and Illinois, which were settled by squatter farmers from Kentucky and Tennessee in the early nineteenth century, the Heartland was developed by pioneers from the Mid-Atlantic states and New England, all of whom were incorrectly dubbed "Yankees." By the Civil War, the area conformed well to the definition of "heartland" found in the *American Heritage Historical Dictionary*: "A central region, especially one that is politically, economically, or militarily vital to a nation." The U.S. Heartland gave us the Republican Party and Abraham Lincoln. After the Civil War some residents of the Old Northwest continued their westward migration to Iowa and Minnesota, eventually moving along the upper Missouri River valley to the Dakotas. They were joined by immigrants from Sweden, Norway, and the Ukraine. But for the purposes of this book, the Heartland is most significant also because this is where communal utopianism has thrived.

During the heyday of Heartland communities, all utopias embraced the notion of "journeying," as Robert Fogarty called it. They "struggled to redefine themselves," he wrote, "to secure a collective foothold in the world, and then to announce that they had the truth."[1] In fact, U.S. population movements in the first half of the nineteenth century determined in part that the Heartland would be the center of utopian building. People from the East who had migrated to the opening frontier in order to find a new beginning were joined by individuals impacted by a religious excitement known as the Second Great Awakening, the fervent revival that swept western New York in the 1820s. Religion was a major factor in how utopian community members self-selected their roles.

Yaacov Oved thought that one important common element was what he called "voluntarism."[2] Members joined their chosen community without compulsion because of their deeply held religious or ideological convictions. For some, of course, their commitment was not as strong as it was for others, the core members. Nevertheless, most people who joined a utopian community were committed to holding property in common, to selfless living for the benefit of the community, and to developing new roles for women and different ways to treat children.

Not all utopian communities were tied into religion—some were secular. The former were millennial communities and bonded together in the belief that they must do so quickly in order to prepare for the Second Coming. Spiritual adhesion took priority over economic considerations, although members did adopt communal property. Their leaders claimed a rare charisma in that they were able to have inspirational contact with God. The members' devotional attitude toward the leaders was crucial for the utopia's growth at least, if not for its very survival. In the cases of some utopias, when the leader died, community bonds atrophied and the community also declined or even dissolved.

Secular utopias differed from their religious counterparts in a number of important ways. The catalyst was, rather, the evil of capitalism and the need to respond communally to ameliorate this malignancy in everyday life. They held out, in Horace Greeley's terms, a fellowship of compassionate members where there were "no paupers and no surplus labor . . . [no] inefficiency in production and waste in consumption."[3] The promise was not salvation but the alleviation of financial or social distress. The utopia guaranteed the elimination of the dehumanizing conditions of factory work and at the same time provided security, fraternity, a better education, and moral improvement through communal living. In simple terms, members would become perfect. Secular communities often lacked a charismatic leader, holding together instead through a commitment to egalitarian ideals. In fact, in some cases (as with the Icarians), they survived a leader's abrasive personality and endured because of their ideology. Secular utopias held more unconventional views about the roles of women, sex, and marriage. Although some religious groups such as the Shakers and the Zoarites allowed women to participate in community affairs, their women never gained full leadership or control over the community. The secular utopias gave women more (but still not complete) equality with men. In New Harmony and the Fourierist phalanxes, women enjoyed a more emancipated role than their counterparts in American society.

Yet serious contradictions were endemic in both religious and secular societies, except perhaps within the Hutterite Bruderhofs (see Chapter 6). Members were torn between a commitment to communal life and a recurring assertion of individualism. Communalism was gradually subverted by outside opportunities such as high wages or cheap land or the attraction of the American way of life (as with Amana and Bishop Hill). Artistic creation was sometimes impressive (as seen in the Shaker music and the Nauvoo theater) but always narrowly focused on community ideals. Some utopias promised an emancipated role for women but, ironically, in practice kept them in traditional gender roles and politically subordinated to men. Other communities viewed children with compassion but sometimes saw them as a source of dangerous temptations, in that their parents experienced a special love for their own progeny rather than a complete devotion to the society. Secular communities wanted their children to be educated and adopted innovative ways to accomplish this end, but often the community ended up indoctrinating its children in communal values. Thus, the fraternity promised in the utopian communal lifestyle was at times undermined by the very humanity of its members.

Despite these weaknesses and contradictions, however, for over a century the Heartland saw the "persistence of community," to borrow Timothy Miller's apt phrase. Miller identified six essential qualities that were shared by all these utopias. First, members had a sense of common purpose and a sense of separation from American society. Second, they voluntarily accepted some level of self-denial and suppressed individual choice for the welfare of the group. Third, the utopians lived together in a defined geographic proximity. Fourth, all communards relished the personal interaction of sharing. Fifth, they adopted a community of goods, some communities for a longer period than others. The sixth element in Miller's analysis was that (except for some Fourierist phalanxes), the communities were viable societies "that managed to get off the drawing board and into real existence" and "keep the world at bay."[4] That the element of separation recurs in these descriptions further emphasizes its importance to the communal lifestyle.

A different form of communalism appeared throughout the United States in the last half of the twentieth century in the form of intentional communities and hippie colonies. In the 2000 edition of the *Communities Directory,* George Kozeny described the first as "a group of people who have chosen to live or work together in pursuit of a common ideal or vision." Intentional communities "come in all shapes and sizes," he observed, "and display an amazing diversity in their common values, which may be social, economic, spiritual, political, and/or ecological."[5] Members shared many of the qualities of the earlier secular utopias in that the community served as a refuge from the norms of American life. However, entries in the 2005 edition of *Communities Directory* show that the Heartland contained a mere scattering of utopias. The hippie colonies, according to Miller, were "the countercultural encampments that thumbed their collective noses at the conventional American society and were regarded both with fascination and with loathing by members of the very Establishment that they rejected." Hippie colonies congregated on the Pacific coast and in the Southwest. The appendix in Miller's book *The 60s Communes* lists only about 10 percent of hippie colonies as being in the Heartland, and all of them have sparse information available for scholars. In the Heartland the "persistence of community" waned even though it thrived in other parts of the nation.[6]

Why this phenomenon? Unfortunately, there is no definitive answer. Striking testimony to the paucity of recent utopian building in the Heartland is the fact that only five intentional communities (touched upon in Chapter 8) lasted long enough to leave a viable historical record. They provide indisputable evidence that the era of extraordinary communal living was over.

THE EVIDENCE that the era of vibrant communalism had come to an end by the Great Depression is further reason that there was a need for a definitive compilation of the history of Heartland utopian communities. This book is not a new theoretical analysis of utopia communalism but, instead, a chronological study of the unusual proliferation of communal societies in the Heartland, incorporating recent scholarship and set in a sequential arrangement. The story here begins with the Shakers, the best-known communal religious movement in nineteenth-century America. The Shaker community originated in a revivalist English group in New York in the 1770s and took root in New England before coming to the Heartland. Creating and maintaining celibate "families," these agricultural communes were located mainly in Ohio and Indiana.

The next utopian communities (see Chapter 2) appeared at New Harmony, Indiana. The first was started by German Separatists led by Father George Rapp, who purchased land on the banks of the Wabash River in 1814. For a decade over seven hundred hardworking immigrants, known as the Harmonists, cultivated prosperous farms and built a flourishing town. They kept their German language and culture and practiced celibacy. For a combination of reasons, in 1824 Rapp decided to sell his community to the Welsh philanthropist Robert Owen for the then-princely sum of $135,000. Rapp moved to Economy, Pennsylvania, close to Pittsburgh. Owen had first attempted to build his model factory town at New Lanark, Scotland, but ran into financial difficulties in trying to construct other cooperative towns. Inspired in part by the Shakers and the Harmonists, he decided to create a secular, communal, New Moral World in America. In the spring of 1825, Owen arrived at the site, which he renamed New Harmony, and was welcomed by over eight hundred colonists. The very diversity of its members and Owen's chronic absence led to growing internal differences, which convinced him in the spring of 1827 to abandon communalism.

The Heartland was home to other religious Separatist utopias as well (see Chapter 3). In 1844 William Keil, a onetime adherent to Rapp's Harmonist communalism, organized a communal society at Bethel, located approximately forty-five miles west of Hannibal, Missouri. On twenty-six hundred acres some five hundred devout Germans lived "on the Love of God." Informally organized, with no official charter of incorporation, they participated in a community of goods without money or accounting procedures. Like the Rappites before them, they preserved their German heritage, developed craft industries, and farmed. Also like Rapp, Keil was restless, however, and in 1855 moved most of his followers to the Pacific coast and named the new colony Aurora. Here Keil died in 1877, still beloved by his flock. Two years later the community began the liquidation of their assets.[7]

Another Separatist utopia appeared at Zoar, Ohio, in 1817. Originating in the same part of southern Germany as the Harmonists, the Zoarites were poor and started their community with the financial assistance of the Society of Friends (Quakers) in Philadelphia. Led by the charismatic though physically disfigured Joseph Bimeler, they built brick homes that housed up to eight families, all of whom ate in a single kitchen. They struggled economically until 1833, when the state constructed the Ohio-Erie Canal through a portion of their colony, which generated a $20,000 contract. With these funds the Zoarites started several profitable industries and opened a large general store and a hotel. By 1838 the utopia's five hundred residents communally owned twelve thousand acres and boasted a capital wealth of two million dollars. After Bimeler's death in 1853, however, the colony floundered because of poor leadership, providing another example of a utopian community inspired primarily by one personality. By the 1890s the colony was largely a tourist haven and artists' colony. It dissolved in 1898.

The third Separatist utopia appeared north of the Iowa River as a cluster of seven villages known as the Amana colonies. Officially called the Community of True Inspiration, like the Shakers, they were led by a woman, Amana leader Barbara Heinemann, who, aided by Christian Merts, brought about 560 followers to America. They first developed four villages at Eben Ezer, close to Buffalo, New York, and in 1842 they created a prosperous community of goods. In 1854, largely because of the encroaching population of Buffalo, they moved to twenty-six thousand acres in Iowa. At the time they numbered over thirteen hundred communards. Their seven villages were based on manufacturing and agriculture and thrived as a religious utopia until the Great Depression, when they abandoned communalism and reorganized as a joint stock company and a noncommunal religious society.

The last Separatist colony was Swedish. Their leader, the eccentric Eric Jansson, led his peasant flock from Sweden to Illinois in 1845 to avoid governmental harassment because of their religious beliefs. Surviving both cholera and a brutal exposure to the winter climate, they nonetheless persevered. Over the following eight years they built brick structures, which still stand, and thrived as an agricultural commune. But with the murder of Jansson in May 1850, leadership problems infected the community. The Panic of 1857 brought irreversible decline in income and increased the growing debt. Added to these woes was the Americanization of their young people, who, unlike the German Separatists, learned the English language and wore American clothes. By the time of the Civil War, as one student of Bishop Hill put it, they were in "new circumstances to which the Janssonists' religious protest was far less relevant."[8] By 1863 they had dissolved.

Alongside the religious utopias of the mid-nineteenth century, new secular communities appeared: the Fourierist phalanxes (see Chapter 4), and Icaria (Chapter 5). Twenty phalanxes were built according to the design of Albert Brisbane, who brought the ideas of French utopian socialist Charles Fourier to America in 1840 in his book *The Social Destiny of Man*. These were short-lived joint-stock colonies that boasted of being able to solve the problems of an emerging industrial America. In Ohio seven phalanxes were started, all of which espoused lofty goals of prosperity, equality, and expanding roles for women. Some of them also espoused racial equality. Members quickly became disillusioned with the challenges of communal life, however, and most communities dissolved after five years. Indiana saw one such phalanx experiment on 1,045 acres of land in LaGrange County. It began in 1843 and lasted three years. Michigan also saw only one community, the Alphadelphia Phalanx near Ann Arbor on the banks of the Kalamazoo River. Its living quarters were a large frame mansion, and members engaged in farming and milling. But, like the others, the phalanx ran short of food and money, and in the winter of 1845 it disappeared. Between 1843 and 1845, the Prairie State saw five even shorter-lived phalanxes, some of which lasted only months. Iowa, likewise, was home to three small communities in Mahaska, Clayton, Decatur, and Clarke counties. All were short-lived, and beset by squabbles between unskilled workers and artisan members. Some phalanxes were gone within a year or two, and others never grew much beyond the planning stage. Of all the phalanxes, only the Wisconsin Phalanx achieved even a modicum of prosperity, but it also held together for only two years.

Icaria, whose collective life spanned a half century from 1848 to 1898, offered a more radical utopia than the Fourierist communities. Founded at Nauvoo, Illinois, by the French journalist Étienne Cabet, Icaria housed over one thousand communards by the mid-1850s. Its central tenet was the complete abolition of private property and money. Each member paid an entrance fee of $125 and demonstrated knowledge of Cabet's voluminous works, published in Paris. At the height of its existence, Icaria boasted an unparalleled culture for the day. It had the largest library in the state, produced a theatrical play each month, and maintained its own newspaper and school. Money flowed in from new arrivals (about 95 percent of the Icarians were French) and from a distillery and a sawmill. Internal dissension surfaced because of Cabet's absence in France for over two years, and from the dissatisfaction of some women because of their limited role in colony affairs. In 1856 a showdown led to the expulsion of Cabet, along with 219 loyal followers. They moved to St. Louis, where another Icaria lasted until after the Civil War. The Nauvoo utopians relocated to southwest Iowa where they built a flourishing agricultural commune that lasted until 1898.

Contemporaneously, during the last half of the nineteenth century, another important religious utopia appeared in the Heartland: the Hutterite Bruderhofs. These German-speaking religious communities (see Chapter 6) in some ways were reminiscent of the earlier Separatists with their millenarian beliefs. They are considered by some historians to be the most economically prosperous of all the German communities in America. In 1874 about eight hundred Hutterites left the Ukraine for the Dakota Territory in order to escape persecution and to continue their life in a community of goods. Although some fled to Canada during World War I to escape the rabid anti-German hysteria infecting the nation at that time, most eventually returned to the United States.

Three early-twentieth-century Heartland utopias were built near Chicago, called Zion City, the Spirit Fruit Society, and the House of David (see Chapter 7). John Alexander Dowie, an exotic Moses-resembling faith healer, ruled over Zion City, a theocratic community on the shores of Lake Michigan approximately fifty miles north of Chicago. By 1900 over one thousand members of his Christian Catholic Apostolic Church submitted to his all-encompassing rules, living in an elaborate and carefully planned urban center called Zion City. Within three years this center housed eight thousand residents. Dowie owned all the property, arranged the marriages, and prohibited smoking, drinking alcohol, swearing, gambling, and spitting. Zion City's factories and lumberyard shipped products by railroad to Chicago, and the city's retail stores and banks took care of residents'

needs. But within three years Dowie's inept financial accounting led to
bankruptcy, and he fled to Mexico, allegedly to recruit new converts. New
leadership deposed him while he was away. He died in 1907, and afterward
over fifteen hundred people abandoned the City of Zion. Outside investors
purchased its businesses and factories. In 1942 communal ownership of
property was dissolved, and the place became just another mid-American
town, now known simply as Zion.

In 1905 the Spirit Fruit Society moved to Lake County, just northwest
of Chicago, after four years of community under the leadership of Jacob
Beilhart in Lisbon, Ohio. By that time their neighbors had become wary of
their lifestyle of free love and spiritualism. On 909 acres near the town of
Ingleside, the society lived contentedly in a stone mansion and prospered
from dairy farming. Visitors and newspaper reporters were impressed with
their courtesy and politeness. In November 1908, however, Beilhart died
unexpectedly from peritonitis after a ruptured appendix. His followers
never adjusted to the loss. In 1914 they moved to Santa Cruz County,
California. The property there was called Hilltop Ranch, and the society
continued to prosper from dairy farming and a poultry business. In 1930,
with only a few aged members remaining, the group dissolved.

Nearby, one of the most fascinating experiments in Heartland
communalism, the House of David, took shape near Benton Harbor on
the shores of Lake Michigan. In 1903 the leader Benjamin Franklin Purnell
and 385 devotees, many from Australia, formed a community with the
goal of gathering together the scattered remnants of the tribes of Israel
for a millennium. Purnell insisted on celibacy, vegetarianism, abstinence
from alcohol, and uncut hair and beards (for men). The first requirement,
however, did not apply to the leader, who enjoyed sexual relations with
many female communards. Such shenanigans were unknown to most of
the community, whose members lived as brothers and sisters and enjoyed
the community's amusement park, theater, ice cream parlor, baseball team,
and marching band. In 1926 Purnell was arrested for statutory rape and
died before the trial was over. His community continued as two separate
entities. One, under Purnell's replacement, Thomas Dewhirst, kept the
name House of David. The other, under his wife, Mary, called itself the
Israelite House of David Community.

After a hiatus of a half century, Heartland communal life reappeared
in the form of five intentional communities, two of which were Chicago
missionary ventures (see Chapter 8). Mennonite scholar John Miller started
Reba Place Fellowship to replicate a Hutterite Bruderhof in an urban setting
in order to help individuals deal with the isolation of city life. His mission
was located in Evanston, Illinois, and grew to include twenty-one homes
whose inhabitants lived communally. Mostly vegetarians, they earned
income from outside work for a common fund. A rural version of Reba Place

called the Plow Creek Fellowship was founded in 1971 in Tiskilwa, Illinois.

In 1966 the Padanaram Settlement was organized under the charismatic leadership of Daniel Wright, a minister who moved his Indianapolis congregation to a farm near the town of Williams, Indiana. Called Padanaram after a place name in the Book of Genesis, it was a log village of two hundred residents who made a living milling and logging. Men and women had separate tasks because, they believed, God had ordained the subordinate role of women. After Wright's death in 2001 his daughter, Rachel E. Wright-Summerton, became Padanaram's spokesperson. In 2009 it is what is known as an ecovillage. The communal kitchen is closed and people eat in their homes. The community's children no longer attend a communal school. Wright-Summerton told this author in a telephone conversation in March 2007 that Padanaram "continues to be a village of trust."[9]

In 1973 a Chicago businessman, Richard Kieninger, organized the Stelle Community in a wooded area in northern Illinois after he and his followers pooled their money and resources to construct an intentional community in the form of a small city. Numerous industries were started, such as a plastics company, a machine company producing screws, and a print shop. Members abstained from alcohol, smoking, and drugs, and men dressed in coats and ties while women wore skirts and blouses. They opened a holistic health center. Because of their restrictive lifestyle, however, few new members joined Stelle, and its membership stagnated at just over two hundred residents, including children. In early 2000 they disbanded the communal organization. Only vestiges of communal life survive, where about twenty families share a garden and co-op, and once a week one family prepares a meal for all the members. Stelle is best described today as a community of cooperative living, not a commune.

The two Chicago missionary communities, the Olive Branch and Jesus People USA, round out the history of communal life in the Heartland. Rachel Bradley opened the Olive Branch Mission, one of the first rescue missions in America, in 1876 in order to reform prostitutes. In 1995, because of redevelopment on Chicago's West Side, it moved to its present site at South Claremont and Sixty-third Street to serve the city's homeless and addicted residents. Since 1979, under the leadership of Charles D. Cooper, members have lived communally. In 1996 David E. Bates succeeded Cooper and expanded the mission's activities to include eight additional ministries. He also established satellite missions in Jamaica, Kenya, and Burundi.

The Jesus People USA was formed in 1973 when a Milwaukee-based evangelical outreach mission moved to Chicago. Led by a council of elders, the group grew quickly and moved from a church basement to an apartment building at 4431–33 Paulina Street in 1975. Four years later they relocated to larger quarters in an old hotel on Malden Street. Millennialists, they prepared for the Second Coming while tending to the needs of the city's dispossessed. Communards condemn smoking, alcohol, and drugs. Sexual abstinence is required of all unmarried members. Working in groups during the day, they perform assignments in the fifteen ministries listed on the 2007 community Web site. Today, all community members reside in a renovated hotel at 920 W. Wilson, about four blocks from Lake Michigan. In 2006 Jesus People USA had 420 members: 90 couples, 130 children, and 110 single members, as well as visitors.

CHAPTER ONE

Shaker Villages

The Shaker villages, the earliest Heartland utopias, were not indigenous to the region. They were the offspring of Shakers from the Northeast who between 1805 and 1828 constructed communities in Ohio and Indiana. These communards were members of a millennium sect founded by Ann Lee, a poor, uneducated young woman from Manchester, England. Born in 1736, the second of eight children of John Lee, a blacksmith, and his wife, Ann was illiterate and as a child worked in the textile mills and earned money as a cook. At the age of fourteen she learned of George Whitefield's message that a person could be saved if he or she were "born again," and she became obsessed with religion. In 1758 Ann joined the Shaking Quakers, a small sect in nearby Bolton led by James Wardley and known for their violent physical paroxysms, shrieking, and incoherent mutterings called "speaking in tongues." Ann was profoundly moved by Wardley's divination that the "new heaven and new earth prophesied of old is about to come." Then, he said, all "anti-Christian denominations . . . will be swept away."[1]

In 1762 this short, plump, blue-eyed woman with chestnut brown hair married Abraham Stanley, also a blacksmith, and proceeded to suffer years of religious torment. She bore four children who all died in infancy, and she came to believe that these calamities were messages from God that she must confront the evil of lust. As later recounted in her *Testimonies of the Life of . . . Our Blessed Mother Ann Lee,* she went into a deep depression, suffered "bloody sweats," and slept in a bed that was a "couch of embers."[2] Ann told the Shaking Quakers to abjure all sexual relations and focus only on doing God's work, and she encouraged them to denounce the Anglican Church publicly because it rejected the Sabbath.

As a consequence of her attacks upon the church Ann was repeatedly arrested for disturbing the peace and confined in a Manchester jail. During one of these confinements she had a vision where she saw Adam and Eve in coitus and realized that this act was *the* Original Sin. In another revelation Christ instructed her to "hunger for nothing but God" and to lead his mission to the world. She began to see vibrant colors and objects. She totally abstained from sex with Abraham and committed herself to a holy war to combat the Devil's temptations. During a 1774 incarceration, a vision revealed to her that she was "Mother in Christ" and should emigrate to the American colonies to found the "Church of Christ's Second Appearance." In the spring of that year, the Believers (she, Abraham, a brother, a niece, and five relatives) left Liverpool for New York City.[3]

For a while the group scattered, and Abraham finally abandoned his wife. Stephen J. Stein states that the "Shaking Quakers dropped out of sight."[4] Almost nothing reliable is known about them between their arrival in New York City and their move five years later to a tract of land northwest of Albany known by its Indian name of Niskeyuna (at the time called Nisqueunia). Here they built a log cabin and barely survived the harsh frontier conditions. They adopted communal property and, as it was later remembered, started religious exercises that involved dancing, whirling, and falling on the ground. Gradually, reports about them spread through upstate New York.

In the spring of 1780 a Baptist revivalist from New Lebanon, New York, called Joseph Meacham visited Niskeyuna. After lengthy discussions with Ann, he became convinced that her "testimony was the voice of the son of God."[5] In May 1780 he returned to New Lebanon and urged his congregation to go to Niskeyuna and find out for themselves what this communal Christianity was all about. Over the ensuing months a substantial number of them, and others living nearby, converted to the new religion, now called Shakers.

Encouraged by the New Lebanon conversions, Ann went on a mission to bring more members into "Christ's spiritual family." In the fall of 1781, accompanied by James Whittaker and her brother William, she left for a two-year pilgrimage throughout New York, Massachusetts, and Connecticut. They lived in private homes and talked with families or preached in town squares about Shaker Christianity. She began calling herself "Mother Ann" and told everyone that she was the female counterpart of Christ. By the late summer of 1783 the missionaries returned to Niskeyuna, and a year later, when Mother Ann died, Whittaker took over leadership of the community.[6] While the mission did not attract as many new converts as Mother Ann had anticipated, given her success with the Mount Lebanon settlers, it was a significant milestone in the growth of Shaker communalism. Stein believes that it "laid the groundwork for the subsequent numerical and geographical expansion of the sect."[7]

Whittaker moved the community from Niskeyuna to Mount Lebanon and constructed the first meetinghouse there. He organized communal villages in New Hampshire (Canterbury and Enfield) and in Maine (Alfred, Poland Hill, and Gorham). He declared that the "judgment of God is coming and is nigh at hand." In a letter in 1785 he stressed the ascetic essence of Shaker beliefs, writing that he had renounced "all earthly profits and pleasures, all earthly generation, and propagation." Shakers must renounce sex and condemn the ways of world. They must forsake "wicked lives and serve the living and true God." He told his non-Shaker relatives: "[I hate] your fleshy lives, and your fleshly generation as I hate the smoke of the bottomless pit." He told them they were "a stink in my nostrils" and warned that "the day of God's final visitation" was imminent. He admonished them to forsake their "wicked lives and serve the living and true God." Whittaker's harsh attacks ended abruptly when he became ill and died on July 20, 1787, while visiting new converts in Enfield, Connecticut.[8]

At Whittaker's funeral Joseph Meacham, the first American leader, took over. He began in earnest the "gathering" of scattered Shakers. "Although Whittaker had made a limited effort to cluster converts during his brief tenure as leader," Stein wrote, "it was not until Meacham assumed responsibility for the sect that a clear directive to join together was delivered to all members." Citing Mother Ann's vision of the bisexual nature of God and asserting that Shakers were the "visible spiritual family of Christ," Meacham said that leadership must be by a "parental order." Accordingly, he announced that twenty-four-year-old Lucy Wright, Mother Ann's closest companion before her death, was the "Eldress" who would share equal authority with him as co-minister. They would be spiritual parents of the Shakers. But there was more than a theological basis for Meacham's decision. Catherine M. Rokicky observed that "in a community where the sexes were segregated, a separate male/female leadership structure was pragmatic."[9]

Meacham imposed other changes as well. He and Eldress Wright appointed and removed all village leaders, called deacons and deaconesses. Each community (there were ten by 1796 in New York, Connecticut, Massachusetts, Maine, and New Hampshire) constituted a "Family" of between thirty and one hundred adults. Two men and two women were appointed elders, and they assigned all duties and decided what jobs would be performed. At work, there was no physical contact between the sexes. All labor was done for God's glory and the good of the Family. As Lawrence Foster explained, "by removing all but the most basic private property and by removing the competing demands inherent in separate nuclear family arrangements, the Shakers were able to devote their entire lives to establishing their ideal of the kingdom of heaven on earth."[10]

Shakers were sexually segregated all the time, not just at work. Each meetinghouse had sections for men and women with separate stairways. Men and women ate communally but at different tables. Only at "union meetings," held three or four times a week, were they together. Then men and women sat opposite each other on benches and discussed issues of community interest. Children born of Shaker parents before they converted lived in special houses and were separated by sex. Adults supervised and instructed them in Shaker beliefs and practices and taught crafts and skills. Boys attended school in the winter and girls in the summer.[11]

Meacham was convinced that Shakers needed clearly defined rules of membership. So in 1790 he published the *Gospel Orders,* in which he described three classes of members in the United Society of Believers in Christ's Second Appearance. These categories were the Novitiate, the Junior Order, and the Church Order. The Novitiate retained their personal possessions but accepted Shaker religious doctrines and the authority of the elders. The Junior Order members also kept their property but conveyed its use to the Family. The Church Order members transferred all possessions to the Family and promised full commitment to the society. This pledge meant assuming "joint interest" in the community; if they left, they would receive only a small stipend and not be able to sue the Family for the assets they had donated. Individuals in the Church Order could become deacons and deaconesses. Most Shakers, it turned out, qualified for the Church Order.[12]

By 1790 Meacham had developed detailed regulations of daily life also. Adults could have only six hours of sleep and must be at breakfast at six o'clock in the morning. Specified times were set for lunch and supper. He set uniform standards of production for items made in the villages. Guidelines were developed for the treatment of livestock, outside decorations of the buildings, and requirements of health and hygiene. Meacham described Shaker music as "solemn songs," a "mixture of words & unknown sounds of words" sung with a "solemn & melodious Tone." Worship included the "Square Order Shuffle" that, he said, would minimize spontaneous individual jerkings.[13]

As Meacham's health began to decline, he composed a summary of his accomplishments and his thoughts on the succession after his death. He praised Lucy Wright's leadership and their "union & mutual Labours." Theirs had been a "union of the spirit" that had laid the foundations of the church where men and women had "Equal Rights in order & Lots & in the Lead & Government of the Church." At his passing, he stated, she would become what he had been, "the elder or first born." In establishing female leadership of the Shakers, Meacham believed that Wright would have the

"Greatest measure of the wisdom & Knowledge of God For the Protection of soul." At New Lebanon, after a visit to the village at Harvard, Father Joseph—as he was then called—died on August 16, 1796. "The death of Meacham did not mark the close of an era," Stein pointed out. "On the contrary, his consolidation of the Shaker community subsequently made possible a new age of expansion under his successor." This expansion would transform the United Society of Believers from an eastern phenomenon into a church that would proselytize the Heartland.[14]

By 1796 eleven villages had been built in the Northeast, and the task of completing the organization of these communities fell to Eldress Wright. Her first challenge came from Shakers who would not accept female rule, which they sarcastically called "petticoat government." These dissidents wanted the society to follow the "universal sentiment & custom" of binding females according to rules established by St. Paul. One of them, Angell Matthewson, said that "wimmin are fools & that men that are willin to have a woman to rule over them are fools also."[15] Then there were apostates such as Reuben Rathbun of Hancock Village. In 1800 at Pittsfield, Massachusetts, he published *Reasons Offered for Leaving the Shakers,* in which he described naked swimming and men who had "involuntary evacuations" of the "seed of copulation." Mother Ann and William Lee, he charged, had used obscene language and engaged in drunken brawls. Whittaker had committed "whoredom."[16]

Eldress Wright responded to these schisms by starting a recruiting revival in the existing villages and launching a mission to the trans-Appalachian frontier in order to harvest new followers. To lead the revival she told Ebenezer Cooley, a former evangelist, to exhort new Believers to denounce physical pleasures and to submit to the rule of the elders. On January 1, 1805, Wright dispatched Benjamin Seth Youngs, Issachar Bates, and John Meacham to the frontier. Traveling on foot, they stayed in private homes and visited congregations of Presbyterians, Methodists, and Baptists. They preached to men and women struggling against poverty who were separated by the mountains from loved ones in the East. That summer they organized the first Heartland community at Union Village (called Turtle Creek until 1812), located about halfway between Cincinnati and Dayton. In 1806 Union Village Shakers organized Watervliet (Beaver Creek) east of Dayton. Two years later three missionaries founded West Union at Busro, along the Wabash River in Indiana. In 1822 they built North Union, near Cleveland. Finally in 1824 they established White Water. In addition to these Heartland communities, Shakers laid out two villages in Kentucky—at Pleasant Hill in 1806 and South Union in 1807. Within a decade of Wright's death in 1821, when leadership passed to church elders and eldresses, Shakers had increased from 1,373 in 1800 to 2,316. By 1850 there were about 4,000 members of the United Society of Believers in Christ's Second Appearing living in villages spreading from Alfred, Maine, to the western hub at Union Village and on to Indiana and Kentucky.[17]

The villages were agricultural communes committed to transforming the midwestern wilderness into an earthly Kingdom of God where all the unpleasant sights and smells of the farm were eliminated by an obsession with cleanliness. Their basic rule of life was "Clean your room properly," because "good souls don't dwell in filth [and] there is none in heaven." All buildings were plain, without frills, according to their rule that "simple is beautiful." They grew crops for God's glory and to provide the essentials of life, not to make money (which, it turned out, they did anyway). Men made brooms, clothing, and furniture; women put up jams and jellies and grew vegetables and medicinal herbs.[18]

But these religious utopians were not isolationists. They encouraged visitors, welcoming them with cheerful—and often much appreciated—hospitality. They had contacts with other communal utopias. For example, two Harmonists joined West Union at Busro, and the two societies were in regular communication with each other. Shakers from North Union lived for a while with the Separatists at Zoar, and on one occasion the Zoarites nursed Issachar Bates back to health after he broke his arm. Benjamin Seth Youngs proposed that the Shakers unite with the Amana colony because such a step would, he wrote, "please God." But since the Amanites accepted marriage, nothing came of the proposal.[19]

Stein claims that these villages had a "draining effect on the eastern societies." For example, Wright chose the most talented members of the coastal villages to help establish and run the new communities, and the "skills of these individuals were thus lost to the seaboard societies." In addition, eastern deacons and deaconesses became preoccupied with raising money for the Heartland ventures, providing equipment for the farms and workshops, and sending out all kinds of supplies such as medicine and clothing. The total cost of such support by the time of Wright's death was over $26,000. By then the burden had become too much, and the "ministry in the East finally began to refuse the petitions, explaining that the drain was adversely affecting the morale and activities of the eastern Believers."[20]

Union Village was the center of Heartland Shakerdom. It was led by David Darrow who, before he came to Ohio, was the Elder Brother at New Lebanon when Wright selected him to direct the village. He held that position until his death after a long illness on June 27, 1825. The first years were arduous times. In warm months the men cleared the forest and grubbed roots and stumps to plant crops. During the winter they cut the timber into shakes, planks, and clapboards. Women did the cooking and domestic tasks despite an inadequate supply of water at the location. One sister wrote to New Lebanon that she had not had one day of rest since she arrived.[21] As a result of this Herculean effort they completed the elders' house in October 1807. Then they erected a sawmill, a blacksmith shop, and storage buildings. By 1812 they had a meetinghouse and sleeping quarters for the Young Believers, a designation they adopted to distinguish themselves from Shakers in the East, who were called the Old Believers.

The wilderness environment was not the only obstacle Union Village had to overcome. Local hostility and vigilante violence was there from the start. Night raiders threw rocks through their windows and cropped their horses' ears. They burned their preaching stands and the plank seats they had erected for worship. In 1807 the family of a young woman who had joined Union Village set a large grain barn on fire.[22] Nevertheless, the Young Believers persevered. Benjamin Seth Youngs claimed that there were 160 of them living there at the end of the first year. Early in 1812 the ministry reported to New Lebanon that 56 people were housed in one building; 32, mostly the very old and the young, in another structure; and 13 individuals in a third house. A quarter of a mile from the village they built a house where 13 brothers and sisters cared for 80 children.

Watervliet, named after the eastern village, was situated six miles southeast of Dayton and at first was called Beaver Creek, Beulah, and Mad River. In May 1805 Youngs visited a New Light "preaching station" located there. He was accompanied by (among others) Richard McNemar, a Presbyterian minister who had joined Union Village that year and brought his entire congregation with him. When the men arrived at the "preaching station," they encountered the minister, John Thompson, who said he was determined to protect his "innocent lambs" from the Shakers, whom he condemned as "raving wolves . . . that were going about the country in sheep's clothing." But the Shakers, wrote Edward Deming Andrews, "emerged victorious."[23] By 1806 they had converted John Houston, a wheelwright and farmer who owned eighty acres, and then John Patterson, Beaver Creek's first settler, who also had title to a quarter section of land.

The village grew steadily. In 1810 twenty-seven brethren had joined, and that year they put up a log meetinghouse. In sequence, between 1812 and 1814, they built a gristmill, a tannery, and a coopers' shop, a woodenware shop, and a woolen mill. They made wagons, brooms, and ironware. In December 1818 they communalized all property and proclaimed the central canon of the Shaker gospel: "our Lord and Savior Jesus Christ did make his second appearance, by his Spirit, first in Ann Lee, whom we acknowledge to be the *first Mother* of all souls in the work of regeneration, and the first spiritual head of the Church of Christ then in the body."[24]

In 1822 Union Village was responsible for founding North Union near Cleveland. Ralph Russell, a native of Warrensville, had visited Union Village and converted to Shakerism. He was convinced of the need to create a village in northern Ohio from which he could reach new converts in that part of the state. He returned to Warrensville and with the help of some relatives and friends started a new settlement. His log cabin, which was among seven cabins at the place, became the center of a small settlement some 240 miles from Union Village. The settlers called it the "valley of God's pleasure" because of a vision Russell had of a ray of light that "rose in a strong erect column and became a beautiful tree."[25]

Union Village missionaries Richard McNemar, Richard W. Pelham, and James Hodge soon arrived at North Union, purchased additional land, and dedicated it as communal property. They also held the first religious services in Russell's cabin, and three of his brothers became Shakers. In 1826 a stonemason, James Sullivan Prescott, came there to help construct the meetinghouse and soon afterward joined the community. In 1828 the eighty-nine members living at North Union signed the covenant and formed a communal society, which over the next fifty years grew to house more than five hundred Shakers and own fifteen hundred acres.

Union Village started Whitewater, located north of Cincinnati. The central figure of this village in the early years was Miriam Agnew, a Whitewater resident who had become a Believer in 1822. She received Darrow's approval to return home to preach the Shaker gospel and told him that the people gave her a warm welcome. After George Blackleach came from Union Village to assist her, thirty new converts were added. Earlier, in 1818, Darrow had sent McNemar and Calvin Morrell to a New Light congregation located at Darby Plains seventy miles north of Union Village and organized a small group of Shakers who were constructing a meetinghouse. These men found the community accosted by unfriendly neighbors and troubled by persistent illness and legal problems over land titles. When Darrow received the optimistic report from Agnew he decided to relocate the Darby Plains settlement to Whitewater. But the arrival of these people only caused difficulties. Food was now scarce, and the illnesses troubling the Darby Shakers now infested the Whitewater village. Only direct assistance from Union Village enabled the community to survive the early years.[26]

In June 1808 Shaker missionaries arrived at Busro Creek, sixteen miles north of Vincennes in the Indiana Territory. Nine months later they converted 110 local residents, named the place West Union, dedicated the land as communal, and began farming, but troubles appeared immediately. Conflicts broke out with the Shawnee Indians, who were openly pro-British on the eve of the War of 1812. In the winter of 1811 a group of 80 Young Believers arrived, bringing the total number of settlers to over 300. Then, with the arrival of 1,400 American militiamen who were quartered nearby and with earthquakes and repeated attacks of malaria, the community—

led by David Darrow's daughter Eldress Ruth Darrow, herself suffering from fever—packed their baggage and livestock and returned to Union Village, passing through the Kentucky villages of South Union and Pleasant Hill along the way.[27]

Heartland Shakers replicated the worship, doctrines, and organizational structure of the eastern villages. They followed the rules for religious services laid down by Eldress Wright and practiced group ritual dancing involving "leaps," where men and women moved side by side without touching, and they minimized the earlier sudden outbursts that had attracted so much publicity. They sang religious songs to accompany the leaps and used prescribed gestures called "motionings" while singing. They abjured instrumentation and sang a cappella using lyrics found in the *Millennial Praises*, a book published in 1813 that had the words for 140 Shaker hymns. The lyrics reflected their ideas on Christian love, thankfulness, trust, union, and order. They celebrated the connection between Jesus and Mother Ann as "the blessed Son and Daughter, Completely join'd in one." Other songs condemned the anti-Christ and its false gospel or described non-Shakers as "illegitimate offspring" of carnal sex whose parents "wax wanton . . . as all carnal creatures will do."[28]

Heartland ministries were, like their eastern counterparts, divided into Families of between thirty and one hundred adults led by two male and female elders chosen by the New Lebanon hierarchy. The elders had absolute authority to rule, which meant listening to confessions, conducting meetings, preaching, and deciding on admission of new members. They determined work assignments, assigning some tasks exclusively to men and other jobs only to women. The elders appointed trustees to supervise the community property and conduct business with outsiders. To accomplish this second task, the trustees were permitted to leave the village in groups of three for up to four weeks and had the authority to make decisions for the good of the community. All their travel expenses were paid by the village.[29]

In addition to the trustees' business contacts with outsiders, the Believers undertook a vigorous commitment to attract new members. Among their main targets were individuals who had become dissatisfied with the Protestant sects. Richard Pelham was a typical convert. Born in Indiana in 1797, at the age of eleven he moved to Lyons, New York, to live with his uncle after his mother died. There, after attending a Methodist revival, he joined the church. However, by the time he became an adult he had left the church and traveled to the Heartland to find a more purified religion. He arrived at Union Village in 1822 and made his confession to the elders. That year he helped Ralph Russell establish North Union and, the following year, assisted Miriam Agnew in organizing the Whitewater village. He became a prominent spokesman for Shaker beliefs, and five years before he died in 1873 published an influential pamphlet titled "A Shaker Answer to the Oft Repeated Question: What Would Become of the World If All Should Become Shakers."[30]

Luther Gould was another example of a dissatisfied Protestant who turned to Shakerism. He was born in 1798 in Connecticut and, like Pelham, lost his mother as a youth. Then his father remarried and had the entire family join the Presbyterian Church. But young Gould was preoccupied with his soul's salvation. After a Shaker met with him and explained their gospel he became increasingly interested in their beliefs. Finally, at the age of forty-three he joined North Union, where, according to his testimony, he "thought himself fully in the light of true salvation."[31]

Individuals who had special skills and crafts essential to the village economy were another focus of Shaker recruitment. One such person was James Prescott. He was born in 1803 in Lancaster, Massachusetts, and was raised in a strict Congregational family. He became a stonemason and practiced his trade in Hartford, Connecticut. In July 1826 the Shakers at North Union hired him to lay the foundation of their meetinghouse. While there he studied their theology, and that fall he converted. He became the Second Elder of the village and for the next fifty years was in charge of the school and served as a legal trustee for the community.[32]

All converts had to pass through the Gathering Order, the door to "the true Church of Christ upon Earth." This was not a decision to be made quickly because the Shakers discouraged impulsive decisions that would not last. The members of the Union Village, for instance, insisted on caution and deliberation before entering the Gathering Order. Only after passing through that order would the individual become a member of one of the three gospel orders described by Joseph Meacham in 1790. Some individuals lived in the villages but never became Shakers. Then there were special residents called Winter Shakers. These men and women came to the village in the fall and stayed until spring. While there they performed essential economic tasks and received shelter, food, and clothing. John Parks of Union Village was one such individual. When he left the community the residents simply explained that "he never was anything of a Shaker." One student of North Union claimed that some recruits were not in the least bit interested in their religious ideas but were merely "in want of a second shirt, and almost as destitute of principle."[33]

Young people were allowed to stay in the village until they reached twenty-one years of age. Then they had a choice between two options. They could move through the door of the Gathering Order and become a member, or they could leave. Before they could join the community, however, they had to demonstrate that they sincerely wanted to be a Shaker. In addition, they needed the consent of their parents or guardians to take the step. If they chose to leave they would receive a portion of their parent's or guardians' property. Many young people entered a village because they needed shelter at a time when there were no social welfare services to help them out. "The Shakers willingly offered such youths a home, family, and structure," Rokicky wrote, "when they might have felt uncertain about the future." Orphans were a special type of resident because Shakers openly advertised that they had a duty to provide for the care of the "fatherless."[34]

Not all children behaved as expected. Some found the Shaker religious practices absurd and ridiculed them. Others resented the strict daily routine. So, the elders established procedures on how to disinherit "disobedient and rebellious" young people who did not "subject themselves to our lawful authority."[35]

Another problem involving children was the effort by relatives to get them released. One such episode occurred in December 1813 at Union Village. James Bedle, who had once lived there, left his wife in the village and bound his four children who remained there as indentured servants to Peter Pease. Afterward, Bedle tried to take them away a couple of times but failed. Finally, to avoid further conflict, the elders allowed the two youngest to be removed (against their will). The two oldest siblings and their mother then left the community. A more serious problem arose in 1819, also at Union Village. A young woman named Phoebe Johnson and her brothers and sisters had joined the village with the permission of their parents. A few years later Phoebe's mother died, and as a last request she asked that they remain in the village to be raised by Shakers until they were adults. The father initially promised to support this request. But a hostile local newspaper, the *Western Star,* published inflammatory articles advocating mob action to free them. In August several hundred men, including the father, attacked the community and assaulted Shakers with clubs and whips. The children were released but some of them chose to remain.[36]

Initially, Heartland Shakers had a casual attitude about the education of their young residents. They did nothing about developing standards other than to have separate day schools for boys and girls, with rudimentary instruction in reading and writing. As in the East, these academic subjects, however, were subordinate to an emphasis on character building and self-discipline. Moreover, Shakers never felt higher education was necessary, and some agreed with Harvey Elkins that it filled "the brain with sawdust." The first attempt to improve academic standards began in 1821 when New Lebanon elders assigned a former teacher, Seth Y. Wells, with the responsibility of developing rules of instruction for all the villages. Two years later he published *The Summary View of the Millennial Church,* in which he stated that teaching of Shaker values must be combined with classes in mathematics, chemistry, geography, and music. He wrote that intellectual talent was God's gift and should be developed to the fullest. He also felt that

Shaker schools must be open to non-Shakers and, consequently, become public institutions subject to regulation by state laws and inspectors. "Now," Stein observed, the "Believers no longer dismissed education as unimportant; now they eagerly sought to improve their schools."[37]

At about the same time that Heartland Shakers implemented Wells's reforms in education they adopted new doctrines on marriage. In the eastern villages, if the wife became a Shaker and the husband did not, she had to continue to live with her husband until he agreed to let her enter the village. If it was the other way around, and a husband wanted to join without his wife, Shakers allowed him to leave his spouse and take the children, if they were willing, with him into the village. In the Heartland reciprocity was the rule. If one partner converted and the other did not, then they should "make a just divide of their interests." Under such circumstances, questions concerning both children and property had to be resolved in a mutually acceptable way. The Shakers did admonish the nonbelieving spouse, though, not to try to stop the other partner's commitment to act "according to his or her own faith and sense of duty to God."[38] James Prescott, in his *History of North Union,* told of a William Andrews, who, in 1825, joined the village and brought his family with him. But soon afterward, "he now became as though he had none, according to St. Paul's injunction . . . he now put away the office of a wife and became a brother in the Lord." But the account ended happily when the wife and the four children accepted the gospel and "the wife . . . became a sister in the Lord." Another case had a less fortunate ending. When O. Wheeler joined North Union in 1825 he brought his three children with him. His wife, however, refused to join, and, Prescott wrote, "a mutual parting and separation took place . . . growing out of a change of religious sentiments of one of the parties, which resulted in breaking up of the family."[39]

In 1807 the Ohio legislature passed a statute that dealt with men who refused conjugal relations by joining a religious sect that required celibacy. If this happened, the woman could sue in the Court of Common Pleas for support, and the court would determine the amount she should receive. The husband lost all authority over his children, and the court further determined what support he must provide for them. The law forbade the husband to interfere with the court's ruling. There was also a penalty clause in the statute. Any person who persuaded a husband to join a sect, and thereby to abandon his family and renounce his marriage, could be fined up to five hundred dollars.[40] This law, whether it was intended that it do so or not, improved the legal status of women, because in early nineteenth-century divorce law, a woman had no claim to her husband's property or custodial rights to the children.

When marriages broke up, violence against Shakers sometimes erupted. For example, in August 1810, one of the most notorious episodes took place after James Smith, Jr., joined Union Village and his marriage to his wife, Polly, was dissolved. When he refused to surrender their children to his wife, she appealed to her father-in-law, Colonel James Smith, to retrieve them. The colonel then published a scathing polemic titled *Shakerism Detected, Their Erroneous and Treasonous Proceedings and False Publications, Contained in Different News-Papers, Exposed to Public View, by the Depositions of Ten Different Persons, Living in Various Parts of the States of Kentucky and Ohio.* He charged that the Shakers brutally abused children by whipping them and refusing to provide them with a basic education. He stated that Elder David Darrow used community resources to live a lavish lifestyle. In response to this tract, a mob of five hundred men made up of apostates, relatives of Shaker converts, Presbyterian ministers, and local drunks stormed the village. At one o'clock in the afternoon of August 27, 1810, the mob sent in a committee of twelve men to discuss the situation with the elders. The committee was led by Presbyterian minister Matthew G. Wallace, who told the officers that the good people in the area were convinced that Shakers threatened civil and religious liberty. Wallace said their neighbors were aware that Shakers held some youngsters by force. He demanded the release of several children (including Polly's) who had a parent or grandparents demanding their return. He insisted that the Shakers stop recruiting new members. The elders stated that if the children wanted to leave they could do so. They invited the committee to search the village to see if any children were held against their will. During the inspection the committee discovered that all the children were content to live in Union Village. When the committee members returned to the mob and reported their findings, the mob dispersed.[41]

Some neighbors took the issue of captive children to court. In 1812 Nancy Dunn petitioned the Ohio Supreme Court to order the Union Village Shakers to surrender her married daughter, Sarah Naylor. Dunn claimed that Naylor was held illegally and was being deprived of her liberty. The elders responded that Sarah, called Magy by the Shakers, had voluntarily joined Union Village a few years earlier and could leave anytime she wished. They informed the court that Sarah had visited Nancy Dunn several times and had voluntarily returned to the community. They called Dunn's charges "groundless slander." The court ordered the issue to be decided by a jury. At the trial Dunn admitted that she had visited her daughter frequently and found that she was well treated. She confirmed that Sarah had visited her at home occasionally. But she insisted that her daughter wanted to leave the Shakers and the elders refused to let her go. They testified that Sarah had, in fact, married John Naylor of Cincinnati twelve years earlier, and with his consent, she had left Union Village. Naylor, under oath, said he had married Sarah and was supporting her financially as best he could. Based on this testimony, the judged dismissed all charges against the Shakers.[42]

Heartland villages, contrary to the charges leveled against them, were egalitarian and open societies. Almost all new members agreed to community ownership of property, became Church Order members, and lived in a society where "no man has right of the things he . . . calls his own, but they have all things common." Regardless of how much property one surrendered to the village "all should have just and equal rights and privileges, according to their needs."[43] A Shaker could leave any time he or she wished and redeem the property surrendered upon joining, conditions usually put in writing when they entered. Most of the time, these individuals just took the tools of their trade, clothing, and cash. Other conditions included a pledge to work freely for the good of the society and a promise not to bring any charges against it for work done while he or she lived there.

The Shakers, as Rokicky put it, "succeeded at institutionalizing the concept of community-held property and establishing dynamic villages that changed with the economic realities of the times."[44] Heartland villages were started by an initial grant of land by converts. For example, North Union began with land donated by five men, three of them brothers, which had seven log cabins on the property. Within four years these Shakers had built their meetinghouse and then added several frame buildings, barns, and a gristmill. In the workshops they made brooms, brushes, and tools. They later added a woolen factory, a tannery, and a blacksmith's, as well as a school, an office, and several dormitories. The mill, built in 1843, was the centerpiece of North Union's economy. Located on the bank of a creek, it was four stories tall with a basement made of sandstone and an exterior of wood. It ground flour and made feed for the livestock. Their neighbors used the mill for the same purpose, for a fee, and it became known as the most efficient mill in the area and a main source of income for the Believers.[45]

Further information on this economic expansion came from the numerous visitors who took detailed notes of the successful industries and of their vigorous daily life. Such accounts of North Union described a prosperous sawmill putting out an ample supply of lumber. They told of a woolen factory, like the mill rising to four stories, put up in 1854. Its top floor had a powered spinning jack and looms. A lower story had an iron lathe, used to make broom handles—probably their main, if not their most vital, manufacturing operation.[46]

Shaker women made items for sale outside the village. Women of North Union made towels from flax and used yarn from the woolen mill to knit stockings, mittens, and gloves, which they sold for six dollars a pair. They canned and preserved fruits and made apple butter, catsup, horseradish, and dried pumpkin. They were responsible for what was called "indoor work," cooking and serving food, and doing the washing, ironing, and mending of clothes. North Union had piped-in water to help with the chores in the laundry. The women did all the daily cleaning in both the women's and the men's sides of the residences and taught in the girls' school. Women developed excellent medicines from herbs and pioneered techniques in collecting, drying, and packaging. By 1825 Union Village had the largest herb industry in the state. And from these herbs, Shakers made extracts, oils, distilled flavoring, and fragrant waters.[47]

The role of women increased in importance when a wave of spiritualism, starting in the eastern villages, spread to the Heartland. It was a time known as the "Mother's Work" revival, and (compared to the Gathering Order revival of the 1820s) women more freely expressed their excitement. The revival started in 1837 at Union Village when Elder Freegift Wells urged everyone to confess their sins. Then, in July 1838, members of this village traveled to North Union to spread the revival. Here Eldress Lucy and Sister Vincy told about their deep spiritual anxiety and displayed bodily movements. Young girls between ten and fourteen years of age entered into trances and saw visions. One woman spoke in three different languages, one right after the other. One contemporary recounted that young girls "were taken by violent aspirations of supernatural power and carried away in vision into the Spiritual World, saw and conversed with Angels, and departed spirits, some of whom they once knew in the body."[48] In August 1838 one young man and several women went through involuntary spasms. During the early 1840s three women at North Union—Lucretia Sutton, Charlotte Hart, and Merch Sawyer—were intermediaries for Moses. Through them he commanded, "I want you to be willing to suffer, for Mother [Ann] does love souls that are willing to suffer." He further told them, "I hate the half-way Shaker; I hate false Believers." Abraham spoke through Sutton: "So fight, fight on . . . and overcome all evil and Mother will crown you with endless love." Through Sutton, Queen Elizabeth of England told them to stress simplicity: "I have possessed much of the treasures of earth. But they never done [*sic*] my poor needy soul any good." At Whitewater the spirits of George Washington, Thomas Jefferson, and the Indian chief Powhatan gave instructions. Washington informed one man that Mother Ann had blessed him and that soon all the Brethren would receive this gift. Jefferson admonished them to obey the principles of their gospel and thereby receive rewards in heaven. Powhatan revealed that other Indian chiefs had been "gathered into Mother's gospel, and they are living souls, and they send their everlasting love and blessing to you."[49]

The Mother's Work revival had abated by the mid-1840s, its energy largely spent. One reason it slowed down was that some Shakers admitted they displayed the excitement "because of the notoriety they received for any manifestations they displayed." By that time, also, some of the messages were controversial and within the villages caused discord between those who would accept them and those who would not. For example, one of the messages received by Sylvester Graham—that Shakers should renounce meat, alcohol, tea, and coffee—not only caused divisions in the Heartland villages but resulted in trouble in the East. Elder Freegift Wells of Union Village journeyed to Watervliet, New York, in 1843 "after seeing the divisions over the dietary question in Ohio" and asked them to reject the vegetarian diet.[50]

Since the villages were as self-sufficient as possible, they engaged in a number of agricultural activities. They planted orchards, berry bushes, and grape vines. At North Union, one of the original land grantors, Elijah Russell, looked after their most important product, apples, the surplus of which they sold in the Cleveland area. Russell kept a close eye on the trees that grew peaches, pears, plums, and cherries. He developed effective grafting skills to improve the quality of the ones that were planted in poor soil.[51] Also at North Union, Samuel Russell purchased the best breeds of dairy cattle from across the United States and England to build one of the largest dairy farms in Ohio. The men tended to over eleven thousand silkworms, whose silk the women reeled and spun into cloth. Union Village grew sweet corn, potatoes, barley, oats, rye, peppers, mangoes, apples, tomatoes, and cucumbers. It produced sugar from maple trees, gathering as much as five thousand pounds annually and, like North Union with its apples and sugar, sold the sugar for a profit to settlers living between the village and Cincinnati. Union Village also raised bees and tended livestock, especially hogs. At Whitewater they raised hogs and grew corn and broomcorn and planted apple and peach trees.[52] In all this activity the Shakers were as ingenious as their eastern counterparts. At North Union they were able to dam the creek traversing the land to power their three mills. Daniel Baird of North Union invented "Babbit Metal," an alloy soft enough to reduce the friction caused by bearings made of harder metals and thereby to prevent overheating.

Despite the prosperity of the Heartland Shaker communities, by midcentury their ranks began to decline, with the erosion probably originating during the wave of spiritualism. The Mother's Work revivals caused the villages to close their meetings to the public, and more than ever they "secluded themselves from the rest of the world and suspended all regular outside contacts." They gave their villages new, more spiritual names. For example, Union Village became Wisdom's Paradise, with its Jehovah's Chosen Square. Recruitment of new members, so vital during the formative years, all but stopped. And, for a society built on human compassion and concern for others, Heartland Shakers, like their counterparts in the East, were unexplainably oblivious to the great moral and political questions emerging in the 1850s over the future of slavery.

They were simply "unresponsive to the coming of a war that decided that question, a war that imposed new difficulties for them." During the conflict they stuck to their pacifism and refused to support the Union cause or to serve in the military. This neutrality caused Union forces "to pilfer their villages for food and supplies and to confiscate their animals and wagons for military use."[53]

After the war, divisions grew among those who still remained committed to the Narrow Path. During the last three decades of the nineteenth century, known as the "Time of Transformation," controversies developed over socialism and feminism. On one side were those who agreed with the progressive leadership of Frederick Evans of Mount Lebanon on these issues. On the other side were the followers of conservative Elder Harvey L. Eads, of South Union.

The postwar years began auspiciously, however. In 1871 at Lyceum Hall in Cleveland, Evans addressed a standing-room-only audience made up of Shakers, mostly from North Union, and Spiritualists. He gave a rousing sermon that caused listeners to twist and jerk in ways reminiscent of the paroxysms of the earlier years. He called the Shakers the "root" and the Spiritualists the "branches" and said that when "ye see the branches flourish, ye may know the *root* is holy."[54] Despite the success of this revival, the Spiritualists never joined with the Shakers, whose numbers shrank precipitously. New admissions fell off and most of the elderly died. Increasing numbers of young people left the villages.

The same year as the Cleveland revival, Evans, an Owenite and social reformer before he joined the New Lebanon village, started a publication titled *The Shaker,* in which he urged a commitment to socialism, pacifism, and temperance. He organized missions to the laboring classes in the eastern cities, but his message seemed irrelevant to most American workers. He launched an effort (which failed) to invite Americans to stay at Shaker villages just to enjoy their congenial way of life. Two years later Evans added feminism to his agenda. He changed the title of the magazine to *Shaker and Shakeress* and appointed Antoinette Doolittle as his coeditor. In this position, she encouraged sisters to submit essays and poetry. The magazine published articles by Shaker women that challenged the theological justification of female subordination. Ruth Webster of Union Village denied that women were responsible for Adam's fall and hence accountable for human sinfulness. Martha J. Anderson from Mount Lebanon argued that Mother Ann wanted to release women "from the thralldom of sin and set her in her proper place as the helpmeet and co-worker with man in all the duties and services of life."[55] Recognizing that about 75 percent of Shakers were women, Evans argued that the sisters simply had to take over the jobs and leadership positions formerly held by men.

Elder Eads vigorously opposed such activism and departures from Shaker tradition. A personification of the rigid Shaker, he insisted that they must retain traditional sex roles and remain separate from nonbelievers. He said that America, then in the midst of the Industrial Revolution, was now more corrupt than ever before and more alien "to the simple pastoral ideals of the founder's heavenly garden village." Most Shaker women agreed with Eads and remained in the domestic chores, subordinate to male leadership. "They continued to make pies, bake bread, churn butter, can fruits, care for the sick, clean the buildings, and wash the clothes. They sold comestibles such as pickles, jams, baked beans, horseradish, and applesauce. They knitted sweaters, shawls, and mittens and worked the [appropriate] craft shops."[56]

ONE AFTER ANOTHER the Heartland villages closed, like those in the East. North Union dissolved in 1889, White Water in 1907, Watervliet in 1910, and Union Village in 1912. South Union disbanded in 1922. Some remaining members, like those of Union Village, went to homes for the elderly such as the Methodist Home for the Aged in Cincinnati, where they were provided care in return for assigning all real estate to the home. In the East, Ethel Hudson, the last resident of Canterbury, New Hampshire, died in 1992. Only Sabbathday Lake, Maine, endured into the twenty-first century, and it survives as a museum. Visitors pay five dollars a ticket to examine the dozen white-painted frame buildings clustered around a forty-eight-room brick dwelling house. It houses a dozen adults, segregated by sex, who sleep, dine, and work largely oblivious to the curious tourists who have come to examine the last vestiges of the United Society of Believers in Christ's Second Appearing.[57]

CHAPTER TWO

New Harmony

At the same time that the Shakers were constructing their garden villages, two different communitarian ventures appeared one after the other on the banks of the Wabash River at New Harmony, Indiana. George Rapp's Separatist community was religious, like the Shakers; Robert Owen's utopian socialist experiment, which followed, was America's first secular utopia. First of all, between 1814 and 1824 Rapp developed a flourishing town of craft industries and nearby productive farms. Then Owen purchased the community from Rapp and turned New Harmony into a "model village," a prototype alternative to exploitative capitalism.

The history of New Harmony began in 1785 in the southern Germany duchy of Württemberg when the twenty-eight-year-old Rapp broke away from the Lutheran Church and gathered between three and four thousand followers under his ministry, to await an imminent Second Coming of Christ. Called Separatists, they were mostly small-scale farmers and simple townspeople who were deeply critical of the basic teachings of the Lutheran Church and saw its clergy as corrupt and immoral. They believed it was wrong for the church to collect taxes, and that violence in any form (especially war, of which the church approved) was an abomination.[1]

In 1798 Rapp published *Articles of Faith,* a book that summarized his beliefs and instructed the Separatists to be tolerant and honest, and to live a life of simple piety. There must be no infant baptism or confirmation. They should take oaths only to God. He advocated, but did not require, abstinence from sexual intercourse because Adam had been created "biune," without sex organs. However, in the Fall, these organs appeared in him and in Eve and this resulted in an alienation from the Creator, or the "loss of universal harmony."[2]

In 1803, after Rapp preached to a large crowd near Knittlingen, the government summoned him to Maulbronn for an inquiry and confiscated the *Articles of Faith* and other Separatist books. Rapp concluded that his congregation would probably lose in this confrontation with the state and decided to emigrate. He told his followers to liquidate and then pool their assets and to follow him to safety in the "land of Israel" in the United States. That summer, while his followers were complying with his instructions, he and three companions sailed for Philadelphia, where, in December 1804, he purchased five thousand acres thirty miles north of Pittsburgh.[3]

By February 1805 seven hundred Separatists had moved there and signed the Articles of Association of the Harmony Society. In these articles they agreed to give their possessions to Rapp and a small group of communal officers. These officers would direct the daily life of the colony, as in the supplying of food and clothing, organizing instruction for the children, and seeing to medical treatment. The document designated February 15, the day the articles were adopted, as their anniversary, or "Harmonie Fest."

Rapp was a benevolent but dominant ruler and saw to it that everyone wore simple clothing and worked hard. In 1807 he instigated celibacy and dissolved all marriages. Couples could still live together but only as brothers and sisters.[4] Harmony Society prospered. Living in 130 log buildings (later brick-and-frame buildings), they cultivated two thousand acres and ran a profitable flour mill and sawmill, along with a tannery, a distillery, and a woolen factory. Not everything went smoothly, however. Their neighbors resented the competition these diligent Germans brought to the area. The lucrative Pittsburgh market for their goods involved using an expensive water connection. There is some evidence that Rapp had always planned to build a more isolated community farther west, where the Harmonists could await the millennium without distractions. For a combination of reasons, therefore, in the summer of 1814, with $100,000 realized from the sale of the Pennsylvania property and for $2 an acre, he purchased federal land in the Indiana Territory. Eventually Rapp owned thirty thousand acres of well-watered fields and abundant woodland in both Indiana and Illinois and controlled over seven miles of the Wabash River. Rapp called his community New Harmony.[5]

Unfortunately, the new locale was at the time a swampy flood plain, a breeding ground for mosquitoes and malaria. As the pilgrims from Pennsylvania began to arrive, sickness swept through the settlement and 120 communards died. Wolves preyed upon their livestock. Under Rapp's leadership they drained the swamps and constructed living and working quarters. Within two years they had a vineyard, and as Rapp wrote to a friend, they looked forward to the chance "to make of a wild country, fertile fields and gardens of pleasure." They built a forge to make bricks for their houses, workshops, school, and tavern. They constructed a large mansion for "Father" Rapp, as they addressed him.[6]

The centerpiece of the community was a labyrinth of shrubs with a central shrine for meditation. They buried their dead in a cemetery in unmarked graves (not in family plots), located according to the day the individual died. In 1822 they constructed a large cruciform church with twenty-eight support columns and a balcony to serve as a platform for their orchestra's concerts. The stone lintel of the door was embossed with a golden rose, the symbol for them of the coming millennium. They used the same symbol as a trademark on all their products, mainly pottery, rope, leather goods, whiskey, and woolen and cotton cloth. They opened outlet stores in nearby towns and sent agents to cities in twenty-two states and ten foreign countries. New Harmony soon became the center for frontier settlers to purchase supplies, grind their grain, and transact banking business.[7]

Work began at five o'clock each morning and ended at sundown. Men wore the same simple blue denim clothing they had donned at the Pennsylvania settlement, and the women wore skirts of various colors, scarves, aprons, blouses, and Normandy caps. They marched back and forth to their jobs to the music of their orchestra, and men and women worked side by side in the fields and shops. Women brought food to everyone from a central kitchen five times a day. The meals were a substantial combination of meat and vegetables.[8]

Rapp captured the essence of communal life in a small book that the community press, run by physician Johann Christoph Mueller, published in German in 1824 and in English the following year. Titled *Thoughts on the Destiny of Man, Particularly with Reference to the Present Times*, the book described New Harmony as a place "where those who occupy its peaceful dwellings are so closely united by endearing ties of friendship, confidence and love, that one heart beats in all, and their common industry provides for all. Here, the members kindly assist each other, in difficulty and danger, and share with each other, the enjoyments, the misfortunes of life; one lives in the breast of another and forgets himself; all their undertakings are influenced by a social spirit, glowing with noble energy, and generous feeling, and pressing forward to the haven of their mutual prosperity." Rapp preached Sunday sermons on topics such as brotherly love, self-sacrifice, humility, and self-criticism. He insisted on an evening confession to him of any faults committed during the day.[9]

Education was a priority. They had kept their children out of schools in Germany because they felt the schools indoctrinated and corrupted them. But now New Harmony's prosperity allowed them to create their own educational system, which eventually included about one hundred children, those born before the rule of celibacy took effect, and those of new members. Indeed, Rapp wrote that "the proper education of Youth is of the greatest importance to the prosperity of any plan, for the melioration of mankind." Teachers conducted classes for children aged six through fourteen six days a week. Three days the classes were in German, and the other days in English. Mueller was the headmaster, and he was aided by the colony innkeeper, Frederick Eckensberger. Subjects included mathematics, singing, religion, geography, history, natural history (or science), and German and English grammar. At age fourteen the boys became apprentices in the various crafts or in agriculture, and the girls were trained in sewing, spinning, weaving, and housework. Sometimes, though, teenage girls were given special training beyond the traditional areas. For example, Gertrude Rapp, daughter of Johannes and Johanna Rapp (one of the last children born, in August 1808, just after the community adopted celibacy), lived with her aunt in the Shaker village at West Union in order to master English. She was a gifted musician and sang in the girls' quartet and gave piano concerts. As an artist, she drew sketches, painted in oils, and made wax flowers. In her twenties she managed the Harmonist silk industry and was highly praised for the fine cloth it produced.[10]

New Harmony's vigorous cultural life centered on prose and poetry, music, and gardening. A collection of their verses and short essays appeared in 1826, titled *Fiery Coals in the Ascending Flames of Lust for the Elusive Sophia*. The collection extolled their joyous hope for the millennium. As one of the pieces put it: "People of Harmony, you should be content with the present age, for a better future is near at hand. In that distant time to come, the entire earth will bloom, as a garden of God; the ennobled and improved man shall live in peace with his brothers; lambs shall feed with wolves, and babies play with young lions; and freedom, truth, justice, love and goodness will be commonplace on the beautiful earth."[11]

Music was a vital part of community life. It was stressed in the school and in the form of either choral or instrumental concerts, and, historian Karl J. R. Arndt believed, "helped foster group cohesion, provided a means of personal expression, and [provided] a constructive form of recreation for the society's young people."[12] In 1820 they published a hymn book entitled *Harmony Songbook Written by Early and Modern Authors*. Mueller composed a number of its hymns, the most popular of which was "Through Fallen Church Windows." As music director, Mueller organized concerts, arranged pieces for the orchestra, supervised rehearsals and gave vocal lessons and instruction in instrument playing. He purchased a piano and even considered buying an organ that would have cost $7,000.

Gardening was just as important as poetry, verse, and music. Behind each building was a formal garden. There was a community botanical garden and a greenhouse to grow plants not indigenous to the area. By 1824 New Harmony, then one of the largest towns in Indiana, was a thriving community of 180 buildings with well-kept fields and vineyards, profitable industries, and a vibrant cultural life.[13]

The Harmonists were soon involved in local politics. Father Rapp's adopted son, Frederick, was a delegate to the state of Indiana's constitutional convention in Corydon and became a leader in public efforts to select Indianapolis as the location for the permanent capital. He served on the convention's militia committee and was responsible for putting a provision into the constitution that allowed conscientious objectors to pay a fine to avoid military service. The senior Rapp loaned the new Indiana state treasurer $5,000 to underwrite expenses. He stated that New Harmony's male residents would vote as a block to support their favorite candidates for state and federal office. Rapp kept up regular contact with other religious utopias. They were in touch with the Shakers at West Union, and some New Harmony parents, like the parents of Gertrude Rapp, sent their children there for instruction in English. There was serious talk of a merger of New Harmony and West Union, but nothing came of those discussions. Rapp gave money to the German colony of Zoar, in Ohio, to help it through its first difficult years.[14]

Much of what we know about New Harmony comes from visitors' accounts. John Woods, an Englishman, described their gardens and vineyards in detail. The English traveler Richard Flower was impressed by the German commitment to hard work, as compared to the lackadaisical attitude he found among frontier Americans. Morris Birkbeck, from the experimental agricultural colony of Prairie Albion across the river in Illinois, wrote that New Harmony's success was due to the "association of numbers in application of good capital," although he commented despairingly on what he called their "disgusting superstition" in religious matters. A third English traveler, known only as Mr. Courtney, was impressed with the school as "well conducted by a respectable tutor, . . . all clean, neat and orderly, . . . a most pleasing, peaceful and active scene."[15] And even the famous Lord Byron touched upon New Harmony in Canto the Fifteenth of *Don Juan*. He wrote:

> When Rapp the Harmonist embargo'd marriage
> In his harmonious settlement (which flourishes
> Strangely enough as yet without miscarriage,
> Because it breeds no more mouths than it nourishes,
> Without those sad expenses which disparage
> What Nature naturally most encourages)—

Why call'd he "Harmony" a state *sans* wedlock?
Now here I've got the preacher at a dead lock,
Because he either meant to sneer at harmony
Or marriage, by divorcing them thus oddly.
But whether reverend Rapp learn'd this in Germany
Or no, 'tis said his sect is rich and godly,
Pious and pure, beyond what I can term any
Of ours, although they propagate more broadly.[16]

Troubles appeared amid this concord, however, coming both from their neighbors and from members of the community. American backwoodsmen began to resent New Harmony's wealth, its political power, and its celibacy. One of them even asked the state legislature to make celibacy illegal, observing that "it is shurly not Right that those who are man & wife should not Enjoy [each] other as such [just to] please the old gentleman." Others were jealous of the colony's control of such a long stretch of the Wabash River. Some Indiana citizens resented the block voting of the New Harmony men in elections. In 1820 a riot broke out in the streets of New Harmony town between the frontiersmen and the communal men. The sheriff, a frontiersman, arrested nine of the Americans and charged Frederick Rapp and Frederick Eckensberger with assault.[17]

Beginning in 1818, when a large group of new emigrants from Württemberg arrived, tension mounted within the utopia. These arrivals had less of the zeal than the original Separatists, and some of them refused to accept celibacy. So Rapp reluctantly married several couples. He began making individual contracts with new members that contained nothing about the return of property if they decided to withdraw. Rapp thought that without such information individuals would be reluctant to leave New Harmony. As Arndt put it, Rapp "was closing the door on compromise in the face of disgruntled members and the rising generation."[18]

By 1824 more problems arose within the community, most of them about economic matters. For reasons still unknown, Rapp shut down the colony textile mill and consequently had to lay out money to buy cloth from the Inspirationists at Amana, Iowa. By then he realized that he had overextended himself in purchasing the thirty thousand acres, because more tolerant treatment of religious dissenters in Germany had resulted in fewer immigrants to New Harmony than he had expected. It became evident that the sandy soil in the area was not as well suited for grape cultivation as they initially had believed. The lucrative urban retail markets of St. Louis, Cincinnati, and Pittsburgh were so distant that shipping costs seriously eroded any profits they might make. Rapp became convinced that the only way to keep the community cohesive, and to maintain discipline and obedience to his rule, was to start over again. He believed that any weakening of these two factors "could seriously undermine his leadership." Finally, Rapp was worried about the upcoming millennium date he had set of September 15, 1829, based on the Sunwoman of Revelation, found in Revelation 12:6. What would happen if the day came and nothing occurred?[19]

In the winter of 1824 he announced that, according to the Sunwoman of Revelation, they must now "flee into the wilderness" to build another utopia. He sent Frederick up the Ohio River to find a new location close to Pittsburgh. For $10,000 he purchased one thousand acres, twenty miles south of the original Harmony Society. In August, Father Rapp hired Englishman Richard Flower (father of George Flower of Prairie Albion) to find a buyer for New Harmony. So Flower returned to England, where he met with Robert Owen. The men agreed on a price of $135,000 for the entire community—180 buildings, the adjoining twenty thousand acres of land, and established industries and equipment.[20]

As the Harmonists prepared to leave the Wabash River valley, Rapp predicted that the new community (which he called Oekonomie, or Economy) would be the place for the Second Coming. There he would build "a city in which God would dwell among men, a city in which perfection in all things was to be obtained." He wrote his son that "the true and divine human form will again appear and has really appeared. . . . Thus under a beautiful and clear sky, it will develop to that beautiful form of new and loftier plains." By June 1825 they had relocated. After buying 2,186 more acres for $33,445, they gathered to await a millennium that never happened.[21]

While the Harmonists were preparing for the end of the world in Pennsylvania, back at New Harmony Owen was organizing a "model village" to show the world how to live without the evils of the Industrial Revolution. In fact, by the time he arrived at the Wabash River site he had already built a utopia, a model factory town, at New Lanark, Scotland. Owen was born in 1771 in Newton, Wales, the son of a blacksmith and postmaster, the sixth of seven children. At the age of ten he moved to London to live with an older brother and work as a shop assistant for James McGuffog, a wealthy linen draper. In 1784 he obtained a position with Mr. Satterfield, a Manchester wholesale dealer. During his time with Satterfield, the young Owen was shocked by the dehumanizing conditions in the city's cotton factories. It was an experience that launched him on a lifelong crusade against the exploitation of workers, against clashes between rich and poor, and against avaricious individualism.[22]

In 1789 Owen started his own business, making the frames that were used in the manufacture of ladies' hats. After this enterprise went bankrupt in 1791 he rented a building in Manchester and started a mechanized factory to spin cotton. The spinning operation was extraordinarily successful because he used high-quality American Sea Island cotton. Within a few years he was purchasing raw cotton at five shillings a pound and selling the spun thread for nine pounds eighteen shillings a pound weight. After amassing a large fortune in the cotton-spinning business, Owen began construction of his model town at New Lanark, southeast of Glasgow, Scotland. Arthur Bestor, Jr., wrote: "It was there that [Owen] initiated the experiments in factory reform that gradually evolved into experiments in comprehensive social planning. . . . It was there that he finally made his decision against programs that looked to a gradual amelioration of existing society and in favor of those that proposed communitarian transformation of it. . . . It was from New Lanark that he first projected his ideas to the world at large."[23]

Owen's reforms were dramatic. He stopped employing children under the age of twelve. He built new housing and paved the streets. New Lanark had a store where residents purchased food, clothing, and whiskey. Factory foremen kept detailed records of performance and rated workers as "bad," "indifferent," "good," and "excellent." At night police patrolled to prevent crime. In 1816 Owen opened the Institute for the Formation of Character, which included a nursery school for any child aged from one to five. Children from six to twelve attended the day school, after which age they worked in the factory for ten and three-quarter hours a day. Instructors trained them on the "play principle," where they abjured discipline and instead used "steady kindness" to teach, without textbooks, by lectures in history, geography, chemistry, and "economic facts." They also used pictures and wall maps. When not in school, the children sang in the community choir and marched in close-order drill dressed in loose-fitting kilts. Owen also had an evening school for adults in the institute. New Lanark grew and prospered.[24]

In 1818 Owen publicized his communitarian ideas in *View of Society.* He argued that human problems were caused by the environment, not free will, and that it molded initiative and formed character. He claimed that an aristocratic upper class should not be allowed to live off the labor of the working majority. He demanded support for compulsory education for all children.[25] In London newspapers such as the *Times* and the *Morning Star,* Owen proposed organizing cooperative communities made up of residents from all levels of society, from paupers to aristocrats. Living and working together in these communal utopias they would receive whatever they needed from "the general store of the community." In his 1820 *Report to the County of Lanark,* he wrote that "individual accumulation of wealth will appear as irrational as to bottle up or store water in situations where there is more of this invaluable fluid than all can consume."[26]

Owen's ideas received widespread attention in the United States. Cornelius Camden Blatchly, head of the New York Society for Promoting

Communities, included selections from Owen's writings in his book *Essay on Commonwealths*, published in 1822. The president of the Philadelphia Academy of Natural Sciences, William Maclure, organized an "Owenite Club" in 1823. But Owen himself showed little interest in this American audience until a number of developments converged on him, encouraging him to abandon his "communitarian dream" in the British Isles and to look to the New World as a place for his utopia.[27]

After almost a decade of promoting his ideas he began to realize that he would never be able to raise enough money to build cooperative villages in Scotland or England, and that his fortune ($250,000) would cover the cost of less than one village. In addition, by 1824 some of New Lanark's residents began to resent Owen's proscription against teaching religion in the institute. Other employees were frustrated with his being absent from the town most of the time. A typhoid epidemic made some individuals question the efficacy of his insistence on hygiene. So, when Richard Flower visited him at New Lanark in August that year and offered him the town of New Harmony for $135,000, to be paid in two annual installments, he "succumbed so readily to the lure of cheap western land without considering the difficulty of assembling upon it a population appropriate to his purpose."[28]

Within a month Owen was in London preparing to depart for America. On October 2, 1824, he sailed from Liverpool, accompanied by his son William and his devoted Scots follower Captain Donald MacDonald. On November 4 they landed in New York City and that evening met with Blatchly's Society for Promoting Communities. During the next week Owen became acquainted with noted educator John Griscom, a professor of chemistry at Columbia College, who introduced him to that college's faculty. Owen next met with David Hosack, vice president of the College of Physicians and Surgeons, who asked him to speak to its faculty about his views of society. Owen talked with other luminaries such as John McVickar, author of *Outlines of Political Economy;* William Harris, president of Columbia; its future president Charles King; and Trent Irving, the brother of Washington Irving. He then boarded a steamboat to Albany to visit Governor DeWitt Clinton, who gave him letters of introduction to Thomas Jefferson and Andrew Jackson. Back in New York City until November 18, 1824, he went through another round of introductions. Then he moved on to Philadelphia, where, between November 19 and 23, he was introduced to William Maclure and James Rush (son of Dr. Benjamin Rush) and lectured to enthusiastic audiences at the Franklin Institute and the Athenaeum. Then, at Washington, D.C., on November 26, Owen met with President James Monroe, Secretary of State John Quincy Adams, and General Andrew Jackson. Along with his son and MacDonald, he departed for New Harmony on November 28, going by hackney coaches to Hagerstown, Maryland, and then west by stagecoach on the National Road to Pittsburgh. When they arrived there on December 3, waiting to greet them was Father Rapp, then at his new community of Economy.[29]

Traveling by boat down the Ohio River, they arrived at New Harmony on the afternoon of December 16. Frederick Rapp, in charge of the community's business affairs, escorted them on a weeklong inspection of the town. By New Year's Eve Owen admitted to William "that he had decided on the purchase."[30] On Monday, January 3, 1825, Owen took title to 180 buildings and twenty thousand acres. Then, that afternoon, he left for a three-month tour to recruit settlers and to get financial backing for his utopia. On February 17, he was in the nation's capital just after the House of Representatives chose John Quincy Adams as president. He gave two addresses in the Hall of Representatives in the Capitol. The first one, on February 25, was attended by the president-elect. The second time, on March 7, Adams and this time also James Monroe listened to Owen's three-hour speech. The *National Intelligencer* printed the full texts of both discourses. In March, he visited Jefferson and Madison at their Virginia homes and then returned to Philadelphia.

He arrived back at New Harmony on April 12, 1825, where the newly arrived colonists welcomed him. Two weeks later Owen presented them with a constitution, the first in an ongoing list of such documents that Owen would give to the farmers, adventurers, and drifters who gathered on the banks of the Wabash to build his New World utopia. At the time the town included brick-and-frame homes, dormitories, two churches, a lecture hall, four mills, a textile factory, a tanning yard, mechanics' shops, and a distillery and brewery. Owen confidently expected that such accommodations would provide all the facilities, tools, and necessities of life for his utopia.[31]

He called it a "Preliminary Society" and stated that three years would be required to advance from this stage to a fully collective society. During the transition, New Harmony would be in a "half-way house" condition with himself as its "trustee," assisted by an executive committee. Each member could keep their personal possessions but would have free room and board. They would, however, have to purchase household furniture and tools. Annually, community profits would be divided according to a formula of "whoever worked more received more," minus whatever amount of goods that individual had taken from the community store. Each adult was credited with $80 in the store's books as a maximum amount that could be spent. Medical treatment and education were free. The Preliminary Society document had no requirements for admission.[32]

On June 5, 1825, Owen left the colony for a six-month tour and appointed his son William in charge, to be assisted by MacDonald. First he went to Pittsburgh, then on to Niagara Falls, New York. He crossed the state on the Erie Canal and arrived in New York City on July 4. After brief stops at Philadelphia and Boston he embarked for Liverpool and docked there on August 2, 1825. He traveled to New Lanark to make arrangements to bring his family to America. In November he returned to Philadelphia to advertise for more colonists. Assisted by Maclure, he personally recruited teachers, scientists, and artists, who then traveled with him down the Ohio River aboard what they called later the "Boatload of Knowledge," along with $15,000 worth of supplies.[33]

By the time Owen reached New Harmony on January 12, 1826, the press had become strongly critical of his views on religion. While he was sailing from New Lanark to Philadelphia he composed an open letter, which was published soon upon his arrival. In it he condemned all religions because, he said, they indoctrinated bigotry and hypocrisy. He denied the concept of original sin and postulated that it was the environment that caused human depravity. In a lecture at the Franklin Institute, he rejected the idea that the Bible was the word of God. The *New York Advertiser* sarcastically observed that any man "who can invent anything more absurd, more extravagant, more irreligious in its principles, or more mischievous in its tendency . . . must be possessed of no ordinary capacity." But Owen was oblivious to these developments and remained convinced that thousands were ready to follow him in the transformation of society.[34]

William tried to govern the community while Owen was gone, but with little success. Following the Preliminary Society document, he encouraged open admissions. Consequently, by the fall of 1825 New Harmony was a hodgepodge of divergent and sometimes hostile cliques. The economy collapsed, because under William's weak leadership just 140 of over 800 adults were willing to work in the community's crafts, industries, and agriculture. By Owen's return, just three shops were still operating. Since only 36 men went to the fields each day, the once bountiful farms had deteriorated to the point that William had to purchase food from outsiders in order to feed the community. Only Robert Owen's pledge to offer his own money as a subvention kept the colony solvent.[35]

Most residents were living in a fool's paradise, however, and believed that now, with the senior Owen back in charge, they would quickly realize his vision of a new moral world. William Pelham, coeditor of the *New-Harmony Gazette*, printed bucolic letters to the editor that described an atmosphere of friendship, cooperation, and communal enthusiasm. The newspaper emphasized the community's religious tolerance, noting that even Methodists preached there on Sundays. Its cultural and intellectual life, according to the *Gazette*, was astonishing. Residents attended lectures on science and the arts three times each week. They had regular community dances. Their orchestra gave concerts every Thursday evening. There was a Female Social Society and a Masonic Lodge that had regular meetings.

One thing the newspaper did not exaggerate was New Harmony's innovative system of education. Its two hundred pupils were enrolled in a boarding school and were taught by the intellectuals of the Boatload of Knowledge, led by William Maclure. He drew upon the ideas of Fourier, Rousseau, and Pestalozzi and integrated academic instruction with manual labor. Maclure, who regretted that his education in the classics had left him as "ignorant as a pig of anything useful," believed that children must be taught how to work on the farm and in the factory. Education was not just for children but must continue throughout adult life. Its ultimate goal, Owen's son Robert Dale Owen had written a year earlier in his *Outline of the System of Education at New Lanark,* was to increase "the happiness of the community . . . to raise all classes without lowering any one, and to re-form mankind from the least even to the greatest."[36]

But soon the reality of the emerging difficulties corroded New Harmony's esprit de corps. Economic problems were the first to surface. The annual stipend of $80 per person, given out in weekly amounts of just $1.54, was not enough for most families. The accounting process at the store proved unworkable because it was so complicated. Some individuals grumbled that the amount credited for their communal work in the store's ledger was unfair. Housing was inadequate since the population of Owen's New Harmony was double that of the Separatists, and although buildings could be enlarged this would take time. By the fall of 1825 people were living in the attics of the frame-and-brick buildings or in hastily built log cabins. William, sensing the seriousness of the situation, warned in the *Gazette* that new members who wanted to join would have to wait at least two years before they would have a place to live. Most serious was the fact that many adults just refused to do any kind of work. According to Robert Dale Owen, they had joined New Harmony for their utopian beliefs and ideological discussions, not to do any form of hard manual labor.[37]

Many women became deeply frustrated. They had joined the community in order to realize equality of the sexes. And, at first, they were pleased to be educated the same as men and to enjoy New Harmony's active social life where single women met intelligent young men. But soon, Donald E. Pitzer observed, "domestic chores became the exclusive and expected duty of women despite the guarantee of equal rights." Married women were viewed by Owen as "community wives," and, Pitzer wrote, "their obligations to their own households stretched into tiresome cooking, sewing, and cleaning for the entire village."[38]

Religious questions bothered both sexes. There was a wide gap between what Owen thought of as religious freedom and what most residents of New Harmony believed. Many disagreed with Owen's contention that religious freedom meant open discussion of antireligious ideas and a rational, almost scientific, investigation of revealed religious doctrines.

Others felt there was too much religious diversity in the village. They complained that in the brick Rappite church on just one Sunday, a moral lecturer had the pulpit in the morning, a preacher defended the authority of the Bible in the afternoon, and a Methodist revivalist ranted about sin and damnation that evening.[39]

On the same day he arrived back in New Harmony, and in the midst of this growing rancor, Owen lectured the community on the need to end the temporary Preliminary Society and form a permanent "Community of Equality." Ten days later an assembly of all the adults adopted a position that the transformation should begin "as soon as practicable" and declared the assembly itself to be a constitutional convention to accomplish this objective. Then the assembly appointed William, Robert Dale Owen (the other son), and MacDonald as members of a seven-man committee to write the constitution. They sent it to the editor of the *Gazette,* who published it on February 1, 1826. On February 5, the assembly accepted the constitution unanimously.[40]

In the new Community of Equality there was communal ownership of property. Gone was the cumbersome accounting system, and instead, work supervisors would daily record their evaluations of each person's character and performance. But there were serious flaws in a document so quickly drafted and approved. It did not deal with financial compensation for residents who left New Harmony. There was still a muddy definition of Robert Owen's relationship to the community. He, as the legal owner of the property, had said that he expected to recoup his investment by selling and leasing property to individuals; but the constitution did not cover how and when this was to happen. It said nothing about how future profits were to be shared between Owen and the residents.[41]

On February 22, the *Gazette* printed an article that showed how hopelessly in debt New Harmony was. The editor asked Owen to take control and govern the community for one year, assisted by an appointed committee. Owen agreed. Almost immediately, however, he was forced to deal with three serious defections. The first group consisted of devout Methodists who rejected Owen's "atheism" as repugnant and refused to accept the new constitution because it permitted unorthodox religious opinions. They asked Owen to let them form a separate community, which they called Macluria but which Owen labeled Community No. II. He leased them thirteen hundred acres on which they could build their colony. By the summer of 1826 they had constructed nine log cabins and counted 150 members. However, in late November, Community II dissolved.

Some English farmers from Prairie Albion who had joined New Harmony became so disgusted with its slovenly agricultural practices that they decided to leave and start Community No. III. Owen rented them fourteen hundred acres on which they could scientifically till the land.

About seventy-five members put up log cabins and frame houses on the property, which they labeled Feiba-Peveli. Held together by their English nationalism, they formed a communal bond that allowed the community to survive until the spring of 1828.[42]

The most unexpected defection came from Owen's sons. Early in March 1826, William and Robert Dale and a group of young intellectuals concocted a plan to form Community No. IV. They were fed up with the crude backwoodsmen crowding into the colony and were convinced that only the educated idealists could create the new moral world. They organized themselves into a clique, called the Literati, and wore bloomers as a "badge of aristocracy." In early March, they proposed to the senior Owen that they be allowed to govern New Harmony, eliminate inhabitants who were lazy and irresponsible, and divide it into partitions of men and women firmly committed to its ideals. The elder Owen would have no part in what amounted to a coup d'état. Instead, he offered to give them some forestland where they would be able to "cut down trees and build log cabins as fast as they pleased."[43] Faced with this resistance the projected takeover quickly collapsed.

While trying to deal with these dissensions, on March 18, 1826, Owen offered a new plan to those still living in New Harmony—now called Community No. I. He would sell them the village, valued at $126,520, at 5 percent interest, payable over a twelve-year period. Most members reacted with dismay, if not indignation, at the plan. One man, Thomas Pears, an intellectual from Pittsburgh, stated: "Whatever be the terms, I have no intention of making myself responsible, for I can see no prospect of producing enough to maintain us."[44]

Only twenty-four members accepted it. Owen designated this group as the community's "Nucleus" and gave it full control over the village. For a few months a sense of optimism prevailed. The Nucleus carefully kept the store accounts. They revived cultural activities. They had the schoolchildren help to improve the farms and shops. They ordered detailed reports on those adults who would not work. Nonetheless, the economy remained sluggish. Faced with this fact, in May 1826, Maclure published a letter in the *Gazette* suggesting they organize a federated community made up of independent sections, each of which could exchange their products with the others.[45]

Owen was impressed with Maclure's ideas, and on May 28 the community accepted his plan. New Harmony was reorganized into three units: a School or Education Society, an Agricultural and Pastoral Society, and a Mechanic and Manufacturing Society. The Board of Union supervised their operations. This scheme only complicated matters, however. Maclure, the director of the School or Education Society, would not allow his students to continue to do any manual labor. By summer more problems developed. Owen insisted on keeping personal control of the store and tavern. One member complained that Owen was "shifting into the characters of a retailer and tavern keeper, to save by nine-penny and four-pence-half-penny gains, after the manner of peddlers, the money which he had lost."[46]

Owen retreated. He gave the Mechanic and Manufacturing Society part control of the store and the Agricultural and Pastoral Society full control of the tavern. These two societies then started to quarrel with Maclure and his society, claiming that it was littered with ciphers and snobs. Maclure called them "good for nothings." The fundamental difficulty, as Bestor explained, was that the reorganizations "had siphoned off most of the responsible and devoted members of the community, leaving under Owen's immediate direction mainly the drifters, the parasites, and the fanatics."[47]

Matters worsened in the summer of 1826 when Paul Brown, an intellectual and devoted communist who had published thirty articles in the *Gazette* on economic equality, led a frontal assault on Owen's leadership. He was fed up with the man's incompetence. He branded Owen the "lord proprietor," a "speculator in land, power, influence, riches, and the glories of this world." What really infuriated Brown was his belief that Owen had promised initially to turn New Harmony over to the members and divide it equally among them, and then he had reneged on his word. No true philanthropist could do what Owen was doing, trying to sell the community to its own members. Next, Brown denounced the frivolous socializing that went on. He described some boys as "brutes" who smashed huge holes in the fences so that pigs and cows "ranged at pleasure throughout." Then he went after the editor of the *Gazette,* whom he considered Owen's lackey. Under pressure from Owen, Brown said, the newspaper refused to print any more of his articles. As a result, Brown, imitating Martin Luther, had to post his accusations on doorways.[48]

Maclure emerged as another troublemaker in September. He thought Owen had been mistaken to float the community with his own money because this encouraged idlers to hang on without becoming productive members, which, he wrote, resulted in "nothing but waste and destruction of property" and allowed people "to consume not to produce, money having been substituted for industry, negligence for care, wastefulness for economy." Maclure declared that the school society, which had been subsidized financially by his friends in Philadelphia, was independent of Owen's control. He informed the members of the agricultural and mechanics societies that they now had to pay tuition to enter their children in the school. Both societies refused to comply.[49]

Owen was glad to have Maclure out of his hair so that he could open his own school, one better suited to his ideas of "social education." The children would meet in the town hall three times each week to be taught by teachers whose only qualifications would be "practical experience." As in New Lanark, they would use maps, globes, and visual aids to lecture on trades, occupations, and other "useful things." The pupils would not have to study but would just attend the classes, sit, and listen to the lecture. "By this simple process," he maintained, they "will acquire a better education, and more valuable knowledge than has been given by any system of instruction heretofore put into practice." Maclure ridiculed the plan as "the parrot method" of education. The classes lasted for three weeks until Owen canceled them. At this point Maclure's health broke down, and he left for New Orleans hoping to rest and regain his strength.[50]

After he returned from New Orleans in April 1827, Maclure, thankful to be rid of Owen's eccentricities, turned his full attention to his school. He now opened it free to orphans and to outsiders for an annual fee of $100. He described his educational principles in twenty-six essays published in the *Gazette*. The cornerstone of his pedagogy was the Pestalozzi theory that children should be taught by experience. There was to be a school for children aged two to five who would be housed in the Harmonist Community House with room for more than one hundred pupils. Here "teachers such as Marie Fretageot and Eloisa Buss Neef taught them to share communally, live humanely, and think freely." For children aged six to twelve, there was the "higher school" where teachers under the direction of Joseph Neef led classes in mathematics, science, mechanics, language, writing, art, music, and gymnastics. In the evenings these teachers lectured to adults on subjects such as natural history and science. Maclure created a vocational school for eighty students, mostly boys, with the goal of teaching them a useful skill. In this part of Maclure's educational plan, called the School of Industry, according to Pitzer, he "introduced the trade school to the United States."[51]

In the *New Harmony Disseminator,* he wrote that "We will endeavor to prove that children can educate, clothe and feed themselves by their own labor when judiciously applied to produce articles of real value." They were taught such skills as printing, carpentry, farming, woodturning, blacksmithing, shoemaking, wheelwrighting, and other useful trades. Girls studied sewing, cooking, millinery, and other homemaking skills. Maclure then made arrangements to visit Mexico to recruit more students and left Fretageot in charge. He never returned to New Harmony. He stayed in Mexico until 1835, then he went back to Philadelphia where he died in 1841. Nevertheless, Bestor concluded, during these years "he continued to support generously the educational enterprise he had founded at New Harmony."[52]

Owen now entered the final act in what Bestor called the "tragicomedy at New Harmony." He called for another reorganization, his fifth. He wanted the agricultural and mechanics societies dissolved and a committee made up of himself, William, and three others to govern the New Harmony Community No. I. The community was to be subdivided by occupations, with each unit paying a designated fee "toward the general expenses of the town." Each unit would govern itself and determine how to distribute its goods. For the outlying communities, he wanted "to encourage such of the members as could not be usefully employed in the Town, to settle in some of these detached Communities according to their respective predilections." The village would supply such provisions as were necessary for them "to form societies of common property, equality, & *kindness.*"[53]

It was a pipe dream. "Not a single group went out from New Harmony as a community," Bestor wrote, "and Owen was in reality entering into arrangements with unknown persons at a distance who proposed to come as colonists." Even the editor of the *Gazette* lamented that New Harmony "is not a community" but a hub around which other colonies had formed. Paul Brown was furious. He predicted a "doomsday." Owen, he said, was delusional. These outlining colonies were phantoms, and "no trace of an inhabitant, let alone a community" could be seen out there.[54]

To make matters worse newspapers, beginning with the *Indianapolis Indiana Journal,* had started to reprint parts of Owen's July 4 oration that appeared in the *Gazette* on July 12, 1826. Entitled "A Declaration of Mental Independence," Owen cited three "monstrous evils that could be combined to inflict mental and physical evil." These were private property, the "absurd and irrational" systems of religion, and conventional marriage. The last evil was especially pernicious because it "obligates the contracting parties to do what they may not be able to perform and because it marks a disposition to enslave one-half of our fellow creatures." He described the kind of marriage he wanted as a "natural marriage" in which the husband and wife had an equal opportunity for education and to acquire "an accurate knowledge of themselves and of human nature," where only "intimate sympathy and unaffected congeniality, founded on a real knowledge of each other" existed. Such a union, Owen said, was impossible in the present society. The editor of the *Indiana Journal* commented: "If we are allowed to judge of the moral character of the New Harmony society, by the licentious principles of their founder and leader, it would be no breach of charity, to class them all with whores and whoremongers, nor to say that the whole group will constitute one great brothel."[55]

Without warning on Sunday, May 6, 1827, Owen delivered his "Farewell Address," and the *Gazette* printed it three days later. The reasons for his decision to abandon his utopia were by this time compelling. He had not only lost $200,000 in less than two years, he finally recognized that the colonists were not the compliant Scots workers he had known at New Lanark, and they would never commit themselves fully to his view of communal living. He observed that "too many opposing habits and feelings" had appeared in the village to permit "a community of common property and equality" to develop. He had been unable to get rid of the undesirable colonists because of "the expense of their removal." Part of the blame for New Harmony's difficulties he placed on Maclure. He said that if the "schools had been in operation upon the very superior plan upon which I had been led to expect they would be," perhaps they might "have succeeded in amalgamating the whole into a community." Owen then traced the history of New Harmony from the Preliminary Society to the spring of 1827. He admitted his lack of understanding of how to administer a model village and acknowledged that he had really operated on trial and error. Ever the undaunted optimist, he ended on a positive note. He described New Harmony as "greatly improved lately" and said that the fields had been "put into a good state of cultivation, and . . . [were] well fenced." There was "every appearance of abundance of fruit, all kinds of food and materials for clothing, and no want of industry to preserve the former and to manufacture the latter." He closed by announcing his intention to dispose of his holdings by selling lands to individuals at bargain prices or for rent by long-term leases.[56]

The next day, on May 7, Owen gave his valedictory. He asked his followers to express "honesty of purpose" and have "devotion to the success of each and all communities." He cautioned obedience to majority rule. He turned control over to his two sons and said he was leaving $3,000 to cover expenses. Many New Harmony residents stayed on and either purchased or leased property and worked as free-enterprise artisans and farmers. But New Harmony as an experiment in communal living was finished. Owen departed on June 1, 1827. He returned to England to continue the life of a reformer and philanthropist until his death in 1858.[57]

NEW HARMONY failed as a utopia because of the sheer diversity of its population. Members of the village had no prior experience with communal living and as a result, sociologist Rosabeth Moss Kanter believed, had "no basis for knowing whether they could live together in community, and no necessary commitment to a set of unifying ideals." Moreover, with Owen subsidizing the enterprise, "they did not even need to be committed to building a community." Owen conceded as much when, back in England, he allowed that the village had been a "premature" attempt "to unite a number of strangers not previously educated for that purpose, who should carry on extensive operations for their common interest, and live together as a common family." Brown, however, believed that Owen himself had added to the problem. He had permitted too much dancing and frivolity and done nothing about the constant "clamor, disaffections, and calumny." But Brown, too, thought that the residents were veritable strangers to each other despite all the meetings and various means of recreation.[58]

Some blame Owen's naïveté and the frivolousness of his attention to the community. Robert Dale Owen wrote a valedictory editorial in the *New-Harmony Gazette,* which his biographer called the "official explanation of the New Harmony experiment." Robert Dale felt that his father was guilty of an "inexcusable" lack of careful planning. He had failed to appreciate the antisocial circumstances of the community's quickly admitted inhabitants, and their "habits" were "too great an obstacle" for the community. Also, his father was slow to recognize that New Harmony could never be economically self-sufficient. Finally, his son reflected that New Harmony was corroded as a communal society because, in the United States at the time, wages were too high and land too cheap to allow a feeling of mutual cooperation to take root and flourish.[59]

CHAPTER THREE

Other Separatist Communities

Bethal, Zoar, Amana, Bishop Hill

The Owenite fiasco at New Harmony had no effect upon the Heartland's subsequent experiments in religious utopias. The Separatists of Bethel (1844), Zoar (1817), Amana (1854), and Bishop Hill (1846) continued virtually unchanged the Heartland's millenarian communitarianism. In fact, the German community at Bethel, Missouri, was a direct spin-off, if not a consequence, of Father Rapp's move back to Pennsylvania.

Bethel

During the seven years after Father Rapp relocated his flock from Indiana to a 3,186-acre site at Economy, Pennsylvania, the "city in which God would dwell" prospered. Here the patriarch led a flourishing community of seven hundred residents awaiting the Second Coming set for September 24, 1829. Rapp, then in his seventies, was described by visitor Duke Bernard of Saxe-Weimar as having "blue eyes overshadowed by heavy eyebrows . . . full of fire and life . . . who spoke with a Swabian dialect with some English mixed in." The duke left a bucolic account of daily activities. He portrayed young girls singing in the workshops and mills and decorating the machines each day with fresh flowers. He commented on the "neatness which universally reigns" among the town's residents and on their "order and discipline."[1]

Another visitor, the German economist Frederick List, noted how they steadily increased their wealth by the addition of winemaking, whiskey distilling, silk weaving, and the making of hats. He reported on their large warehouse filled with manufactured articles and stocked with food and clothing. He pictured in detail Father Rapp's forty-five-room home, called the Great House, a music hall, a schoolhouse, a museum, a post office, an apothecary, a brick church with a huge steeple, and eighty-two brick-and-frame homes. The community was proud of their eighteen-piece orchestra, which gave regular concerts. One of its outstanding musicians, Dr. Johann Christoff, composed most of its music and with the aid of an assistant, an Englishman named William Peters, expanded its repertoire to include operas and choral music. The years 1817–1832, Yaacov Oved observed, "were the most intensive and fruitful years for the orchestra."[2]

But the year 1832 saw signs of dissension and the beginning of William Keil's utopian experiment at Bethel, Missouri. Then, for the first time, members openly criticized Rapp's leadership, complaining that he was cheating the society. Celibacy became a controversial issue. Once Rapp had imposed celibacy as being necessary for the coming millennium, he banished all who would not obey the decision. However, in 1826, he himself began a sexual relationship with Hildegard Mutschler and after six years the affair had become an open secret. Some accused Rapp of hypocrisy. More disillusionment appeared when the day of the millennium, September 24, 1829, arrived and nothing happened. Rapp postponed the event until 1836.[3] Then, when a man claiming to be the Count de Leon joined the community along with fifty of his disciples, the problems escalated into a schism.

While living in Germany in the summer of 1829, the "count" sent Rapp a letter in which he claimed to be the "anointed of the Lord, the Lion of Judah," who had gathered a small sect to prepare for the millennium. He asked permission for them to join Economy and help prepare that community for the 1836 Second Coming. Rapp welcomed them enthusiastically. The count and his companions arrived in 1831 and were given rooms in the Great House. In reality, however, he was unfortunately not a nobleman but a religious mystic and entrepreneur named Bernhart Mueller. After only a few months in Economy he claimed that celibacy, the "crucifixion of the flesh" as he described it, would end with the millennium. By 1832 some residents wanted him to lead the community, not Rapp. The insurgency reached a climax in March 1832 when Rapp offered to pay the count $105,000 if he and his 176 dissidents would leave. The count accepted the bribe and purchased land on the Ohio River ten miles north of Economy to start his "New Philadelphia Society." Karl Arndt believed that this crisis was the turning point in Economy's history. Although it "officially endured for seventy-four years after the 1832 schism, the Count de Leon affair marked the beginning of the end."[4]

That spring the count moved his entourage to the New Philadelphia Society. With Rapp's money they built a village that was a replica of Economy. But Mueller was a poor leader. He even tried an unsuccessful raid on Economy to get tools and supplies. He filed frivolous lawsuits against Rapp to get more money. Finally, in 1834, the frustrated count left the society with some of his original followers and started a community at Grand Ecore in Natchitoches Parish, Louisiana, where he died in 1836. After this exodus some of the remaining residents of the New Philadelphia Society reorganized under William Keil and eventually relocated to Bethel, Missouri.[5]

Charles Nordhoff remembered Keil as "a short, burly man, with blue eyes, whitish hair, and white beard" who "seemed excitable and somewhat suspicious." He was a Prussian tailor, born in 1812, who came to New York City in 1838 and then moved to Pittsburgh with his family where he called himself Doctor Keil and practiced naturopathic medicine. Soon he gave up medicine and became a Methodist evangelist who preached about an impending millennium. He attracted a group from the New Philadelphia Society and converted immigrant Germans near Pittsburgh. He also ministered to the German Methodist Church at Stewardstown, urging the congregation to withdraw from the world and use the Bible as the sole guide to life.[6] "The plan to establish a colony developed gradually over the next few years," A. E. Schroeder wrote, "as Keil sent some of his young followers out to carry his message to surrounding states." Finally, in 1844 he decided to build, forty-five miles west of Hannibal, Missouri, a new utopia based on the concept of Christian equality and sharing. Keil and his followers moved to a twenty-six-hundred-acre site located adjacent to a wagon road that originated in Hannibal. As one of the original settlers, Jacob Miller, remembered: "We threw our farms, our savings and all into the treasury and had no promise save bread and water and peace with god." By the end of the summer of 1845 almost five hundred colonists were living there.[7]

Keil named it Bethel, meaning "the House of God." Without rules or regulations other than that members should obey his orders, it was "one of the most informally organized of the Utopian communities" established during the antebellum years. Keil never asked for a formal charter of incorporation from the state because he believed that living in the colony should be voluntary; so was attendance at church services held every Sunday where, as was the custom with all Separatist worship and later with the Hutterites, men and women sat on separate sides of the room. Keil owned all the land in his name. There were no accounting records kept and no money was ever exchanged inside the colony, although Keil did occasionally employ outside laborers and paid them wages.[8]

His two rules on admission were casual. He emphasized living a moral communal life based on unselfishness and the Golden Rule. He said that members should care for each other more than for themselves.

Anyone who agreed with these simple precepts was provided housing, food, clothing, and medical care. He even welcomed individuals with no religious beliefs, although such people seldom stayed for long. Every new member, however, was required to put all of their property and money into the common treasury. They could leave Bethel at any time. But, as stated in a contract signed by each person upon joining, if they left, they could not count on a "large requital, because the purpose of the Society is not to lay up treasures . . . [but] we shall find a way to deal with the brother, that we might abide in love." Keil allowed every resident to work at whatever tasks they thought were best "for the common good."[9] The Bethelites did not celebrate any of the traditional Christian rituals except for Easter, a "May Fest," and Christmas. Keil marked his birthday of March 6 with a festival of music and dancing and a banquet. He honored July 4 with food and festivities. The colony had a thirty-piece cornet band led by druggist Conrad Finck that gave concerts in the community and in surrounding towns.[10] Their living quarters were austere, without curtains, carpets, or stuffed furniture. Women wore calico every day of the week and a sun bonnet in the summer. Men wore nondescript ready-made clothing. Keil, in his sermons, stressed the contrast between Bethel and the outside world of distortion and corruption.

Bethel, although starting with subsistence farming, soon developed profitable industries such as a sawmill, a gristmill, a tannery, and a sewing shop. Some men were skilled cordwainers who crafted deerskin leather gloves. Others manufactured farm wagons and sold them to the thousands of Americans coming through the community headed for Kansas City and the Oregon Trail. Their most flourishing industry was the distillation of corn and rye whiskey for markets in Hannibal and Quincy, Illinois. Keil lived in a three-story mansion located on a hilltop a half-mile east of the village. He named it Elim after the biblical oasis that was a camping spot for the Israelites fleeing Egypt for the Promised Land. Its third floor was his office, where he resumed his medical practice and looked after the health of Bethel residents. Its second floor was a thirty-six-by-sixty-foot room that served as the community banquet hall, dance floor, and meeting room. Keil, his wife, and their nine children lived on the ground floor. The basement stored thirty barrels of wine. Another imposing structure was "Das gross Haus" (The Great House) on the corner of First and Main streets. This multipurpose building was the colony storeroom, a hotel for visitors, and a dormitory for unmarried men. Within ten years Bethel boasted a community of 650 orderly and prosperous Germans with assets estimated at $200,000 and landholdings of over four thousand acres.[11]

However, Keil, like Rapp at New Harmony thirty years earlier, became restless. He fretted that if the community wished to remain separate from the outside world it must leave the increasingly settled part of Missouri. He knew that the completion in 1852 of the Hannibal & St. Joseph Railroad, which crossed the state just thirteen miles south of Bethel, would bring a large American population to the area. "And who knew what temptations or corrupting influences might seduce the simple Bethelites," Snyder observed. Keil complained in a letter written in October 1855 that their children now had too many outside contacts and were growing up "in a blasphemous and unspiritual life."[12]

These circumstances prompted Keil to send a nine-man scouting party to Oregon to find a place to relocate his utopia. They located a thirty-two-acre tract for sale near the mouth of the Willapa River, close to the present-day town of Raymond. Keil decided to purchase the land. But just before 150 Bethel pioneers were ready to leave for Oregon in the summer of 1855, Keil's oldest son, eighteen-year-old Willie, died of malaria. Prior to his death he begged his father not to leave him behind. Keil placed the corpse in a tin-lined coffin filled with alcohol and loaded it onto the colony ambulance, which was converted into a hearse. So began the five-month trek to the Pacific where, in November, Keil buried Willie in the forest.[13]

He named the colony Aurora, after one of his daughters. Eventually, 252 colonists (about half of Bethel) migrated there, most by wagon, but some by ship around South America. Keil left thirty-seven-year-old Andrew Giesy Jr. in charge in Missouri. By 1872, with the arrival of new immigrants from Swabia, Bavaria, and other parts of Germany, Aurora had over one thousand communards, and Keil owned twenty-three thousand acres of land. Men worked at various crafts, just as at Bethel, and the women made cloth, candles, and straw baskets. As before, all products were placed in a communal storehouse either to sell to outsiders or to serve as a stockpile from which members could take whatever they needed. As before, there was no money, and life was simple and pleasant. But in 1877, when Keil died, the trustees of both Aurora and Bethel agreed to dissolve the societies. In June 1879 they decided to sell the assets of both communities, valued at $109,000. The sale was finalized by 1883, and Aurora (then with about 250 inhabitants) and Bethel (with 100 citizens) continued on as incorporated villages.[14]

Zoar

From the same part of southern Germany that provided most of the colonists for Rapp's settlements in Indiana and Pennsylvania, religious dissent and political oppression in Württemberg caused another exodus of Separatists to America to build their communal utopia at Zoar, Ohio. In the summer of 1817 three hundred men, women, and children from that principality, joined by some from Baden and Bavaria, crossed the Atlantic under the spiritual leadership of Joseph Bimeler (Bäumeler), a charismatic crippled hunchback with a protruding eye. He had initially gathered his people together in a refuge along the southern border of Württemberg, in order to avoid arrest for their pacifism and their refusal to pay taxes and to send their children to Lutheran schools. Their religious beliefs outraged the Lutheran clergy. These Separatists, like the Rappites, condemned all church ceremonies and denounced all the sacraments, especially baptism. They were chiliasts and predicted that the Second Coming of Christ would occur in 1836. They accepted marriage, though they believed that sexual abstinence provided a better spiritual life. When the authorities pursued them, they petitioned the royal minister to relocate to Brandenburg. He denied the petition. They then asked for permission to leave the country and the government accepted this request.[15]

Since most of the families were poor, only a handful of them had money to pay for ship passage, but those with funds placed them in a communal pool to finance the group's expenses. Even so, by the time they reached Antwerp, the port of embarkation, they still were unable to purchase tickets for everyone. Fortunately, at this point some English Quakers and members of the Society of Friends in Philadelphia agreed to pay for the cost of the crossing, roughly $18 per person.[16] They were billeted in the steerage with livestock and suffered dysentery and other illnesses, but they finally arrived in Philadelphia in August 1817.

The Quakers arranged temporary housing for them while they searched for a place to live. The English Quakers had sent money to help them finance their relocation, and a Committee of Fifteen led by John James would provide them with whatever they needed.[17] Bimeler tried to find land in Pennsylvania but the price per acre was too high. Then one of the Philadelphia Quakers, Thomas Rotch, helped them find land in Tuscarawas County, Ohio, near Canton, for $3 an acre. Through a merchant and land agent called Godfrey Gaga, Bimeler made the purchase. With a loan of $5,000 from the Quakers, he acquired fifty-five hundred acres for a total of $16,500. In the early fall of 1817, accompanied by a few men, he inspected the site and built a few log cabins.

In November 1817 the first contingent of Separatists left Philadelphia and traveled by wagon over the National Road across Pennsylvania to central Ohio. Bimeler named the place Zoar after the biblical town to which Lot had fled after the destruction of Sodom. They started to construct more homes and awaited the arrival of the rest of the immigrants. Meanwhile, in Philadelphia, the Separatists worked as day laborers or house servants. Some Quakers criticized Bimeler for moving so quickly to Ohio and told the Committee of Five that Bimeler had too much control over his followers. As a result the committee decided not to give him the promised money but to divide it up equally between all the adult members of the community. Even so, some Zoarites began to worry that Bimeler's holding the Ohio land in his name as a trust meant they would lose the land if he died. So Bimeler agreed to sign a testament giving the land to the community if the Quakers would pay for a gristmill and a sawmill.[18]

Most Zoarites, however, ignored such carping and prepared for the relocation. One of them, Hanna Fisher, said that "they are determined to see for themselves" the "land of Promise." By the spring of 1818 membership had declined to 53 men, 104 women, and 68 children. One of the first actions Bimeler took at Zoar was to install communalism because he recognized that because of the advanced age or sickness of some of the men they "could not earn enough money to support their families" by working as fieldhands on nearby farms. In addition, if some of them were working as laborers on farms dispersed throughout the area they were unable to worship together. Accordingly, in April 1819, they signed a communal agreement called the Articles of Association.[19]

This document named Johannes Breymaier, Joseph Georg Ackerman, and August Huber the first directors or "trustees." Bimeler was the general manager and signed all business and legal agreements. In 1824 they revised the articles to expand his authority and named him the community arbitrator. The 1819 document gave the directors control of the children but prohibited them from assigning any of them to outsiders as apprentices without the consent of a majority of the community. New members were admitted by approval of the directors and a two-thirds approval of the society. All property was under the control of the directors. Women had the suffrage. Zoarites adopted celibacy as the best way to limit growth and keep down expenses under their dire economic circumstances. Consequently, "at Zoar, unlike at the Harmonist colonies and Bethel/Aurora, communalism and celibacy were practical, not religious, matters."[20] Ten years later, when the community stabilized economically and began to prosper, its members abandoned celibacy without much discussion. Nevertheless, if one found a mate outside the colony, then he or she had to leave.

In 1833 the state legislature incorporated the village as a "body politic" called the Separatist Society of Zoar. The village held all property in common and conducted business as a corporation under Ohio law.[21] The village's incorporation prompted the Zoarites to revise its 1819 Articles of Association. Members were now divided into novitiates and full associates. Those in the first category served a one-year probation during which time they kept their personal property. When, upon approval of a majority of the community, they were admitted as full associates, they had to turn over all their property to the community. All children of the full associates could automatically become full members at the age of eighteen for females and twenty-one for males. Nordhoff found that "about half of their young people, who have grown up in the society, become permanent members . . . and as many young men as girls."[22]

The governmental structure was changed to have one of the three directors elected annually and their responsibilities were specified in detail. They controlled the property, decided work assignments, and provided each member with lodging, clothing, and food. Bimeler continued as general manager. The directors ran the colony school and appointed its male and female teachers, called "overseers." The directors determined a curriculum that included "scientific branches of knowledge but also gradually training them to performing the diverse branches of manual labor." The communards pledged to "bind ourselves to obey all the commands and orders of the trustees and subordinates, with the utmost zeal and diligence, without opposition or grumbling; and to devote all our strength, good will, diligence, and skill, during our whole lives, to the common service of the Society and for the satisfaction of the trustees."[23]

In Sunday services they sang hymns and listened to Bimeler's "discourses." These were unwritten sermons, which he claimed were inspired by the Holy Ghost. Young men of the community, the first being Johannes Neff, transcribed these sermons from memory, and this record made it possible in 1853 for them to publish *The Discourses.* The book was essentially a summary of Zoar's beliefs. Bimeler admonished his flock to avoid all established religions and to condemn sacraments like baptism and communion as "useless and injurious," to maintain an inner morality and prepare for the millennium by subordinating themselves to God. He said that "all intercourse of the sexes, except what is necessary to the perpetuation of the species, we hold to be sinful and contrary to the order and command of God. . . . Complete virginity or entire cessation of sexual commerce," he said, "is more commendable than marriage." Zoarites must never take oaths or send their children "into the schools of Babylon." The adult men "can not serve the state as soldiers, because a Christian can not murder his enemy, much less his friend." Like the Quakers, Zoarites should never show deference to any human, only to God.[24]

Zoarites lived in brick homes that usually housed eight families. At seven o'clock in the morning they had breakfast in a single kitchen, went to work, and returned there for lunch at noon and dinner at six in the evening. There was no communal dining hall. To obtain food supplies, each home had a representative go daily to the communal storehouse, dairy, and bakery to get supplies in their "distribution rooms," where they presented the clerk their house number. Children stayed with their parents until they were three and then lived in communal houses, one for boys, another for girls, under the care and direction of an adult—a practice that continued until 1845. That year the seventy children started to live in the multifamily homes of their parents. Until they were fifteen years of age they attended classes in a two-story brick schoolhouse that was a part of the county school system. The curriculum included reading, writing, mathematics, German, and English, but no manual training. Their parents had the duty of teaching the boys a trade and the girls household skills.[25]

In 1833 good luck helped bring economic prosperity. The state of Ohio hired colony men to help construct the Ohio-Erie Canal, a portion of which bisected the colony, with a contract of $20,000. This money enabled them to liquidate their mortgage and to start several industries—a foundry, a water-powered milling factory, a stove factory, a dye house, a distillery and cider press, and a tannery. They built two blast furnaces where they made pig iron and castings. A large general store stood at the center of the town and across from it a hotel that housed eighty guests, usually canal passengers who, by 1835, were stopping off to visit as tourists.[26]

By the time the canal was completed, Zoar had become a largely self-sufficient community. It produced all of its food except for coffee, tea, and rice. William Alfred Hinds in his *American Communities,* published in 1878, described "immense fields of corn, wheat, oats, and other crops." They raised over a thousand sheep and seventy-seven cattle. Hinds wrote about a community formal garden, similar to the Rappites' one at New Harmony, with a center "surrounded by a thrifty well kept cedar hedge; from which radiate twelve triangular beds, in which one may notice the familiar petunias, balsams, verbenas, amaranths, dahlias, geraniums, etc." Zoar manufactured all its clothing except for some dresses and men's hats. Craftsmen made all the furniture in the cabinet shop. The tin shop turned out their kitchen utensils. The blacksmiths made their farm machinery. They crafted their own ceramics and pottery. By 1838 Zoar had over five hundred residents, owned twelve thousand acres, and had an estimated wealth of $2 million.[27]

Nordhoff, however, was condescending about their bland cultural life. He thought them simple German peasants who were "unintellectual" and whose leaders were unconcerned with the beauty and comfort of "a higher life." He ridiculed the town's lack of foot pavements and "regularity of design." Houses were shabby and "for the most part in need of paint." He complained that "there is about the place a general air of neglect and lack of order, shabbiness . . . which shocks one who has but lately visited the Shakers and the Rappists." Zoar had no library and forbade the reading of fiction, newspapers, and periodicals. Still, Nordhoff wrote, "considering the dull and lethargic appearance of the people, I was struck with surprise that they have been able to manage successfully complicated machinery, and to carry on several branches of manufacture profitably." What he failed to appreciate was that Zoar's thirty-man brass band, similar to the one at Bethel, gave regular concerts of secular and religious music both within the community and in nearby towns. And Peter Bimeler, the grandson of the founder, had a pipe organ installed in the flour mill where he worked as a supervisor.[28]

Joseph Bimeler died in 1853, and his position was taken by Jacob Sylman, later by Christian Weebel and Jacob Ackerman. Unfortunately, just as in the case of Economy and Bethel/Aurora, the successors could not replace the charismatic founder. Community cohesion began to weaken as young people left the colony. Some of those who remained—such as Levi Bimeler, another of Joseph's grandsons—turned on their parents and made fun of their religion. Levi also condemned their communalism as "a good thing in the interior of Africa, but in the center of the highly civilized state of Ohio it is an outrage."[29] The Civil War further divided the society. Some, being pacifists, denounced the conflict; some young men, because of their passionate opposition to slavery, enlisted in the Union Army.

The Industrial Revolution changed the nation's economy, and Zoarites could not compete with the cheaper factory-made articles. They shut down the dye house, woolen factory, stove foundry, and shoe shop. In 1884 a railroad station opened in Zoar and made the place a tourist haven. "Each week, hundreds of visitors arrived from Akron, Canton, and Cleveland," Catherine Rokicky observed. They expanded the hotel to accommodate these visitors, many of whom stayed for weeks during the summer. Alexander Gunn, a Cleveland businessman and agnostic who moved to Zoar to live, wrote: "The hotel is crowded today with cheap merry-makers, who come in buggies with their girls and have dinner, roam about the village, and drive home in the evening."[30] Artists from Cleveland made Zoar their summer home.

In March 1898 the 222 remaining members of the Society of Separatists of Zoar voted to dissolve the community. By that time most of them had renounced communalism and accepted individual ownership of property and private enterprise. They elected three commissioners to supervise the process. They gave each adult $200 in cash and a share of the property worth $2,000. Some property they set aside as a cemetery, town hall, and meetinghouse. Individuals could keep private belongings such as clothes and furniture. The families that remained continued to live in their multifamily homes. Most residents sold their inheritance and left. The Society of Separatists of Zoar ceased to exist on December 4, 1900, and Zoar became just another incorporated village. Today the Ohio Historical Society operates the Historic Zoar Village and its extensive restoration program.[31]

Amana

Amana, a cluster of seven small villages located along the Iowa River, was the last Heartland utopia built by German Separatists. In 1714 Eberhard Ludwig Gruber and Johann Friedrich Rock, in the town of Himbach, founded the Community of True Inspiration. They believed that God revealed his word through a *Werkzeuge* or an inspired overseer. Both men claimed that they were such instruments, although Rock felt he had closer contact with the Divinity. Gruber was the theoretician who developed rules of daily life and worship. Rock traveled "wherever and whenever the Spirit of the Lord moved him, proselytizing and holding together the scattered congregations of the faithful." By the time of Rock's death in 1749, they had preached their revelations throughout Germany, Austria, Switzerland, and eastern France.[32]

Their message was similar in many ways to that of the other Separatists. They condemned the Lutheran Church as corrupted by useless rituals and excessive financial support through taxation. Only God's word as revealed by a Werkzeuge and the Bible should be followed. As the number of True Inspirationists grew, they were harassed by the authorities. They were arrested, flogged, and had their property confiscated.[33] Under such pressure in the last half of the eighteenth century their numbers began to decline.

The Community of True Inspiration did not revive until 1817 when Michael Krausert, a tailor from Strasbourg, converted to their beliefs. Although he was not immediately accepted as a Werkzeuge, he exhorted a recommitment to Inspiration and the literal interpretation of the Bible. A year later he was joined by Barbara Heinemann, the illiterate daughter of an innkeeper in the Alsatian town of Sulz, after Krausert told her she would soon have the gift of inspiration. In 1823 she married a schoolteacher named George Landmann.[34]

At that time Christian Metz became the leader of the Inspirationists. This twenty-seven-year-old carpenter who lived at Ronneburg Castle near Buedingen, in Hesse, had already gone on a mission in Alsace and Switzerland and "proved to have exceptional leadership abilities and emerged as the central figure of nineteenth-century Inspirationism."[35] In 1833, working with Barbara Landmann, Metz leased several estates near Ronneburg and started to gather together his scattered Inspirationists. When these followers (mostly artisans and merchants) moved there, they continued in their trades and businesses or found jobs on nearby farms. They worshiped as a religious sect but did not form a communal society.

For a decade the magistrates badgered these Separatists because they would not pay taxes, would not send their children to public schools, and refused to take oaths in court. When the rents for their property were increased, Metz urged emigration to the United States. His followers agreed with him. This decision changed the history of the Community of True Inspiration because it compelled its members to adopt communalism. Until then they had lived as families in small congregations on the Hessian estates. But now, immigration to America imposed new conditions. "Since they spoke only German, they felt tied together for practical purposes in order to make a living in an English-speaking land." In addition, their persecution by the authorities, "coupled with the sense of mission that accompanied the prospect of immigration to America, created in the

Inspirationists a high level of religious enthusiasm." So, these Separatists, whose numbers Nordhoff estimated to be about 560 individuals, pooled their assets. Some of them were wealthy and donated large amounts of money to the common treasury. Nordhoff reported that "one person gave between fifty and sixty thousand dollars; and others gave sums of from two to twenty thousand dollars."[36]

In September 1842, Metz and four men departed for America where, at Buffalo, New York, they purchased four thousand acres for $10 an acre. They named the place "Eben Ezer," after the first book of Samuel, which means "Hitherto hath the Lord helped us." During the following year about seven hundred men, women, and children emigrated to Ebenezer. Metz divided it into four villages: Middle, Upper, Lower, and New. He felt that the building of Ebenezer required communalism, and when a minority wanted to retain private property he said that a divine curse would afflict them. They recanted. In January 1846 Metz proposed a constitution that created a community sharing all assets and governed by sixteen trustees. These officers provided housing, food, health care, and a small allowance to purchase personal items at a village store. Everyone worked without pay. Families owned their furniture and household property.

Andelson believes that communalism "permitted the Inspirationists to embark on a rapid and impressive program of building and economic development at Ebenezer."[37] They reaped large profits from selling farm produce and woolen goods to the Americans in the growing cities of Buffalo and New York City. In addition, the colony had a calico print mill, three sawmills, two gristmills, and an oil mill. Among its adult males were carpenters, masons, blacksmiths, saddlers, locksmiths, soapmakers, watchmakers, shoemakers, tanners, coopers, wagonmakers, butchers, bakers, and basketmakers.

Although life in Ebenezer was comfortable, Metz became concerned when Buffalo's municipal boundaries expanded to the edge of the community. In 1854 he sent two men to Kansas to see if new land could be found. Unfortunately, this was during the bloody Kansas civil war over the expansion of slavery, and they concluded it was too dangerous to move there. He then dispatched another advanced guard to Iowa, and they found twenty-six thousand acres for sale in land traversed by the Iowa River. Metz christened the place "Amana," taken from the vista from the Song of Solomon: "Come with me from Lebanon, my spouse . . . look from the top of Amana." Within a decade, over thirteen hundred Separatists, including new arrivals from Germany, were living in the community, and it had been given a charter from the state incorporating it as a religious communal association.

Metz—and Barbara Landmann, who succeeded Metz when he died in 1861—replicated Ebenezer's village structure. They created seven villages about one and a half miles from one another. Main Amana was the largest, followed by East Amana, Middle Amana, High Amana, West Amana, South Amana, and Homestead. Each village had residential buildings that contained four family apartments. They had several communal kitchen/ dining buildings, a general store, a school, a meat market, a bakery, and barns. Amana's economy was a combination of manufacturing and agriculture. The colony had five flour mills, two woolen mills, and a sawmill, all run by water from a seven-mile canal from the Iowa River, as well as a calico textile print shop and a tannery. Homestead had a railroad station. Amana's agriculture was also diverse. For their own consumption and for sale outside the colony, they grew onions, potatoes, celery, hay, barley, wheat flour, and corn meal. They raised cattle, sheep, hogs, and poultry.[38]

Nordhoff visited Amana in 1874 and described a vibrant and prosperous community of 1,480 people living in well-built houses of brick, stone, or wood. The houses were "very plain," he wrote, "each with a sufficient garden, but mostly standing immediately on the street. . . . They use no paint, believing that the wood lasts as well without." A bell summoned everyone to a kitchen/dining building (Main Amana had fifteen of these for its 450 residents). One Inspirationist told Nordhoff that they segregate men from women at meals to "prevent silly conversation and trifling conduct." They also divided the children by sex in the village school where, from age six to thirteen, they attended class from seven o'clock until eleven thirty in the morning. Then, after lunch at eleven, they returned to school until three o'clock. Subjects included musical notation, crafts, arithmetic, English, and writing. At the age of fourteen boys went to the factories or farms, and the girls sewed or worked in the kitchen or the gardens. The adults frowned on high school education or college degrees. A man haughtily told Nordhoff: "Why should we let our youth study? We need no lawyers or preachers . . . . What they need is to live holy lives, to learn God's commandments out of the Bible, to learn submission to his will, and to love him." Out of necessity, however, they sent some young men to college to be trained as physicians, pharmacists, and dentists. Amana had no libraries and allowed only a few newspapers to be sold in the colony. Eleven times a week they attended church services where men and women entered from opposite doors and sat apart from each other on benches. Children sat in the rear of the building. However, Amana was not a closed society. Anyone could leave if they wished because, as Metz stated, "A doorway to the world is always open for those who do not wish to obey."[39]

When Barbara Landmann died in 1883, Amana reorganized. The Thirteen Trustees chose a president and together they ran the colony. Women did not vote or hold office. Each village elected a foreman who organized and supervised the work and gave an annual report to the trustees. Adult men received an annual stipend of between $40 and $100 according to need. Women were given only $25 to $30, according to need, and children from

$5 to $10. Each family pooled these funds, and the head of the household purchased what was needed in the village store.

Amana was a patriarchal community. One of its maxims was the command "Fly from the society of women-kind as much as possible, as a very highly dangerous magnet and magical fire." As for dancing, "at the best there is sin." Women wore no jewelry, kept their hair tied back and concealed with a black hat and "sad-colored little shawl." They wore "dingy colored stuffs, mostly of the society's own make, cut in the plainest style, and often short gowns, in the German peasant way." The community discouraged teenagers from having contact between the sexes and tried "to hide the charms of the young women, to make them, as far as dress can do so, look old and ugly, and to keep the young men away from them." On Sunday afternoons they allowed teenagers to take leisurely walks in the fields, but boys and girls walked in different directions. Men could not marry until they reached the age of twenty-four, and when they did, the couple was considered to be "less spiritually minded" and were punished by placing them "down into the lowest, or the 'children's order,' for a year or two, until they had won their slow way back by deepening piety." Apparently, most young people accepted these rules and practices because, in contrast to the Zoarites, they were content to remain in Amana's cocoon of security, regularity, and peacefulness.[40] As evidence of this conformity, data show that Amana's population declined only slightly over the years— from 1,813 in 1880, to 1,722 a decade later, to 1,770 in 1905. Only in the twentieth century did it begin to fall off, reaching a low point of 1,365 at the time of the community's dissolution in 1932.[41]

This is not to say that within Amana there were no strains or discontent, but most of them were minor. For example, a family might stop eating in the village kitchen and have meals together in their apartment. Some young men wanted to be allowed to play baseball or cards. Individuals began to acquire a taste for possessions such as bicycles, musical instruments, brighter women's dresses—some of which were housed in village stores to be sold to visitors. But the trustees issued orders not to be tempted by such "worldly" things. Jealousy arose over what some saw as partiality within an egalitarian society. For example, the physicians were allowed to have automobiles, and business managers had larger allowances than farmhands because of their "need" to dress like outsiders. "One young man, directed by the council to attend pharmacy school, left the society when the elders denied his request to go on for a medical education."[42]

As time passed, the community's isolation began to fade. By 1900 most Amanites spoke English, and the young people had become exposed to American culture. Men began to wear the same clothes as midwestern farmers. Women wore conventional American blouses and skirts and abandoned the earlier covered hairstyle. By the 1920s unmarried men had cars with radios. And without a successor to Barbara Landmann, the religious zeal of the first generations began to wane. However, such changes did not threaten Amana's existence as a communal society. It was the Great Depression of the 1930s that caused its dissolution.

Even before the stock market crash of 1929 and the ensuing collapse of the American economy, Amana found itself in trouble. When dye from Germany was cut off during World War I, Amana's profitable calico print works shut down. Declining farm prices throughout the country in the 1920s hurt its most important income. Its woolen mills suffered a cutback in production. At the same time expenses increased. Wages for the hired hands, who were essential to run the farms, rose. When a fire gutted their mills they had no insurance to repair the damage.[43]

The Great Depression ravaged Amana's economy and forced the community into bankruptcy. By 1931 its debts were over $500,000. To meet this crisis the trustees appointed a committee to evaluate the situation. In May 1931 the committee distributed a questionnaire to the 917 adult community members. They were to vote on two choices. They could "go back to the old lifestyle of denial wholly and completely," or they could end religious communalism and reorganize as a joint stock company, with guaranteed salaried work for all adult Amanites, and continue as a noncommunal religious society. In all, 75 percent voted to accept the second option and go through the "Great Change." By May 1932 the trustees had divided Amana's $2 million assets into stock shares with each share valued at $50. This formula provided 1,200 nonnegotiable shares to every adult. Trustees divided another parcel of shares to buy homes and livestock "according to different criteria and the majority [32,400 shares] were distributed according to seniority." From that point in time, Amana has existed as two entities. The Amana Society is a joint stock corporation that operates a business for profit. The Amana Church Society retains the old ways of religious service and the burying of the dead in uniform gravestone plots in Amana cemeteries.[44]

Bishop Hill

In the spring of 1846, four years after Metz and the future Amanites left Germany for Buffalo and eventually Iowa, Eric Jansson and his band of Swedish refugees embarked for the United States from the port of Galfa, Norway. Over the following two years these peasants of Uppland and Hälsingland emigrated, traveling via New York City and the Erie Canal and then by steamer to Chicago. Finally, on foot, they arrived at their Illinois site in July. Although an estimated one thousand persons left Sweden at the time, because of disease among the aged and the children and the fact that they could not speak English, only four hundred of them finally made it to the Heartland prairie.[45]

Jansson, described by Nordhoff as "a man of some energy," was sketched by Alice Felt Tyler as a person "of middle height, pale with sunken cheeks, long prominent teeth, and a scarred forehead, hypnotic blue eyes, and twitching facial muscles." After his conversion following a fall from a horse in 1830, when he heard God's message, this twenty-two-year-old radical castigated the Lutheran clergy as "pillars of hell" and "arch purveyors of the devil." Jansson became one of the "readers" of Bible study groups in the northern agricultural provinces of Sweden who, like the German Separatists, wanted to purge the Lutheran Church of its overemphasis on ritual, its worldly aspects, and its links to government. Unlike in Germany, however, some Lutheran clergy "welcomed the readers movement as a means of purifying the church from within, and there was little reason at first to view it as a separatists movement."[46]

But Jansson had radical ideas that got him and his followers into trouble. He preached "perfectionism," or the belief that once saved a person could live a life free of sin. He stated that those who were saved could never sin because "He who is born of God cannot sin, and he who sins is of the devil." He thought himself the vicar of Christ who would rule over his followers during the millennium and establish the kingdom of God on earth. His flock agreed with him. One woman said that "Eric Jansson is as good as God." In 1844 his followers burned Lutheran books in a number of "glorious jubilees." They refused to attend church. They went on hymn-singing marches through the towns of Alta and Forsa and prayed aloud in front of clergymen's homes for the salvation of the occupants.[47]

After the police arrested Jansson twice in 1845 and confiscated the property of some of his followers, Jansson sent a friend, Olof Olsson, to America to find a refuge. Olsson met with a Swedish Methodist minister in Victoria, Illinois, and through him purchased land twelve miles north of the town. Since some of the Janssonists were too poor to pay for passage to America, they pooled all their assets in a communal treasury. "Thus from scriptural example and circumstance the principles of communism were adopted by the Janssonists to be continued during the entire existence of the colony."[48]

The winter of 1845–1846 was horrific at Bishop Hill (named after Jansson's birthplace in Biskopskulla in Uppland province). They had no time to build cabins and had to live in dugouts cut into the sides of a ravine that bisected the site. They arrived too late to plant crops and there was no local source to buy provisions. Almost every morning they buried their dead without proper religious services. By spring over one-third of the colonists had perished, including Jansson's wife and two of his children.[49] When warmer weather arrived, the survivors went to work with stupendous energy. A visitor who arrived in June 1847, Anders Larsson, reported that the Janssonists had constructed a flour mill, two sawmills, a brickworks, a tannery, a roofing-shake facility, and workshops. With planting still going on, they had "over 400 acres in wheat, 700 acres in corn, 3 to 400 in barley and oats, and many hundreds of acres in potatoes."[50] They were also actively involved in surveying the future town, which was to have eighteen houses, all the same size, on each side of a town square, as well as an orchard and a large church.

Jansson governed the community along with twelve appointed "apostles," and one of his first priorities was to educate the children in the English language. His next major decision was to impose temporary celibacy in order to keep the population small enough to get by on the short food supply. For three years, while the order was in force, only three children were born in the colony. In 1849 when the food crisis passed, he reversed himself and reinstated marriage, pairing off couples "regardless of personal likes or dislikes" and marrying them in group ceremonies. When the U.S. census marshals visited the community in 1850 they recorded 406 residents. But by that time new emigrants from Sweden, "encouraged if not misled by letters of the colonists sent to friends and relatives," started to arrive. The Illinois state census of 1855 showed that the population had doubled.[51]

Bishop Hill's most important income came from selling linen, carpets woven from flax, and broomcorn. They bought several hundred head of Durham cattle, well-bred to graze on prairie pastures, from the Pleasant Hill, Kentucky, Shakers. A labor force of men and women organized in teams planted the crops. Olof Olsson Krans depicted this communal agriculture in his oil paintings such as "Sowing the Seed" and "Women in a Row," which today can be seen in the Bishop Hill Museum. The same process of planting was described in 1936 by Minnie C. Norlin, in a biography of her mother who was a member of the colony. Norlin told of women taking up positions at the end of twenty-four rows of markers held at the other end by men. Each woman "had folded up one corner of her apron and tied it securely, making a little bag. This held the seed corn. With a hoe, in rhythmic time she made a hole and dropped in the seed. The marker was then moved ahead for the next hole and thus this human check-row planter moved steadily on."[52] Fifty young men and the same number of horses and plows worked the cornfield. Groups of between thirty and forty men drove the oxen and milked the cows.

With money from these communal efforts, within eight years they constructed a ninety-six-room dormitory named Big Brick, a hotel, a wheelwright's shop, a bakery, a blacksmith's shop, a meat house, a brewery, and the Steeple Building, which served as an apartment house and an administrative headquarters. A German visitor, Baron Axel Adelsward, wrote: "They seem to live contended and happy. . . . They are capable and hard-working, and to join together, as they have done, is a sure way to amass wealth in America, although it seems to me they can have precious little joy for their riches." Jon Wagner has written: "Thus in 1850, Bishop Hill had taken its place alongside such thriving communal groups as Amana, the Shakers, Oneida, Zoar, and the Harmony Society, and it might have seemed that it, too, was destined for many decades of communal prosperity."[53]

This optimistic picture changed abruptly, however, with Jansson's murder on May 13, 1850. The previous year an American named John Root had married Jansson's cousin, and for a while the couple lived in the community, though Root never did become a member. He soon chafed at its regimented life and left, with his bride. Jansson pursued the couple with a posse and forced the woman to return to the colony. Root then formed his own posse and threatened to set fire to the buildings unless his wife was returned, but when Jansson refused to surrender her, Root never carried out his threat. In May, for different reasons, the two men happened to be in court at the Henry County seat in the town of Cambridge. During a recess, Root went outside the building and, seeing Jansson seated at a table through an open window, shot and killed him. Jansson had predicted, years before, that he would rise from the dead, like Christ. So his followers placed his corpse on the altar of their church and kept a three-day vigil expecting the miracle to occur. When nothing happened they buried him in the colony cemetery.[54]

The Janssonists chose a former "reader" in Sweden, Jonas Olsson, as their new spiritual leader, and Olof Johnson to be in charge of business matters. The two men, along with four trustees, continued what Wagner termed "administrative communalism" for the next eight years. In accordance with a revision of their charter made in 1854, all land and property was held in common. Individuals who left Bishop Hill would be reimbursed for work they had performed while living there. These were years of prosperity. The community's landholdings increased to over 11,500 acres, altogether valued at $400,000. Its population increased to over seven hundred. The colonists completed construction of a schoolhouse, twenty-two barns, and outbuildings that included ice houses, a sorghum house, a gold shop, and the Red House. They erected a picket fence around an oak-grove central park and placed a gazebo in the middle of it. The Janssonist settlement of Krusbo, located at the eastern end of the colony, became the center of their pasture complex and the manufacturing of cheese. And at Victoria and Centerville, about fifteen miles away, they operated coal mines. Letters sent to relatives in Sweden were replete with glowing accounts of satisfied communards. One wrote that they "live in splendidness [sic] without any worldly cares." Another commented that "I work with many dear brothers, and one encourages the other with God's words." Still a third colonist remarked that "all people are friendly and religious [and] like to carry our burdens for us."[55]

Beginning in about 1859 things began to change, however. One controversial issue to emerge was that of celibacy. That year some Janssonists returned from living with the Shakers at Pleasant Hill and proposed that marriage be abolished. They wanted the Janssonists to live like the United Society of Believers in Christ's Second Appearing. Although the historical evidence is sketchy, most likely celibacy "was strongly endorsed but not formally required by Olsson and some other leaders, and . . . this provided a focal issue—and a nice bit of scandal—for dissenters, who were inclined to exaggerate its importance." The Panic of 1857 seriously weakened the market for the colony's products and made it difficult for them to pay their existing debts. Then the colonists found out that, for the past five years, Olsson and Johnson had secretly spent $98,000 speculating in railroad and bank stock, most of which was by then worthless. A spiritual problem arose. Unlike the German Separatists, the Swedes "increasingly immersed themselves in material pursuits to the apparent detriment of religious concerns." The character of Bishop Hill had changed from the original gathering of poor, pious peasants to a community of prosperous businessmen. And as one visitor remarked, "they now pay less attention to religion and more to industry." Finally, it seems that the Janssonists by 1860 had become Americanized. Again, in contrast to the German Separatist utopias where the German language and culture were kept intact, the Bishop Hill colonists quickly abandoned their native language in order to learn English. They purchased household furnishings in American stores in Galva and Victoria. They wore American clothes. Furthermore, the conditions that gave rise to their communalism in Sweden just were not present in America. Or, as Wagner put it, "they had scarcely formed themselves as a society before they found themselves in new circumstances to which the Janssonist religious protest was far less relevant." In 1860 the adult males voted to dissolve the community.[56]

During the next two years, they inventoried colony property, real estate they owned in Galva, and the Galva and Victoria coal mines. They listed their total assets as valued at $846,278. By 1863 only two hundred Janssonists lived at Bishop Hill. When Nordhoff came there in 1870, he wrote that it was "slowly falling into decay." He was surprised that its residents were so reticent about their communal past. During the last half of the twentieth century, however, much of Bishop Hill has been reconstructed by the Bishop Hill Heritage Association and the Old Settlers Association, with money given these organizations by the state of Illinois and private benefactors.[57]

IN CONCLUSION, these four Separatist communities represent a continuation of the religious utopianism seen at the Rappite experiment in Indiana. They all had similar practices of belief, daily life, sexual behavior, and cultural life that first were described by visitors to New Harmony. They represented the epitome of sectarian communalism in the Heartland before the Civil War. Only one other such community would appear after the conflict, and this was the Hutterite Bruderhofs in the Upper Missouri Valley. While the separatist communities represented a continuation of the religious communal tradition begun at New Harmony, the secular counterpart seen there under Owen had its latter-day imitators in the Fourierist Socialist utopias started in the Heartland in the 1840s and 1850s.

CHAPTER FOUR

Fourierist Phalanxes

During the years that the Separatists of Bethel, Zoar, Amana, and Bishop Hill were building their communities in the Heartland, some twenty Fourierist phalanxes continued the secular utopian vision of an ideal alternative to the exploitation of commercialism that Owen first attempted at New Harmony. Albert Brisbane was Robert Owen's successor as the leader of utopian socialism, and his message was inspired by the French theorist Charles Fourier. Brisbane first absorbed and then edited Fourier's radical ideas on the progress of civilization and, in the opinion of Carl J. Guarneri, then "created a burst of Fourierist activity . . . almost overnight."[1]

Fourier described his social philosophy in excruciating detail in three massive books, the *Theory of Four Movements and of General Destinies* (1808), *The Loving New World* (1816), and *The Industrial Associations of the New World* (1829). He castigated modern society as hopelessly corrupt, surviving only through deceit and the exploitation of the working classes by the leaders of "commercial capitalism." He argued that society could be saved only by a total restructuring that would replace deceit and corruption with cooperation. The process, he calculated, would involve the creation of cooperative associations that would progress through thirty-two stages over eighty thousand years to reach the final stage of Harmony. Here, Fourier predicted, mankind would enjoy "mature happiness" and live in ideal communities called phalanxes for sixty thousand years.[2]

The phalanx was a four-thousand-acre community, housing 1,620 people in a huge single building, which, in Fourier's mind, resembled the royal palace at Versailles. Its central structure, the phalanstery, was linked by corridors to "galleries of association," areas for meetings and living quarters for children and the elderly. Separating these two galleries from the phalanstery shielded them from the promiscuous sex enjoyed there by the adults. Property was not communal, however. Members invested money in shares of stock and received interest from them. Labor was seen as an investment in the phalanx, and adults worked at a variety of rotated assignments in agriculture, orchards, and shops where they developed talents suited to their personalities and abilities. Individuals voluntarily formed "groups," which were then organized into a "series" that concentrated on one task. Duties were rotated every two hours. Everyone was provided a minimum wage and health care. Eventually, in Harmony, some two million phalanxes would be built, and humans, by then having grown "long and useful tails," would exist in a utopia with an "Italian climate" devoid of distinction between rich and poor, and surrounded by cuddly animals.[3]

Brisbane was the son of a wealthy New York land agent. He met Fourier in 1833 while he was traveling in Europe, and when he returned to Manhattan the following year he started a newspaper, the *Phalanx,* and translated Fourier's books. In 1840 he published his version of Fourierism in *The Social Destiny of Man, or Association and Reorganization of Industry,* an amalgam of Fourier's ideas and Brisbane's own concoctions. Basically, Brisbane simplified the Frenchman's complicated theories and eliminated the parts on sexual relations and human tails. Instead, the American emphasized that Fourierism was the way to reform capitalism and eliminate poverty. Guarneri called the book "the most complete and authoritative account of Fourierism to appear in English in the 1840s."[4]

Horace Greeley, editor of the *New York Tribune,* financed Brisbane's periodical, the *Future,* published in the fall of 1840. It was dedicated to the "cause of Association and a Reorganization of Society." Greeley also hired Brisbane to write a front-page column for the *Tribune.* And in 1843 Brisbane gathered together a collection of these columns in a pamphlet entitled *Association, or a Concise Exposition of the Practical Part of Fourier's Social Science.* He then embarked on a lecture tour that attracted enthusiastic audiences. By this time he was the head of a national Fourier Association, which included many prominent Americans, and had seen the first American phalanxes started in New York, Pennsylvania, and the Heartland. Over the next three decades phalanxes opened also in Ohio, Indiana, Illinois, Iowa, and Wisconsin.[5]

Ohio

THE MARLBOROUGH ASSOCIATION

In 1841 at the town of Alliance, located fifty-one miles southeast of Cleveland, the Marlborough Association was formed on two farms donated by Edward and Abram Brooke to demonstrate that communal living was the only way to improve the condition of wage laborers. Each farm had a house, a barn, tenant houses, and livestock. But difficulties appeared immediately, since most members were poor workers who had no experience in farming. Also, they had no money to buy the tools to make the community a financial success. But they were undaunting. They constructed a large building as a communal residence in which each family had an apartment. Unfortunately, a tract of land separated the two properties, and foolishly they agreed to an exorbitant price to purchase this tract from the owner and overnight incurred an enormous debt. But for a while the members lived a congenial life, working hard, and gathering on Sundays to discuss communal matters.

They drafted a constitution that included communal ownership of property and Fourier's work series system. Some members, such as Abram Brooke, insisted upon no compromise with capitalism and demanded pure communism. He left the community the following year to start an experimental community on sixty acres in Clinton County, which, he advertised, would provide all the necessities of life. However, he never attracted enough members and confessed in a letter published in *The Harbinger,* Brook Farm's semi-monthly magazine, that only two families were living there. Back at Marlborough, the arrival of new members disrupted its modest rational life. They "did not have the same ideals as the founders, and some entered out of selfish motives." In 1845 the community dissolved.[6]

THE OHIO PHALANX

In 1844 Pittsburgh Fourierists organized the Ohio Phalanx (also called the American Phalanx) when they purchased twenty thousand fertile acres in Belmont County on the Ohio River, for $69,000 with no down payment. They were able to do this because the owner of the land, James Shriver, allowed them to build on his property expecting (wrongly, it turned out) to collect rent. Its leader or "despot," Elijah P. Grant, was a graduate of Yale and a lawyer, a doctrinal Fourierist dedicated to building a "genuine Fourier Association" in the Heartland. In September 1843 he attended the Western Fourier Convention at Pittsburgh where he started to recruit what soon became a group of thirty adults who would live in his utopia. By January 1844 they had pledged $40,000, and within a year they committed another $100,000. The property seemed auspicious since more than six hundred acres were under cultivation and the land contained timber, coal, limestone, and sandstone, and was located seven miles from the National Road. It had two houses and ten log cabins. The communards planned to add a dwelling large enough to house twelve families and to build a school, a hospital, a nursery, and a central phalanstery. Morale was high because they were convinced they were creating, as they described it in the *Phalanx* in December 1843, "an industrial army, which, instead of ravaging and desolating the earth . . . shall clothe it luxuriantly and beautifully with supplies for human wants."[7]

In March and May 1844, Grant advertised in the magazine for recruits. He asked applicants to submit information about their age, occupation, the size of their families, and the amount of money they would commit to the community fund. He set a minimum donation of $100 for single men and $200 for those who were married. An admission fee was $5 for men, $3 for women, and $1 for children. Despite the fact that Grant encouraged only "zealous friends of the cause" to apply, he blithely expected that between four hundred and sixteen hundred people would join the Ohio Phalanx. "Applicants are expected to have their minds made up," he proclaimed, "and to be ready to co-operate at once in the experiment of a Social Reorganization."[8]

As reported in the July 27 issue of the *Phalanx*, at a July 4 speech Grant proclaimed that members were committed to the natural rights of man, which could be secured only "by individual association." He praised Fourier as the "greatest discoverer who has ever existed," who had revealed "the laws of social and industrial order, unity and harmony." He believed that phalanxes were "armies for production . . . marked by peace, plenty, and joy; not by carnage, devastation, and tears." He thought that women were essential to the community since "every joy of man is increased by her participation; each grace and refinement are heightened by her aid; may the day be hastened, when her condition shall really be that which the beneficent Creator intended."[9]

But Grant, like Owen before him, was living in a fool's paradise. Only 120 individuals, most of them poor and without any capital to invest, applied for membership. The Ohio Phalanx was unable to make a single payment on the $69,000 purchase price, and by the spring of 1845 it was in debt to the tune of $4,000 on the interest alone. Grant, "in complete despair," resigned as president and returned to Canton to work in a bank. Upon reflection, he believed that the phalanx failed because many members just did not understand Fourierism and were prone to petty disagreements among themselves, sometimes over religious matters. In May 1845 the Ohio Phalanx dissolved.[10]

THE CLERMONT PHALANX

Cincinnati Fourierists formed a phalanx after they held two conventions in that city in late February 1844 in a Universalist church. Their leader was A. J. Macdonald, a Scots friend of John Humphrey Noyes, who did a study of socialist communities in the United States before his death from cholera in 1854. Macdonald read them encouraging letters from Brisbane and Greeley, and they unanimously voted to form committees to select a site for a utopia in Clermont County. In May 1844 Macdonald took 130 individuals thirty-five miles up the Ohio River on the steamboat *Yucatan* to start the Clermont Phalanx (later The Brotherhood, and Utopia). He purchased one thousand acres of land that was heavily timbered, mostly hickory, black walnut, and sugar maple. The property cost $20,000, but the colonists had only $1,000 as a down payment.[11] Macdonald recorded his impressions the day the group landed.

> The weather was beautiful, but cool, and the scenery on the river was splendid in its spring dress. . . . We reached the domain about two o'clock P.M., and marched on shore in procession, with a band of music in front. . . . [We] then formed a mass meeting, at which we had praying, music and speech-making. . . . Here . . . was all that could be desired, hill and plain, rich soil, fine scenery, plenty of first-rate timber . . . a good commercial situation, convenient to the best market in the West.[12]

Following a festive celebration aboard the steamboat they began the construction of a phalanstery that would serve as a dining hall, with seven rooms for living quarters. For a while morale was high. They acquired cattle, hogs, and sheep and started craft shops for shoes, clothing, and tinworks. They built a sawmill and a gristmill. After one of the members, A. H. Ernst, donated one thousand fruit trees, they planted an orchard. Many individuals were skilled mechanics and experienced farmers. In May 1845 the community advertised in the *Phalanx* for new members "of the right character" to apply, stipulating that if they had large families they must have money "in proportion, and the members must be such as can make themselves useful." By the fall of 1845 the Clermont Phalanx had eighty adults who "ate and worked together and took pride in the practicality of living together and sharing responsibilities."[13]

But financial troubles increased. As reported in the *Phalanx* as early as June 1844: "We had received no account of it lately, and as the last that we had was not very flattering in respect to its pecuniary condition, we should not have been surprised to hear of its dissolution." In the spring of 1845 an Ohio River flood damaged much of the property, and by the end of that year Clermont was in debt to over $15,000. Members had pledged

$17,000 in stock purchases, but the colony had received only $6,000.[14]

As was the case in the Ohio Phalanx, most members had only a vague understanding of Fourier's theories. Macdonald thought that their superficial knowledge was based only on Brisbane's columns in the *Tribune* and that they were "afflicted with an acute but unfocused communitarian fever." Even though they listened eagerly to a speech by the phalanx's president, Judge Wade Loofbourrow, in which he declared that the phalanx was "the fulfillment of the Gospel of Jesus Christ, in the establishment of the kingdom of Heaven upon Earth, the reign of Universal Peace, and the restoration of Universal Unity," this had little effect on communal unity. The basic problem was the fact that the Clermont Phalanx was, in Guarneri's terms, an "unfiltered mixture of strangers," whose differences became acute. They were dissatisfied with living in "circumstances inferior to what they had been used to." Friction led to lawsuits, and in the fall of 1846 the community dissolved. Most members returned to Cincinnati.[15]

Some individuals, however, remained at the property and under the leadership of John O. Wattles organized the Brotherhood, or the Spiritualists Community. When some one hundred new members, some of them Swedenborgians, joined, they continued as an agricultural cooperative until 1847 when another flood of the Ohio River destroyed their buildings. Later, the Yankee printer and inventor who had lived at New Harmony for a while, Josiah Warren, attempted a third socialist community at the Clermont site (this time called Utopia) that attempted significant innovations in utopian socialist theory. He believed that New Harmony failed because of its insistence on a "community of goods" and "combined interests," which impaired personal responsibility and individuality. He felt that a phalanx should be based on "equitable commerce" where individual producers would exchange "labor notes" for what they made instead of receiving money based on the current market value of the goods. There would be no constitution or bylaws, and each member could do as he or she pleased. His community of twenty-four families, each with its own house, opened at the eastern edge of the Clermont Phalanx in July 1847. It lasted as an agricultural cooperative until 1858.[16]

TRUMBULL PHALANX

On November 6, 1843, Pittsburgh Fourierists met in the town of Warren, in northeastern Ohio, to draw up a constitution for a phalanx they named Trumbull. It would be financed by stock shares valued at $25, to raise a capital of $200,000. Anyone could join the association just by buying a share of stock. There would be a board of directors and an elected president, Benjamin Robbins, who advertised in the *Phalanx* that this would be a community of sixteen hundred Fourierists.[17] Next, he purchased 280 acres

eight miles west of Warren, with access to the Ohio and Pennsylvania
Canal and a toll road. Half of the rich dark soil was already cultivated. Also
on the property were a gristmill, an oil well, a sawmill, a double-cording
machine, and a cloth-dressing machine.

Despite Robbins's prediction in the *Phalanx,* only about two hundred
members arrived. They crowded into hastily built sheds while they started
to construct the phalanstery. They also planned to build a church, a
school, a lecture hall, and a library. Organized as work groups, labor was
counted by the hour, and what was owed to the workers was recorded in
an account book. These wages were called "permits," which would be paid
as soon as the community declared a dividend. But even though at the
time of Trumbull's dissolution in 1847 some members were owed $600,
"some of them did not receive as many cents."[18] Special attention was
given to the education of the children in the local public school and in a
phalanx school. Member Nathan C. Meeker and his wife taught traditional
academic subjects, as well as crafts to the boys and household skills to the
girls. Mrs. Meeker helped one woman start a nursery school in her family
apartment, which was "the first in the Western Reserve."[19]

Meeker predicted that the phalanx would cure the ills of civilization.
"Those not accustomed to view the progress of combined labor will be
astonished to see the aggregates," he wrote on August 10, 1844. "My eyes
see men making haste to free the slave of all names, nations and tongues,
and my ears hear them driving, thick and fast, nails into the coffin of
Despotism." Each Sunday they held a social meeting where, according to
Meeker, they "spoke of the near relations they sustained to each other, and
of the many blessings they look to receive in the future. . . . One spirit of
joy and gladness seemed to animate them," he continued, "that they had
escaped from the wants, cares, and temptations of civilization, and instead
were placed where public good is the same as individual good." By the end
of the year the future of the phalanx looked bright. Its president, Benjamin
Robbins, and secretary, H. H. Jones, were confident that the "union of the
Associations" was "a great and noble idea. . . . With each day, we are having
abundant cause to hope for a joyous future. . . . We have harmony within
and sympathy without; and being persuaded that these are sure indications
of success, we toil on, 'heart within and God o'erhead'"[20]

By the summer of 1845 Trumbull was flourishing economically. It
had eliminated $8,000 of its $18,000 accumulated debt. A flour mill was
in operation. Two sawmills annually cut 600,000 feet of lumber worth
$3,000. Each year their shingle-machine yielded $4,000. They had a device
that made wooden bowls, which, they predicted, would bring in $3,000
annually. Blacksmiths, shoemakers, wheelwrights, tanners, and carpenters
plied their trades. They harvested thirty acres of wheat, fifty acres of oats,
seventy acres of corn, twelve acres of potatoes, ten acres of buckwheat,

five acres of turnips, and one acre of broomcorn. Their orchard had five hundred young peach trees and two hundred apple trees. Their livestock included forty-five cows, twelve horses, five yoke of oxen, and twenty-five head of cattle.[21]

Difficulties mounted underneath this bucolic surface, however. One problem was the location. Half the land was a morass and could not be cultivated. A creek ran through the center of the community and, because of constant overflowing, added to the swampy terrain, which became a breeding ground for mosquitoes. Consequently, one resident remembered in a letter written in the summer of 1848, "three-fourths of the people, both old and young, were shaking with [fever] for months together." Largely because of sickness, there were not enough adults to care for the crops, and production declined. "All through the sultry months which should have been their working time," Noyes commented, "they lie idle in their loose sheds, or where they can find a place, sweating and shivering in misery and despair."[22] As early as the summer of 1845 members started to leave. Some left because they had tired of the Spartan lifestyle and a coarse diet without meat. Others left because, as Rokicky put it, they "were fainthearted and could not make some sacrifices." One member, identified only as "J. M.," observed that the "gloom of debt is over them from the beginning. . . . It is a constant question and doubt," he wrote, "whether they will 'SUCCEED,' which means, whether they will barely keep soul and body together and pacify their creditors."[23]

Then there were the "human parasites," as one communard called them, who infested the phalanx. A New Englander who claimed to be a doctor "established a boardinghouse where he fleeced phalanx residents of their money in return for a floor to sleep on and coffee made from burnt bread, then added insult to injury by presenting exorbitant medical bills for treating their ague." Another "keen fellow," both a preacher and a lawyer, was elected the secretary and treasurer and embezzled funds "for his own advantage, which many of the members felt to their sorrow." Many found out that they were just not suited for communal life. As Meeker later remembered in an article for the *New York Tribune* printed on November 3, 1866, they found communal housing lacking in privacy for married couples, the conduct of lazy members was disruptive, and the paltry rewards of communalism were totally inadequate. Their open admissions policy allowed in people who were either sick or impoverished or both, and such individuals were unable to contribute to the operation of the community.[24]

Every day life became more and more contentious. "They are cursed with suspicion and the evil eye," Noyes commented. "They quarrel about religion. They quarrel about their food. They dispute about carrying out their principles." Such tensions point to the fundamental difficulty with Trumbull and the other phalanxes, the gap between their lofty expectations and the reality of communal life. After suffering repeated hardships these "soldiers of despair," as Noyes labeled them, finally realized that the better life was not soon to come. In December 1847 they dissolved the phalanx.[25]

INTEGRAL PHALANX

In June 1845 the *Ohio State Journal* reported that an association had purchased nine hundred acres of fertile land for $45,000 on the Miami Canal, some twenty-three miles north of Cincinnati. It had six hundred acres under cultivation and operated a large flour mill, a sawmill, and a lath factory, all powered by water. The land was owned by Abner Enoch, himself a Fourierist and a member of the community, who donated $30,000 as capital stock to the Phalanx. The association announced that they were going to start a newspaper, the *Plowshare and Pruning-Hook,* as a semi-monthly at an annual subscription rate of one dollar. It boasted in the *Harbinger* in July that, when combined with the fertile soil and the abundance of water power, in "a very few years of judicious industry [such efforts] would place an Association in the West in possession of immense material resources."[26]

Soon after some lawyers joined the community, there appeared "a sudden turn in the story of this Phalanx," involving dissension among some members "who are continually hankering after the 'flesh-pots of Egypt'" and "are ready to abandon the cause upon the first appearance of difficulties."[27] By October 1845 the community had dissolved, and some individuals relocated to the Columbia Phalanx. Others went to Illinois to start over again as the Integral Phalanx, on land fourteen miles southwest of Springfield.

COLUMBIA PHALANX

In the summer of 1845 thirty-two families, most of them from the town of Beverly, organized the Columbia Phalanx. It was an agricultural commune that grew wheat, rye, corn, oats, potatoes, beans, grapes, pumpkins, sweet potatoes, turnips, buckwheat, and flax. In a second letter to the *Harbinger* in October, they announced plans to build a flour mill in Zanesville, and that the town was a profitable market for the community's lumber. The letter also invited new members to join them. But familiar difficulties appeared. Many communards were ignorant of Fourier's ideas and had no clear concept of communal life. Others disagreed with the Phalanx's effort to put into practice Fourier's ideas on racial equality and working on Sundays. For whatever reasons, the Columbia Phalanx dissolved in early 1846.[28]

YELLOW SPRINGS (MEMNONIA)

In 1856 Dr. Thomas L. Nichols and his wife, Mary S. Gove Nichols ("two of the busiest and most colorful radicals of the century," according to Guarneri), fled from their American Hydropathic Institute in the state of New York because of local opposition to their advocacy of free love. The couple had attended a Fourierist meeting in 1848 and believed in the Frenchman's reform ideas, especially in regard to women's rights and sexual freedom. They settled in Cincinnati and purchased land in the nearby town of Yellow Springs and called it Memnonia—or a communal School for Life. The couple embraced Fourierism as the guide to perfection. They claimed that Memnonia "would prepare people for utopia," wrote Catherine Rokicky, and that residents could expect "universal health, intelligence, wisdom, freedom, individuality, equality in relations, purity, life, and happiness. . . . The couple spoke continuously of establishing Harmony at Memnonia and used Fourierism as the guideline to achieve it."[29]

Sexual relations at the colony allowed women to have more than one partner in order to eliminate "possessiveness of love." However, women would have sex only to conceive a child, and sex would never be for physical pleasure alone. According to the community's Law of Progression, couples had to have a three-month time of continence before having intercourse. Other rules required members to bathe daily, drink only water, and accept vegetarianism. They had an educational program that involved courses in Fourierism, mathematics, art, music, science, and foreign languages. Spiritualism, involving regular séances led by Mrs. Nichols, was a part of community life.

Horace Mann, president of Antioch College, opposed the colony and tried to close it down. But it was only after visions experienced by Mrs. Nichols in a séance inspired the couple to convert to Catholicism in March 1857 that pressure from a largely Protestant locality forced them to abandon Memnonia. On March 29, the day the couple were baptized by the rector of St. Xavier College in Cincinnati, the community dissolved. They moved to England in 1861 in opposition to the Civil War. And so, the "Nicholses had traded their communitarian experiment for the centuries-old Catholic Church," Rokicky concluded. And "they gave up free love for monogamy."[30]

Indiana

LA GRANGE PHALANX

Indiana saw the same pattern of creating locally self-sufficient phalanxes as did the Buckeye State, except that here only one Fourierist utopia was built. In the autumn of 1843 local farmers of LaGrange County, numbering about thirty families, began construction of a phalanstery on 1,045 acres of rich land, half timbered and half prairie, purchased for $8 an acre at a site located forty miles from Fort Wayne, close to the Wabash and Erie Canal. By the following spring, twenty more individuals applied for admission. The structure was really an extension of a house already there that was owned by one of the members. It was to be ninety-two feet long and two stories high and have a two-bedroom apartment for each family.

The *Phalanx* on February 5, 1844, printed an account written by W. S. Prentise, the colony secretary, in which he listed three barns, a sawmill operation, and one hundred head of cattle, two hundred sheep, horse and ox teams, and an abundance of farm tools. The colony was chartered by the state legislature, and one of its provisions, interestingly, stipulated that it was forbidden to "contract a debt."[31] Most members were practical farmers, but La Grange also had mechanics, teachers, and two physicians. It held to the proscription on indebtedness and in 1846 was able to produce goods worth over $4,000 from communal labor. By then they had cultivated 250 acres, had completed the phalanstery, and put up a blacksmith's shop, a school, and a refectory measuring twenty-six by thirty-six feet. By that time, too, they had cultivated 492 more acres and converted another 250 into meadow pasture. The farmers worked a ten-hour day and received seventy-five cents per day, payable annually. Ten families were engaged in agriculture and in the fall of 1846 planted 300 acres of wheat. They expected a bountiful crop of peaches and apples from their orchard. In addition, that season they harvested 140 acres of existing wheat, 52 acres of oats, 38 acres of corn as well as "potatoes, beans, squashes, pumpkins, melons and what not." An article in the *Harbinger* on July 4, 1846, noted that the preamble to the phalanx's constitution "shows that their enterprise is animated by the highest purposes." Whatever problems "this little band of pioneers" might face, the article added, they must remember that such burdens "can not be equal to the burdens which the selfishness and antagonism of the existing order of things lay upon every one who toils through its routine. . . . The poorest Association affords a sphere of purer, more honest, and heartier life than the best society that we know of in the civilized world."[32]

Despite such auspicious beginnings, however, for reasons never understood the La Grange Phalanx dissolved at the end of 1846. Two considerations might help to explain the end of the phalanx. Although Prentise noted in the *Harbinger* in the winter of 1844 that a stream ran through the property "falling twelve feet, and making a good water-power," another secretary, William Anderson, confessed two years later that the "domain is as yet destitute of water-power except on a very limited scale." Second, the Indiana community was hit with the same sort of chicanery that plagued the Ohio communities: human avarice. A member named Jones was able to purchase one-half of the community stock, and "he managed trading and money matters all in his own way, whether he was an officer or not." According to A. J. Macdonald, this "has been assigned as the chief cause of their failure."[33]

Michigan

ALPHADELPHIA PHALANX

Like Indiana, Michigan hosted only one effort at constructing a phalanx, which, although as brief as La Grange Phalanx (lasting just three years), was more widely publicized. In February 1844 the *Phalanx* published a notice that a Fourier "industrial Association" had been formed in Michigan "under the most flattering prospects." It had its origins in a convention of fifty-six Fourierists from eight counties who met on December 14, 1843, in a schoolhouse on the banks of the Kalamazoo River near Ann Arbor. After three days the delegates adopted a tentative constitution and sent it to a three-man committee for final revision. The committee presented the document to a second convention that met at Bellevue on January 3, 1844. The convention members approved the document and selected a site for the community in the town of Comstock, also on the Kalamazoo River. They planned to build a brick "mansion" with a cobblestone foundation and to develop "manufactories." Nearby they purchased three thousand acres priced at $32,000, nine hundred of which were fit for agriculture. The goals of Alphadelphia were as lofty as those of the other phalanxes. As one of the officers, Dr. H. R. Schetterly of Ann Arbor, expressed it, they were "desirous of escaping from the present hollow-hearted state of civilized society, in which fraud and heartless competition grind the more noble-minded of our citizens to the dust."[34]

In May Schetterly sent the *Harbinger* a detailed history of the first months of the phalanx. He described the annual meeting in March, where one hundred new members, including children, were admitted. The diverse group included millwrights, machinists, furnace men, printers, manufacturers of cloth and paper, "and almost every other kind of mechanics you can mention, besides farmers in abundance." Nevertheless, in the beginning only two hundred members were allowed to live on the property.[35]

There, while constructing the "mansion," they lived in a frame two-story, 520-foot-long apartment building. Their main activities were farming, building a furnace and a machine shop, and operating an existing sawmill that produced one hundred thousand feet of lumber, to be shipped out on the Central Railroad, which passed through the property. They planted winter wheat and expected a plentiful harvest. Twice a week they had "religious meetings," which emphasized their conviction that "if God be for us, of which we have sufficient evidence, who can prevail against us?" No religious tests were required for membership, however, and anyone who wished could preach, though this was usually done by "one of the printers."[36]

Two years later, the *Harbinger* published an account of conditions at the phalanx described in another letter from Dr. Schetterly. He noted that they had made progress in constructing a seventy-foot phalanstery with small but comfortable rooms. By then membership included carpenters, shoemakers, tailors, blacksmiths, and printers, almost all of whom though "skillful and generally well informed" were illiterate. Schetterly bragged about the "good morality" of the members. But Schetterly also admitted to serious problems. When the initial supplies of food had been exhausted and "these luxuries were all consumed . . . most of the members had to subsist afterward on coarser fare than they were accustomed to." Disgusted at decisions made by the officers in economic matters that proved to be "bad bargains," many "laborers became discouraged and some left." Then, in the winter of 1845, "some of the influential members went away temporarily, and thus left the real friends of the Association in the minority." There was, Schetterly confessed, "a manifest lack of good management and foresight."[37] In the winter of 1847, Alphadelphia dissolved because it was, like the Indiana effort, crippled by the diversity of its membership and their unreasonably high expectations of immediate success.

Illinois

Between 1843 and 1845 five short-lived phalanxes were started in the Prairie State, all of them inspired by the optimistic reports of Fourierist settlements in Ohio appearing in the *Phalanx* and the *Harbinger*. In the *Phalanx* on October 5, 1843, A. J. Macdonald mentioned that a "small Association" had been started in Bureau County but added that "no further particulars" were available. This community was located in sparsely settled north-central Illinois and disappeared the same year it opened. In 1844 the Bond County Fourier Association formed when residents of Greenville, east of St. Louis, raised a subscription of $15,000 to invest in land and livestock. They announced that they were committed to "improving the physical, intellectual, social and moral condition of society." However, no community site was ever located.[38]

In Fulton County in west-central Illinois, the Canton Phalanx was launched in 1845 but dissolved within months. The same year, near Springfield, the Sangamon County Phalanx appeared along Lick Creek and it, too, broke up within months. Some of its members moved to the newly created Integral Phalanx nearby. This last Illinois community was formed at Loami Village under the leadership of John S. Williams, a Cincinnati abolitionist and leader of the Ohio Integral communards who relocated to Illinois.[39]

They purchased 508 acres of prairie and woodland southwest of the state capital. Watered by Lick Creek and a number of springs, the land was well suited to growing corn, at one hundred bushels per acre, that could be shipped to Springfield by barges on the Illinois River, just two miles from the phalanx. Nearby was a steam-powered sawmill and flour mill for their use. In October 1845, Integral's secretary wrote to the editor of the *New York Tribune* that the phalanx expected to buy more adjacent land "at cheap rates." The communards planned to build a storehouse where families could charge the goods they needed. Until the community numbered four hundred persons (as stipulated by Fourier) it would operate temporarily on a system of "hired labor" where each person was fully compensated for their "labor or other services." Under this system each individual would be charged "a fair price for what he receives from the Phalanx; the balance of earnings, after deducting the amount of what he receives [from the storehouse], to be credited to him as stock, to draw interest as capital." Until four hundred members arrived, there would be no constitution or bylaws because such rules in the transition period "will be worse than useless." Unless they strictly followed all of Fourier's rules they would "run into anarchy and confusion, and become disgusted with their efforts, we hope they will have the honesty to take the blame upon themselves, and not charge it to the science of Association." Its ninety-five members stayed together until 1847 when the community dissolved.[40]

Iowa

PIONEER PHALANX

In the summer of 1844 a small group of Fourierists from Watertown, New York, known as the Industrial Association of Jefferson County arrived in Mahaska County, Iowa, nine miles from the town of Oskaloosa, to start the Pioneer Phalanx. They built crude log cabins joined together along the Des Moines River and aspired to create "a little city in the wilderness." In September 1844 the Congregational minister Reverend Benjamin Spaulding, a member of the "Iowa Band" of graduates from Andover Theological Seminary, visited the community and described life there. The residents shared all property communally and ate all meals together. They had a profitable farm and planned to erect a sawmill on the Des Moines River. "They believe," Spaulding wrote, "in common with the founder of their system [Charles Fourier], that most of the evils which we suffer, social and moral, spring solely from the jarring of individual interests, and would at once disappear under a proper organization of society." Their motto was "Love thy neighbor as thyself." But by May 1845 petty disagreements led to the collapse of the experiment.[41]

COMMUNIA

In 1847 a group of German and Swiss immigrants moved to the hills of Clayton County, Iowa, and started a community named Communia next to German farms in the area. At first they focused on agriculture, not industry. All property was held collectively, and the Bible was the guide to daily living. When a Prussian tailor and Fourierist called Wilhelm Weitling arrived in 1851, however, the community changed into a phalanx. He persuaded its sixty-one residents to abandon the emphasis on Scripture and organize a "Labor League" community that would recruit artisans. Their new constitution called Communia the "Working Men's League" and pledged as an association "to carry on . . . every kind of agricultural, industrial, commercial, and other business and to conform and distribute it amongst themselves, according to the proportionate equal interest of all the Members and Shareholders thereof for becoming thereby enabled to promote those interests and to the comfort and well-being of all the Members and Shareholders, to give them benefits in sickness [and] old age."[42]

Soon new members arrived and Communia promised to become "a series of model communities that would offer artisans a haven initially from the vicissitudes of industrial capitalism and later provide the greater society a blueprint to emulate."[43] But nagging personal antagonisms and squabbles, combined with inadequate financial backing and poor business decisions, slowly undermined loyalty to community. Weitling's frequent absences served only to exacerbate the declining morale and growing disillusionment. In 1864, following a protracted legal battle over how to divide Communia's assets, the Clayton County Court dissolved the society.

GARDEN GROVE

In 1848 some residents of the Pioneer Phalanx planned to build a phalanx in Decatur County called Garden Grove. Dr. O. Roberts and William Davis led a group to settle on land purchased from the Mormons. They wanted to give each family forty acres to cultivate and manage for itself and "to have a pleasure house [Phalanstery?] [which had] a dancing and lecture room, a reading room, a bathing room . . . in common." They hoped to "settle a colony of the 'right sort,'" that is, especially of those "who had experience in Community life before." However, Arthur Bestor believes the community never went beyond the planning stage.[44]

HOPEWELL (HOPEVILLE)

In the winter of 1851, a dozen families from Van Buren County, led by twenty-year-old Hiram Lamb, purchased land along the Des Moines River in Clarke County, Iowa. They erected log cabins and expected that the cheap land would be the basis of a prosperous utopia. But individualism prevailed almost from the start. As one member put it, "every man wants to boss his own work and do as he pleased. It was but a waste of time to try to work together, so they soon scattered into farms of their own."[45]

Wisconsin

SPRING FARM ASSOCIATION

At the small town of Sheboygan Falls in 1845, Dr. P. Cady of Ohio led a meeting of ten families who agreed to form an association. The convention divided into two factions: one wanted to settle on the shores of Lake Michigan and the other preferred a remote location on federal land twenty miles from the lake. Only the latter group took any action. Six families, including ten children, pitched tents on the site in February 1846, named it Spring Farm, and declared their goal to be "Union, Equal Rights, and Social Guaranties." The men, mainly blacksmiths, carpenters, and joiners, built a two-story frame building and started to cultivate thirty acres. B. C. Trowbridge, the leader of the community, wrote to Macdonald that the weather "cut off our crops the second year, and left us short of provisions." So, even though the colony was well managed and resolved issues "by mutual agreement," they failed after three years because of "poverty, diversity of habits and dispositions" of the members.[46]

WISCONSIN PHALANX

The Wisconsin experiment was unique in that, at the time of its breakup in 1849, it was the only phalanx to turn over a profit to its membership. Six years before, in December 1843, an ex-spiritualist named Warren Chase convened a meeting at Kenosha to start an association on two thousand acres in Fond du Lac County where the future town of Ripon would be situated. The following spring they drafted a constitution, elected officers, and raised $1,000 in stock subscriptions. They also drew up an act of incorporation, which they sent to the territorial legislature for approval, and "became a body corporate and politic, known as the 'Wisconsin Phalanx.'" A party of eight men with ox teams and cattle went there in late May 1844 to start constructing buildings, and eighty colonists arrived in the fall. The seven-article constitution of the Wisconsin Phalanx allowed only men the franchise, although women served on committees in charge of domestic tasks. Admissions requirements prescribed that a person demonstrate some knowledge of Fourierism, be of good character, and have a skill useful to the colony. New members also had to buy four shares of stock at $25 a share. Apparently, such requirements were prohibitive because Chase reported in a letter of March 3, 1846, that "we cannot receive one-tenth of those who apply for admission."[47]

Following Fourier, they organized into two series, agricultural and mechanical. The agricultural series started plowing and planting right away, and the mechanical series excavated a cellar for the erection of a phalanstery. Article 5 of their constitution read that, each year, out of the total production of the community "shall first be deducted the taxes, repairs and insurance, and the balance shall be divided as follows: One quarter shall be paid as a dividend to the stockholders upon the capital stock paid in; and the remaining three quarters shall be divided among those who perform the labor." By the summer of 1845, 180 members, half of them children, had joined the community, most of them coming from New York and Vermont. Some were Methodists and Baptists and wanted weekly church services. But Chase and others were religious liberals and instead wanted a weekly fellowship meeting and séances. The religious conservatives won out, and the phalanx had regular Sabbath services.[48]

Despite their differences, by 1846 the membership had increased to a total of 259 individuals, who shared a dining hall and a two-hundred-foot phalanstery, called the Long House, that had apartments for families on the first floor and rooms for single individuals on the second. The most significant income came from wheat, along with other agricultural products. By October 1846 they had a sawmill in operation. Communal living was not required. Each family decided whether to use the dining hall or prepare their own meals and whether to live in the phalanstery or in single dwellings that were erected during the first year. "Most of the families," Chase noted in the *Annual Statement of the Condition and Progress of the Wisconsin Phalanx, for the fiscal year ending December 7, 1847*, "choose this mode of living, more from previous habits of domestic arrangement and convenience, than from economy."[49]

Work assignments were classified as "Necessity" (stonework and digging), "Usefulness" (farmwork, shop work, and bookkeeping), and "Attractiveness" (domestic chores and duties of the officers). Workers rotated these assignments, for which they were credited seventy-five cents for a ten-hour day, although some artisans wanted a higher wage. Each evening the group's elected foreman gave out the assignments for the following day. Because the Wisconsin Phalanx prohibited alcohol and profanity, it apparently attracted young parents who wanted to raise their family in a moral environment. Children received a free education until the age of ten in a school taught by women. After that age men taught them academic subjects and manual labor skills and had them do jobs for the association for which they were given credit. A visitor identified only as "Hine" sent a letter to the *New York Tribune* dated July 20, 1847, in which he optimistically reported on "its resources, both physical and moral. . . . Its physical resources are abundant, . . . [and] in a moral aspect there is much here to encourage." The communards were "generally quite intelligent, and possess a good development of the moral and social faculties. . . . They have an excellent school for the children, and the young men and women are cultivating music," he continued. "While writing, I hear good music by well-trained voices, with the Harmonist accompaniment."[50]

Beginning in 1845, however, a series of divisive issues eroded the phalanx. Some members became convinced that the private homes and "unitary living" had to be eliminated if ever a true Fourierist community could be realized. They convinced a majority of the men to pass a rule that everyone had to live in the Long House. Some families left immediately. Then the California Gold Rush seduced others to abandon the phalanx, because, according to Guarneri, "the prospect of easy money proved far more enticing than the difficult process of establishing communal life." Chase expressed his frustration with this exodus in poetry: "Behold the struggle! The mad, selfish rush; For Shining baubles or a beggar's crust! . . .; Shut up the book; talk not of brotherhood; Man lives for self, not for the common good." Rancor developed because "the farmers and mechanics were always jealous of each other, and could not be brought to feel near enough to work on and divide the profits at the end of the year." Some members found work outside the phalanx and "had gained property and become established in business."[51]

By 1849 only 120 members remained, most of them simple farmers and field hands "whose limited intellectual interests left little time for discussions about, or interest in, Fourierism."[52] In August 1849 Chase had the state legislature authorize the "proceedings for closing out, and . . . was given full charge of the business." In April 1850 all the land was sold and the profits divided among the stockholders. Many members became wealthy in the process because "a town site had been laid out between the two portions of [the phalanx,] which enabled [it] to plat additions to what is now the city of Ripon and to sell much of its land as town lots. . . . In consequence, the division was a cheerful affair, the stockholders finding themselves materially better off than they had anticipated."[53] Or, as one anonymous member of the community put it in his *History of the Wisconsin Phalanx:* "Thus commenced, flourished and decayed this attempt at industrial Association. It never attempted to follow Fourier or any other teacher, but rather to strike out a path for itself. It failed because its leading minds became satisfied that under existing circumstances no important progress could be made, rather than from a want of faith in the ultimate practicability of Association."[54]

CARL GUARNERI focused on eight reasons why the Fourierist phalanxes did not survive. First of all, their "pie-in-the-sky propaganda" ignored the harsh realities of life in the Heartland. Next, they purchased too much land—the average was over twelve hundred acres, needed for communal living. To acquire these holdings they incurred crippling debts for which they could not even meet the interest payments. Because of such heavy debts they could not survive even moderate natural setbacks such as frost or fire. All phalanxes to some degree were plagued by squabbles over work assignments or shareholders' rights. Communards were all crowded together, frequently in one dwelling, so they were sometimes devastated by contagious disease. Their admissions policies allowed entry to cranks, misfits, or avaricious men who joined just to make money. And they all suffered from a rapid turnover in communal population. Finally, adding to all these problems was the mounting opposition to Fourierism of evangelical Protestants who claimed that the Fourierists were out to destroy property rights and conventional social values. Well-documented articles in the *New York Observer,* the *Universalist Quarterly,* and the *American Whig Review* attempted to convince Americans that Fourierism was the antithesis of Christianity and "that Associationists were hiding Fourier's most shocking descriptions of life in Harmony, visions that the Frenchman asserted were necessary extrapolations of his theory."[55]

Brian J. L. Berry argued that the creation of phalanxes was "a reaction to the Crisis of 1837 and the deflationary depression of the early 1840s [and] lasted no longer than the depression itself." Guarneri concurred. "As the depression of the early 1840s lifted and the business cycle began its climb," he wrote, "opportunities for employment increased, and workers who had flocked to phalanxes found new options for mobility and security." For a variety of reasons these Fourierist communities never came close to achieving what they had set out to accomplish, which was to change America. "The Associationists obviously failed in their largest intention," Guarneri stated, "to transform American society into a cooperative utopia. And no phalanx lasted long enough or grew large enough to fit the most common notions of success."[56]

CHAPTER FIVE

Icaria

The next Heartland experiment with secular utopias, Icaria, had a much more impressive record in longevity than its Fourierist counterparts. Indeed, historians see Icarian communism—first practiced at Nauvoo, Illinois (1849–1862), then replicated at Cloverdale, Missouri (1856–1866), Corning, Iowa (1866–1898), and Cloverdale, California (1882–1888)—as constituting one of the longest-lived attempts at nonreligious utopian communalism in American history. Utopian communism was similar to utopian socialism, however, in that both were radical alternatives to laissez-faire capitalism. The leader of utopian communism was Étienne Cabet, a Frenchman born in Dijon on January 1, 1782, who, like Fourier, "saw the world around him as riddled with political corruption, merciless exploitation of workers, rampant crime and immorality." Living in Paris and editing the newspaper *Le Populaire*, Cabet castigated the French king, Louis Philippe, for betraying the French Revolution and supporting the "bloody and tyrannical laws" passed by the Chamber of Deputies, which caused many honest Frenchmen to be hauled before military tribunals for any criticism of the government. Cabet was fully aware that he was violating the 1819 penal code, which defined as a felony any published material that caused an "affront to the king [or incited] hatred and contempt of the government." By the time Cabet's articles started to appear in his newspaper, over five hundred press cases had been prosecuted in Paris alone.[1]

Indeed, on February 28, 1834, the police arrested him and arraigned him before the Assize Court of the Seine. The jury found him guilty of sedition. The judges sentenced him to two years in prison and removed all his political rights (voting and publishing) for four years. Under French sedition law, however, Cabet could ask for an alternative sentence of five years in exile. Urged by his friends he requested exile. So in October 1834 Cabet moved to London, accompanied by his wife and young daughter. While there he wrote his magnum opus, *Travels in Icaria*, which was published in the spring of 1839 when he returned to Paris.

In its eight hundred pages, William Carisdall, a fictional visiting English aristocrat, describes a utopian paradise. Icaria, named after its founder the "good Icar," is a nation where all private property and money have been eliminated. An assembly elected by the adult men takes care of every citizen's needs. For example, it daily sends free packages of food and clean clothing to every home. Education is free for both sexes from childhood to the age of twenty-three, and there are also free evening classes for adults. Male and female physicians take care of the sick in sanitary hospitals where music is piped to all the rooms. A factory system uses machines to do all the hard and dangerous work while, as in hospitals, music uplifts the Icarians' spirits. Work ends at noon, and everyone has afternoons and evenings to attend "spectacles" in huge amphitheaters or to go to plays and concerts. The capital, Icara, is a model of city planning and has symmetrical shaded streets and promenades. Icarians have no established religion and only practice the Christian Golden Rule. Carisdall finds no crime, no saloons, or gambling houses. One Icarian, named Valmore, asks the astonished visitor: "What crimes do you imagine we could have today when we have no money, and when everyone has everything he or she could desire?" He goes on to say that one would be insane to want to steal and "how could there even be suicides when everybody is happy?"[2]

Travels in Icaria was a best seller, going through five editions in eight years. With the royalties he received, Cabet reopened *Le Populaire* and started to attack the government for arresting striking workers in Lyons, Belleville, and Rouen, for authorizing police raids on workers' "banquet halls," and for shutting down left-wing publications. Government repression escalated in the summer of 1841 when police arrested 187 individuals and convicted 137 of them of conspiracy to overthrow the government. The episode caused Cabet to publish a pamphlet in September 1841, *Ma ligne droite, ou le vrai chemin du salut pour le peuple* (My right line, or the true course of salvation for the people), in which he cautioned against worker violence because such "useless" acts only give the authorities an excuse to crack down and "to make searches, arrests, and seizures." In *Le Populaire,* which by then was one of France's largest-selling newspapers, he called on his countrymen to "unite for our common defense, let us be brothers in order to save ourselves, let us shun everyone who could alter our unity; let us discuss our doctrines and our principles, for . . . tolerance and moderation." By 1843, as Christopher Johnson has pointed out, Cabet had created a national organization of communists-Icariens in twelve major cities. And by 1845 about one hundred thousand men and women in seventy of France's one hundred departments were Icarians. That year *Le Populaire* enjoyed a record press run of thirty-five hundred copies.[3]

But then, the threat of militant, class-conscious Marxism in France caused the middle class to see the Icarians as dangerous radicals. In 1846 Cabet concluded that the government was about to silence *Le Populaire,* and he became hysterical. He charged that the king had brought the country to economic ruin with "egotism and political indifference." The Chamber of Deputies, he wrote, was controlled by "lords of wealth" who created monopolies, shut down labor unions, and reenacted the notorious press laws to put him and others in jail. "Communists and reformists," he urged, "unite for our common defense." The police arrested him and had him interrogated. This was too much for the fifty-nine-year-old communist. Fearing another exile he decided to leave France. On May 9, 1847, *Le Populaire's* front page read: "Let's go to Icaria!"[4]

His decision was an impulsive one because Cabet had no plans for the emigration; indeed, he had not the slightest idea of where he and his followers were going to settle or how to get there. Almost in desperation he contacted Robert Owen, whom he had met briefly while in exile in England, in hopes that Owen might be able to help. On September 9, 1847, Cabet went to London and met with Owen, who conveyed to him an offer made by William Smalling Peters, an agent for a Texas land company. If the Icarians would erect farmsteads by July 1, 1848, on 3,000 acres near present-day Dallas, each married adult male would receive 320 acres and each single man 160 acres. Cabet returned to Paris and began to recruit Icarians with an announcement in the November 14 issue of *Le Populaire:* "On to Texas!" By the winter of 1848 over five hundred men, women, and children were ready to leave France.[5]

On the morning of February 3, 1848, Cabet escorted the First Advance Guard of sixty-nine men, all bearded and dressed in black velour tunics and grey felt caps, to the docks at Le Havre. They marched onboard the ocean steamer *Rome* and stood at attention on deck. As it left port they bellowed, to the tune of "La Marseillaise," the new Icarian anthem, "Chant du Départ" (Song of departure). The advance guard arrived in New Orleans on March 27 and under their leader, a Toulouse sign painter named Adolphe Gouhenant, boarded a steamboat for Shreveport, en route to their final destination along the Trinity River in Texas.[6]

But the Texas experience was a calamity. The advance guard suffered from dysentery, malaria devastated the campsite, and then cholera struck.

Four men died, one struck by lightning. Their only physician went insane and disappeared. The beleaguered group decided to head back to Shreveport. In October 1848 the survivors arrived by steamboat in New Orleans. There they found 480 Icarians, including children, crammed into two apartment buildings on St. Ferdinand Street. When they recounted their nightmare, some wanted to return to France immediately. Others, however, were determined to wait until Cabet arrived before deciding what to do. The second group prevailed. On the afternoon of January 19, 1849, Cabet appeared in the doorway of one of the buildings. They hailed him as Papa, greeting him as a savior. Pierre Bourg, a thirty-four-year-old immigrant from Lyons, penned in his diary: "For us it was heaven . . . everyone embraced him and shed tears of joy and tears of shock that bathed the face of our venerable Messiah."[7]

Cabet listened with a grim face to the tale of the Texas debacle. He convened a general meeting on January 21, 1849, where he said if a majority wanted to go back to France he would accept that decision "in an instant." According to Cabet's account of the meeting published in the New Orleans newspaper L'Abeille, only a "feeble minority" wished to retreat, and at the end of the second day of discussion, a "great majority" pledged total confidence in him. (In fact, it was only 216 Icarian adults who backed his desire to continue.) Next, he dispatched a three-man committee to find a new place for Icaria. On February 5, the committee returned to New Orleans and reported that they had found an excellent location at Nauvoo, Illinois, the city abandoned by the Mormons two years earlier. Acting on this account, on the morning of February 28, 142 men, 74 women, and 64 children walked up the plank of the steamship American Eagle to journey to Illinois and, in Cabet's words, make another sacrifice "in order to reestablish harmony, union, and unity."[8]

Morale improved almost immediately. Exhilarated by the panoramic landscape of the river bordered by forests and flooded by surging springs, they passed the time in joyful camaraderie, singing the "Song of Departure" and other popular tunes. Cabet wrote that the Mississippi River itself must have been "astonished to hear our Icarian songs." Utopia seemed close at hand. At nine in the morning of March 15, 1849, Cabet led the Icarians up a road to Nauvoo's bluffs and the burnt remains of the Mormon Temple, which, despite the damage, Pierre Bourg described as "grandiose."[9]

Cabet was sixty-one years old. Although exhausted by the trip and "anxieties on the way," he still conveyed "intelligence and even a certain degree of kindness." He found lodging in the vacated Mormon homes and stored the communards' belongings in buildings on the Temple Square. By April 2 he had finished negotiations with three Mormon trustees who had been left behind to dispose of the Saints' properties. He signed a deed for the Temple Square, one block lying west of the square, and one lot lying east of it. On April 8 he received another deed for a mill and distillery located on the banks of the river. He paid $3,000 (one-fourth of the total Icarian treasury of $12,000) for the properties. Then he signed a lease for two thousand acres on which there were four working farms. He leased several large Mormon homes close to the square as temporary shelters for his followers, whom he now called the Soldiers of Humanity. By August 1849 the Icarians were sufficiently established to hold a formal welcoming ceremony on the square for over one thousand non-Mormon residents of Nauvoo. The highlight of the ceremony came with mutual pledges of friendship between Cabet and the Hancock County sheriff, Malgar Couchman.[10]

Over the next two years Cabet supervised the building of his utopia. A disciplined taskmaster, he assigned all duties. Men worked in the various shops or on the farms; women were the cooks, seamstresses, and laundresses. Under Cabet's stern leadership, the Soldiers of Humanity constructed a large refectory, which served as a dining hall and theater. Located next to it were the library, office, and print shop. They had workshops for candlemakers, cobblers, carpenters, wheelwrights, blacksmiths, locksmiths, and mechanics. They had a bakery, a butcher's shop, a ham-curing shop, and a shed to make vinegar. They opened an infirmary and a pharmacy. After a tornado destroyed what remained of the Mormon Temple on the afternoon of May 27, 1850, they used its limestone blocks to build a two-story boarding school. They placed four two-story frame apartment buildings on the northeast corner of the square, where each family had two rooms. Despite the fact that cholera had taken the lives of twenty more Icarians by the summer of 1850, morale remained high. Cabet reported in a pamphlet published in Paris in 1855 titled *Colonie icarienne aux États-Unis* (Icarian colony in the United States) that by July 1852 the utopia had grown to 365 communards (176 men, 101 women, 88 children).[11]

Cabet oversaw not only the construction of his Icaria but the details of its political organization. On February 21, 1850, he instituted what he called "pure democracy" when the adult males unanimously adopted a constitution of 183 articles and sent it to Springfield to have the secretary of state, David L. Gregg, certify Icaria as a corporation. The document designated the community as a "Democratic Republic" with a president, elected annually, and five directors, called *Gérants*, chosen every six months. The Gérants supervised finances and food, lodging and clothing, education and health, industry and agriculture. A secretary ran the office and print shop. A general assembly convened every Saturday in the refectory to enact laws and, every two years, to revise the constitution. The assembly also functioned as a court, to deal with matters of disorderly conduct and immorality. Women attended these meetings but could not vote except in matters "that particularly concerned them." The constitution set up high admission standards. An applicant had to pay a 600-franc (about $12) admission fee for himself or herself and for each child. After a person had lived in Icaria for a four-month probation period, the directors and the assembly would interrogate the individual to see if he or she fully understood Cabet's writings and Icarian doctrines. Then the person could then be admitted by a three-fourths vote. While entrance into the utopia was difficult, it was easy to leave. One had only to send the assembly a written note three months in advance. When he or she departed, each individual would receive one-half of the admission fee in cash (the other half would be in IOUs, without interest), as well as any personal tools he or she had initially brought into the community.[12]

The workday began at six o'clock when a bugler summoned the adults to the refectory for breakfast. After downing soup, café au lait, and bread, each man was given a dram of whiskey. Then everyone went off to their assignments. They returned to the refectory at noon for a hearty meal of meat or fish, potatoes, and vegetables along with beer, wine, and coffee. A modest supper consisted of a thick beef or onion stew and water. The community grew steadily. By July 1854 there were 392 members (184 men, 101 women, 107 children), and the 1855 Illinois state census listed 469 Icarians.[13]

Life on the Temple Square was, in the beginning at least, both genteel and refined, with a social and artistic life superior to anything found anywhere else in that part of the Mississippi Valley. Icarians themselves, in diaries and letters, as well as numerous visitors, described concerts, bucolic excursions along the river, and a vibrant theater. They had an orchestra of thirty-six musicians who, on Sunday afternoons, gave concerts of popular songs and marches. The orchestra also accompanied the theatrical productions, which changed at the impressive rate of one new play a month. Usually dramas, comedies, and vaudeville acts, they were performed on a stage in the refectory on Saturday nights. So many Americans attended that Cabet restricted their number by selling only a limited number of tickets. Members of the orchestra formed a small marching band that accompanied the excursions, called promenades, along the banks of the Mississippi. Jean-Marie Lacour and Pierre Bourg rhapsodically described blissful outings of cheerful Icarians led by "our venerable and venerated patriarch [who] walked with a joyous air in the middle of us, our whole ensemble [forming] an appearance of a large and happy family."[14]

The Icarian library of over four thousand volumes was the largest in the state. Books could be read in the reading room or be taken out on loan. The collection (almost all the volumes were in French) included works on history, biography, ethics, science, and the arts. Icaria published a biweekly newspaper, the *Colonie Icarienne,* whose pages contained news on arrivals, reports from the workshops, accounts of daily life, and letters from friends in France. On Sundays the communards gathered either in the refectory or, weather permitting, in a garden spot located in the center of the square for a lively discussion in the *Cours icarien* (Icarian course). Cabet led these fellowship meetings, in which they explored the meaning of their Icarian principles of equality, fraternity, and democracy—the "intellectual heritage of Humanity," he called them.[15]

Cabet believed that the thorough moral and academic education of both boys and girls was essential to achieve communal growth. He had written in the *Travels in Icaria* that education "is considered among us as the base and foundation of society." At the age of four children were placed in the limestone boarding school located on the southwest corner of the square. Boys and girls slept in separate quarters on the second floor, and classes were held on the first floor. Only on Sunday afternoons could they visit their parents. Adults taught the four-year-old children how to read and write. Then, until the age of fifteen, both sexes were given the same curriculum of grammar, arithmetic, geometry, history, geography, natural history, drawing, music, and English. During the afternoons the boys worked in the fields or workshops and the girls helped in the refectory, the laundry buildings, and the tailor's shop. Cabet ordered the teachers to inculcate a strict code of moral discipline and to have a "punishment room" for difficult children. Here they would be taught separately by a special teacher because they had "shown an uncontrollable disposition and [were] considered a dangerous example" to the community. Émile Vallet, who attended the school in the 1850s, remembered that Cabet himself sometimes lectured on "doing unto others as we wish to be done by." He further admonished the children to "protect, live and work for the feeble, the sick; to forgive; to hold the other cheek when smitten on the one; to be kind, one to another; to love and respect their parents and everybody in general."[16]

But all was not well in Icaria, and the school became an early bone of contention. One of the first ordinances passed by the general assembly in April 1849 required that all children between the ages of two and four had to live in a nursery and could be visited by their parents only on Sunday afternoons. On turning four they moved into the school. Some women resented what amounted to the destruction of their family life. That summer, with some support from their husbands, they protested Cabet's unabashed attempt to "insulate the youngsters from the old world influences of their parents and raise the children to value fraternity over the individual sentimental affections that mothers displayed." Cabet reacted by trying to stop the Sunday visits because the experience, he wrote, would "reverse all the previous educational efforts." He ordered the children to cease addressing fathers as "daddy" and mothers as "mommy" and to simply call them "my parent." Only he should be called Papa. Such confrontations were the main reason some couples left as "angry dissidents."[17]

The dispute over the school led to another gender issue, the denial of suffrage to women. In 1850 a group of Icariennes formed a committee to change the constitution. For seven months they regularly asked the assembly to give women "absolute political equality." They demanded that they "be electors and eligible for all the public functions, even for the *Gérance.*" They argued that disfranchisement was a violation of the Icarian principles of democracy and equality. Cabet dismissed them as "ignorant and obstinate" mothers and warned that they were inciting anarchy. But they persisted. In January 1851, after a protracted three-day session of the assembly over the suffrage question, Cabet received the full backing of a majority of the men. He later commented that "the proposition to revise the Constitution (found to be inopportune and rejected by the majority) was the cause of the general malaise." Consequently, at least twenty women left Icaria along with their husbands.[18]

Other perhaps less vexing gender issues surfaced. Cabet required all women to wear uniforms of dresses, blouses, and aprons made by the tailors and seamstresses. He insisted that women surrender all personal property such as toiletries and jewelry. He was furious when he discovered that some women had kept these items and, "behind the closed doors of their two-room apartments, secretly bedecked themselves in clandestine jewelry parties." Some Icariennes resented Cabet's assertion that a man's "reason" was superior to a woman's "sentiment." On a number of occasions he complained that too many Icarian women were poorly educated and flaunted the dangerous feminine faults of vanity and coquetry. He thought many of them were "demanding, critical, destructive, etc." More shocking was the fact that, in violation of Cabet's proscription of tobacco and alcohol, "some smoked and drank whiskey." These backsliders were accompanied by men who, "not content with the morning dram, had taken to drinking whiskey during the day, and some in huge amounts—as much as four gallons a week." Some men had taken to hiding whiskey bottles in their apartments and pretending to be sick so they could stay there and drink. One man was drunk all the time.[19]

Added to these problems was the physical toil of the strenuous daily work schedule. Infirmary records show a rising rate of sickness, and by 1855 so many adults were ill that the infirmary was half full most of the time. Some men started to complain about the formalities and monotony of the workshops. Visitors detected a growing malaise. One American correspondent from the *New York Tribune* wrote that the Icarians were exhausted from the regimentation and fed up with "nothing to eat but bread and soup."[20]

In 1853 things further deteriorated when Cabet undertook a "great reform" His intention was to restore discipline, but he succeeded only in alienating a majority of the adult men. Standing before the general assembly the afternoon of January 9, Cabet read his new rules of conduct, called the Forty-eight Articles, reminding them of the hardships many had endured during the emigration and lecturing them on their sacred principles. He told them that they must never forget their mission to build an "Icaria in the desert." On February 3, the assembly adopted the new articles by a vote of 114 in favor and 3 abstentions. The document was Draconian. Every new member had to pledge full dedication to the principles of Equality, Democracy, Liberty, and Unity, surrender all belongings to the Gérance, and renounce tobacco and alcohol. Icarians must "vigorously" carry out all work assignments in silence. Everyone must eat what was served without grumbling. Gone were the idle pleasures of fishing and hunting. Everyone must submit to the decisions of the Gérance and obey the president.[21]

Over the next year and a half, the community divided into two hostile camps. The catalyst for the schism—and for Cabet's eventual expulsion—was the system of surveillance that he instituted immediately after the articles were adopted. He created a network of spies in the workshops. "The eavesdropping soon created so much distrust and suspicion that everybody thought someone was spying on them, and most likely they were right."[22]

In the fall of 1854 two members of the Gérance—Jean Paul Gérard, in charge of finance and food, and Alexis Armel Marchand, in charge of education and health—openly challenged Cabet's leadership. They condemned the use of secret informants and told the assembly that Papa was incompetent as an administrator. He was haughty, aloof, and inattentive to the details of running a large community. They argued that whiskey should be allowed in moderation and the same thing with smoking. Silence in the workshops, they said, was absurd. Some men rose to Cabet's defense. Calling themselves Cabetists, they declared full support for his self-sacrificing leadership. He was their salvation and the hope of humanity. Then, in December 1854, Cabet suffered a stroke that left him partially paralyzed and bedridden for almost a year. After a year of rest, his strength had returned enough that he was able to address the assembly, a body that by then was divided into the "Majority" and the other, the minority, made up of Cabetists. Seething with righteous indignation, Cabet harangued the Icarians. How could anyone think Icaria could survive, he asked, without him? Anyhow, he would never leave because he was too devoted to his mission of defending "our women and children, our old folks and our sick, our widows and orphans." He was fed up with all the bickering. The opposition must shut up or leave. He laid down an ultimatum.[23]

Seven conditions must be met immediately for him to continue "to carry the flag of the community" and "to guarantee and consolidate the Icarian way." First, the Cabetists must move against the "systematic opposition" to convince them to follow him loyally. Second, all women must pledge support for him so that he could protect them and the children. Third, everyone must swear a renewed dedication to the Forty-eight Articles. Fourth, he must have absolute financial control over the community since, he said, "it is true that I am alone responsible [and] have all the means to exercise that responsibility." So, he warned, "if you do not want to work to earn your food, I do not have the responsibility to feed you, to provide health care, etc." Fifth, he wanted the power to punish all infractions of the rules and eliminate "all of the disorders and all of the vices that can exist in Icaria." Sixth, he would no longer be bothered with the day-to-day details of running the colony, which, he said, "have made me lose an enormous and infinite amount of precious time [and] have impeded and incapacitated me and caused incalculable injury to the society." He wanted to focus on policy matters and his correspondence. Seventh, he wanted a change in the constitution to give the president a term of four years instead of only one year and the power to dismiss members of the Gérance and foremen of the workshops. The tirade ended and a stunned silence blanketed the room. Gérard stood up and handed Cabet a letter of resignation. He said that as leader of the "systematic opposition" he had no time for an ultimatum. The next day Marchand resigned. Then on Friday, December 21, 1855, Gérard and Marchand led a band of men in a rousing march around the refectory singing "La Marseillaise."[24]

The Majority were the leading men of Icaria, many of them members of the Gérance and workshop foremen, who were supported by the lowest-ranking Icarians who had been given the most menial assignments. Their wives were domineering, seldom pleased, frequently bored, and driven by what Cabet called coquettishness. In fact, they hated Cabet for having destroyed their families by placing the children in the boarding school. The Majority was united by one burning conviction: that to save Icaria they had to expel Cabet and his cronies. The Cabetists were the solid citizens of the community who were satisfied with life in Icaria and with their work assignments. These men were skilled artisans pleased with their status. Their wives were dedicated homemakers who felt appreciated in the communal environment and who, like their husbands, valued law and order and Cabet's firm leadership.[25]

In January 1856 civil war broke out within the community. The two camps sat at opposite sides of the refectory at mealtime and did not speak to each other. The Majority marked off the central garden area as their spot, off limits to the Cabetists. The Cabetists designated a similar grassy area next to the school. Cabet had the print shop publish flyers aimed at imaginary followers in France, in which he described himself as a martyr crucified with insults and outrages. He had seven young men stay with him day and night as a bodyguard. The Majority nailed posters on the refectory door that called Cabet a blockheaded incompetent. They locked the door of the building and yelled that the Cabetists could no longer have communal food and laundry services. The Cabetists attacked the refectory waving spiked poles topped with chunks of bread. On August 6, on Cabet's orders, they broke into the refectory. The next day they grabbed Gérard and tried, unsuccessfully, to strangle him to death.[26]

Fearing physical reprisal by the Majority, Cabet moved to another house located two blocks from the square, which he called "little Icaria," and started another newspaper, the *Nouvelle Revue Icarienne* (New Icarian review). On August 19, 1856, the Majority took over the school and expelled all the Cabetist teachers. Outraged, Cabet sent a Madame Raynaud on a rampage into the square in a horse-drawn wagon yelling "Help! Rise up!" The Majority rushed to the school to save the children. Later they burned Cabet in effigy. They then locked the refectory. This episode was too much for their American neighbors. They called the Hancock County sheriff. He arrived and went to see the mayor of Nauvoo, who then issued Cabet an eviction notice. When Gérard heard about the notice, he convened a meeting of the Majority on September 27. That afternoon eighty-four men and forty-nine women adopted and signed the "Fourth Address of the Faithful Icarians of Nauvoo to Icarians of All Nations." This document charged Cabet with destroying the community by lies and "incessant maneuvers." He had brought financial ruin to the colony by ordering his followers not to go to the workshops or farms. He had used "all the resources of trickery, hypocrisy, and lies to achieve his goal: the annihilation of the community."[27]

Cabet's response was to print a statement entitled *Grounds for which the Minority Demands the Dissolution of the Icarian Community,* on October 8, 1856. He had tried to work with the Majority for a peaceful dissolving of the community, he said, but they refused to cooperate. Instead, they insisted that if dissolution occurred the Cabetists had to forfeit one-half of their reimbursement fees. Five days later he published another statement, announcing that he had sent Théophile Heggi to St. Louis to find a new place for Icaria, that he considered the community dissolved, and that he and his followers were making preparations to leave Nauvoo with the "necessities of life."[28]

That same afternoon he printed the *Declaration of Rights of the Icarians,* in which he listed the new rules for the St. Louis Icaria, giving himself complete control. As president for a four-year term he would appoint all officers, convene and adjourn the general assembly, issue edicts as law, and control all finances. He would make all work assignments and run the community school. Whiskey and tobacco were forbidden. Anyone who joined his Icaria had to pledge faithful adherence to its principles and promise to reside in the community for three years. Icarians must practice "good manners, temperance, solicitude, order, economy, organization, discipline, and solidarity."[29] Seventy-one men and forty-four women signed Cabet's *Declaration*. But more than that (as Cabet recounted in *Départ de Nauvoo du fondateur d'Icarie avec les vrais Icariens* [Departure from Nauvoo of the founder of Icaria with the true Icarians], published in Paris in 1856), the Cabetists praised him as the true "founder of Icaria," who was dedicated to "democratic and Icarian principles." He had inspired "confidence without limits" to remain committed to the ultimate goal "to continue the true Icaria."[30]

On October 20, 1856, Cabet wrote his valedictory, "Adresse du citoyen Cabet aux Icariens en France sur la séparation et le départ pour St. Louis" (Address of Citizen Cabet to Icarians in France on the separation and departure for St. Louis). His "oppressors" had won, he confessed. Tyranny had inflicted "violent oppression" upon his followers, and they suffered "inhuman barbarity" in being denied the necessities of life. Their opponents had condemned them "to die from hunger and the cold" while they lived in "abundance, profusion, in drunkenness and vice." Gérard and Marchand were "abominable ingrates," demagogues motivated by sensuality, materialism, and egotism. Nevertheless, even at the end of his career, Cabet remained "attached indissolubly" to the dream of an Icarian utopia. "Get ready," he exhorted, "prepare yourselves to come and join us [in St. Louis]. . . . Hope, therefore, for trust and fraternal dedication." On the morning of October 15, 1856, a procession of thirty-four men, women, and children crossed the broad river plateau filled with vacant Mormon homes and shops and boarded a steamboat for St. Louis. A week later another group of ninety-five Cabetists left Nauvoo. On October 30, Cabet, accompanied by twenty-two men, fourteen women, and twenty-two children, departed Illinois.[31]

The Majority left behind, consisting of 219 Icarians, had the last word. On October 25, 1856, they printed *A Resolution of the General Assembly of the Icarian Community for the Expulsion of Cabet*. He had violated the constitution and laws by inciting "violent demonstrations of the men of his party." He deliberately "with all his might endeavored to bring forth a financial crisis in the community." He had "authorized and favored the stealing by his partisans of tools, books, musical instruments, drugs, account books, registers . . . belonging to the Icarian Community." He had ordered his followers "to refuse to perform their daily labor." He alone was responsible for "stirring up a kind of civil war in the Community." Therefore, "Étienne Cabet member and President of the Icarian Community is hereby expelled from the said Community."[32]

By Friday, November 6, 1856, all the Cabetists had arrived in St. Louis and found lodging in three rented buildings in the New Bremen section of the city. The next morning, after breakfast, Cabet suffered a fatal stroke. After laying out the corpse for one week of mourning, a cortege of ten men led a procession to inter the casket in the Old Picker Cemetery in south St. Louis. On December 2, Jean Pierre Beluze, Cabet's son-in-law, announced in Paris: "Brothers! It is necessary to add one more martyr on the long list of those who have died in the service of the People and of Humanity. . . . Citizen Cabet, the venerable Founder of Icaria, is no longer."[33] Without Cabet, the Icarians both in St. Louis and in Nauvoo gradually changed their lifestyle. The Cabetists, led by a thirty-five-year-old lawyer named Benjamin Mercadier, within three years voted to eliminate communism and adopt capitalism. And after the Majority relocated from Nauvoo to southwestern Iowa in 1860 they became a small, culturally impoverished, agricultural commune.

Mercadier's first report, published in Paris in February 1857, described the Cabetists' precarious situation. They were crammed into three buildings located about a mile apart from each other. They had no furniture, no coal or wood for heat, and were "without tools, belongings, with little money, with our old people, our nursing infants and numerous children." Some "were sick, others infirm, all were exposed to the many inconveniences of a large city [that] they knew nothing about and whose language was foreign to them."[34] But they made the best of what they had. Mercadier sent the men into the city to find whatever work they could find as tailors, shoemakers, and carpenters. The women earned money as cooks, dressmakers, and domestic servants. By February they had purchased furniture for the two resident buildings and tables and chairs and dinnerware for the third and largest building, the refectory. They started small workshops where they made barrels and furniture for sale in town. They enrolled the children in the nearby public school, but Mercadier appointed two adults to give them "Icarian instruction" in the evenings and on Sunday afternoons.[35]

Fortunately, Cabet had brought a wooden press and type with him, so they immediately started a weekly newspaper called the *Nouvelle Revue Icarienne* (New Icarian Review). Charles Mesnier, a fifty-seven-year-old musician, organized an orchestra that gave weekly concerts in the refectory. On February 3, 1857, they enjoyed a banquet in the refectory to celebrate the departure of the First Advance Guard to America in 1848. They put on small skits, also in the refectory, a weak imitation of the plays that had been presented at Nauvoo. They gathered in the evenings for a soirée, to discuss the day's events and the news from Europe that could be found in the city's newspapers placed on racks for reading in the refectory. With a chest of medicines brought from Nauvoo they were able to recover from their initial sicknesses. Only their financial condition remained precarious. Mercadier's report conceded that they were barely able to pay their bills.[36]

From the day he assumed leadership, Mercadier searched for a better location. He found one in the spring of 1857 six miles west of the city at a thirty-nine-acre former resort spa located along the Pacific Railroad. Called Cheltenham, it was a "charming parcel of prairie and woods, of white and green buildings, and along a small river traversed by a fine bridge."[37] St. Louis banker Thomas Allen offered him the property for $25,000, with $500 down and the balance due in ten annual payments at 6 percent interest. Allen must have been leery of Mercadier's ability to meet these terms because the mortgage stipulated that if he defaulted on just one payment the bank could sell the property. After paying the $500 there was just $59 left in the communal treasury. On May 8, 1857, the Icarians moved to their new home.

The ensuing months were euphoric times. Mercadier wrote to Beluze that they had "won out thanks to [our] activity and good organization, escaping the misery [of] the retreat from Nauvoo and the sudden death of [our] leader." He predicted a continued "state of well being" and "new enterprises in the general interest of the Icarian cause."[38] And for a while they did replicate the communal life they had known in Illinois. Tailors, cobblers, and coopers crafted their products in workshops. Carpenters, tailors, and blacksmiths contracted work from outsiders. Most women were seamstresses while some found jobs as domestic servants. The property contained a large stone house; they converted the upstairs into apartments and used the first floor as a refectory. The three other frame buildings were living quarters where, unlike at Nauvoo, families could stay together. In the basement of one of these buildings they opened an infirmary. Without horses and mules, they never planted crops but they bought a cow and several pigs. On Sunday afternoons their orchestra gave concerts in the dining room, and they continued the tradition of the evening soirée. In the same room they performed plays and skits.

Mercadier revived the Cours icarien and encouraged group participation with "heart and spirit." In sequence he had the adults discuss an assigned topic. Then they read and analyzed passages from Cabet's writings. Next, he had the children recite stories their parents had taught them. Finally, a concert ended the meeting. But Mercadier was often didactic. He tolerated no tardiness or lethargy. Icaria, he preached, "will be . . . saved by our perfections and lost by our imperfections." Icarians, he said, must be sober, temperate, and fraternal and engage "according to one's strength" in useful work. Women must avoid "those resources that are particular to the facial care and coquetry that the community cannot satisfy." Still, he confidently asserted at one of these sessions that "we have only to continue in the path which we followed [and] the Icarian cause will realize all the benefits which we expect of it."[39]

Cheltenham gradually sank into a financial morass, however. Hundreds of working days were lost when many Icarians came down with malaria and dysentery because of a mosquito-infected river bisecting the colony. Mercadier reported that "veritable epidemics" hit almost every family.[40] In his February 1859 *Lettre circulaire* (Circular letter), published by Beluze in Paris, he admitted that their income barely met expenses and there was nothing left to send to the banker. More alarming, the document showed that their revenue was steadily declining and that he, like Cabet, kept no account books. So, Mercadier never knew exactly how much money was coming in and going out. He wrote that "no one disputes the advantages" that would ensue if one knew "of the gains and losses of the Community, for the order, the management, and the knowledge of what happens."[41]

These financial problems were exacerbated by a blowup over Mercadier's leadership. It was prompted by a shocking change that he proposed. Cheltenham, he suggested, should abandon communism. He wanted them to become capitalists and sell their products at a maximum profit in St. Louis. Icarians, he argued, must "study commerce," know "how to make contracts, learn to buy at the lowest price and sell at the highest." Workshops must "manufacture on a large scale," and the men must "work quickly, not waste a single moment." Commerce, unfortunately, "has been neglected too much in the community," and this "has been a big mistake." Now, he concluded, "we must be familiar with the commodities and raw materials provided by the markets of New York, England, France, Paris, Rio de Janeiro, Buenos Aires, etc."[42]

A revolt began in November 1858 and continued over the next fifteen months, led by a volatile cap maker from Colmar named Vogel. He insisted that the general assembly eliminate the existing office of president and that the community be governed by a weak executive and a board of directors. In stormy debates throughout the winter sessions of the assembly, accusations flew back and forth between Vogel with his "dissidents" and Mercadier's supporters. Mercadier himself charged that Vogel had insulted Cabet's memory by demanding a "parliamentary government." A tailor named Dieuaide backed Vogel, arguing that the existing government was not a democracy but an aristocracy. He pointed out that Cabet's concentration of presidential power at Nauvoo had only been a temporary expedient to save the colony from disintegration, "an exception" he called it. But Mercadier wanted "to make the exception the rule." Titus Uttenveiler, a forty-year-old German from Dittenhausen, denounced Mercadier's "single direction" and his arbitrarily laying down of communal rules. The man, he said, simply had assumed "too much responsibility." Another dissident, Salarnier, added that "the People lay down the law, they alone [have] the executive power to enforce it."[43]

Mercadier presented the assembly with letters from thirty French Icarians that condemned any change in the presidency as an insult to Cabet's memory. On February 17, 1859, Mercadier called for and received a vote of confidence from a majority of the adult males. Then he had them pass a new set of strict rules akin to Cabet's *Declaration of Rights.* Tobacco and whiskey were forbidden. Everyone must toe the line and obey the decision of the president and the board of directors. The dissidents refused of course. Vogel said it was intolerable for him not to smoke his pipe or have a drink of whiskey. Then, when Mercadier pushed the change to capitalism, Vogel and forty-three adult males packed up and moved to St. Louis. Mercadier was only too glad to be rid of them. These "non-Icarians," he declared, were ignorant of Cabet's principles. They were "transient Icarians" who had joined the community only to enjoy themselves and not to try to build it.[44] But, as Prudhommeaux concluded, the rupture "was a terrible blow for the colony." The dissidents walked off with $1,800 worth of clothing and tools and $744 in cash and IOUs. Only ninety-three adults remained at Cheltenham, and they were unable to earn enough money to pay the bills. On January 3, 1860, Mercadier detailed their predicament in a letter to Beluze. He lamented that the creditors were closing in, and that the coming year would "be grave for us." He confessed that they still had to pay the owner of the New Bremen properties $1,300 in back rent. The next mortgage payment of $1,500 was due the following month, and Mercadier confessed he had just $300 in cash and $235 worth of unused credit with local merchants. But he must have concealed these facts from the Icarians because they went right on living as before. They dug irrigation ditches to drain the swampy areas close to the river. They planted trees and installed a new pump to bring fresh well water to the refectory.[45]

When the Civil War broke out in April 1861, twenty-six men, including Mercadier, enlisted in the Union army. Union troops were billeted at the colony in May, which imposed an enormous burden on Cheltenham's food supplies. Panic gripped the community. All work ceased. Banker Allen threatened foreclosure. By November 1861 their food was gone and they were out of cash. That month, nineteen more men went off to war, seduced by a promise of 160 acres of tillable land under the pending Homestead Bill and an annuity of $414. In December 1862 Mercadier, now back at Cheltenham, admitted that "the American war hit like a low blow."[46] Four men with their families left for St. Louis. By the fall of 1863 Icaria had only twenty-one men, twenty-nine women, and thirty-two children. Mercadier himself had rented a house in St. Louis. On a bleak afternoon in March 1864 his successor, a thirty-four-year-old tailor from Tallard called Arsène Sauva, gathered together the remnant (eight men, seven women, and a few children) for a final meeting in the stone refectory. Afterward, some Soldiers of Humanity followed Mercadier to St. Louis. Others, such as Sauva, traveled north to southwestern Iowa to join the rump remnant of the Nauvoo Majority, which had relocated there in 1860.

The Nauvoo Icaria, after the exodus of the Cabetists, had been left woefully undermanned and economically crippled by the Panic of 1857. There were just eighty-three men to run the workshops and the farms. Its profitable distillery, which accounted for half of the community's annual income, was left with one person to run it and had to shut down. Beluze informed them that, since they had expelled Cabet, they could have no more financial support from Paris. Because of the economic panic, creditors were demanding larger payments on a debt that had risen to over $32,000.[47] In an April 1857 session of the general assembly, the men elected Marchand as president, voted to dispose of all property at a public auction, and chose Gérard as trustee in charge of the process. The auction was held in August 1859, and the editor of the *Hamilton, Illinois, Representative* reported that "the Temple block, with the four frame buildings . . . and the mill and appendages" were sold for over $21,000. Using this income as collateral, the communards secured a loan from William Shepherd, a railroad investor and banker from Jerseyville, Illinois, for the remaining debt of $11,000. Then they assumed a mortgage of $3,875 for thirty-one hundred acres of federal land in Adams County, Iowa.[48]

Marchand organized the community for relocation by dispatching an advance guard of fourteen men and four women to the remote site. At the time the place was unsettled prairie, and the town of Corning, the Adams County seat, had just a few dozen homes. The nearest supply base, St. Joseph, Missouri, was seventy miles away. By the fall of 1860, a disappointing small number of Icarians, 61 of the 239 Majority, had moved to the place. They erected seven log cabins for families and a larger cabin for single men. They put up a log refectory, which became the colony kitchen and dining room as well as its washhouse, bakery, grocery store, and library. Log workshops were built for making wooden shoes, sewing, and blacksmithing. On the Nodaway River they put up a flour mill and sawmill, and nearby a barn, pigpen, and chicken house. The 1860 census listed 366 acres of cultivated land and 2,759 acres of prairie and timber. They had farm machinery valued at $1,258, and 19 horses, 35 dairy cattle, 37 "other cattle," 29 oxen, 130 sheep, and 300 pigs. In addition to what was itemized in the census, they harvested 2,495 bushels of corn, 500 bushels of oats, 300 pounds of wool, 250 pounds of butter, 30 tons of hay, and some sorghum molasses. However, there was no nearby market for any of these products, and consequently by 1862 their debt had increased to over $17,500.[49]

Ironically, the Civil War—the event that caused the demise of the Cheltenham Icaria—in fact saved the Corning community. Only two men joined the Union army; the others stayed at Icaria and worked to supply the troops. For Union purchasing agents, this was the only place north of St. Joseph to acquire food for the soldiers and grain for the horses and mules. And the Icarians demanded premium prices. Consequently, their "Statement of Revenue . . . Since 1860," published in 1867, showed that they had paid off all creditors and liquidated the mortgage except for about $800.

By 1870 Icaria was in full bloom. They had 400 acres in corn and wheat, 400 in pasture and timber. Livestock numbered 40 horses, 140 cattle, and 600 sheep. They were shipping these products to Omaha by a new railroad, the C. B. & Q., which crossed the northern edge of Icaria. By that year all the log structures had been replaced by attractive frame buildings. American visitors, such as Alcander Longley, C. A. White, Charles Nordhoff, and Oneidan William Hinds, all curious about this village of wooden-shoed French farmers, came to the colony and transcribed their impressions and observations. These accounts, plus the published reminiscences of Marie Marchand Ross, the daughter of Alexis Armel Marchand, provide a detailed picture of life in the utopia.[50]

Icaria was now a prosperous community, governed by a general assembly, a president, and four directors. Before the arrival of new members in 1876, they enjoyed an ambiance of conviviality. Marchand was no Cabet. He saw his responsibility just to be the representative of the colony to outsiders and not to enforce his ideas upon the community. Albert Shaw found him "serene and kindly in manner, lofty in his standards of right and duty, almost a mystic in his devotion to communism and the welfare of mankind . . . a true type of altruist." Sauva, just after he arrived from Cheltenham, wrote that "our system is pure democracy and we experience no difficulty in its application. . . . Our officers are elected to execute the decisions of the General Assembly and have no other power." However, the women, just as in Nauvoo and Cheltenham, could vote only on special questions—admissions, constitutional changes, and the director in charge of housing and clothing.[51]

Just as in Nauvoo, Icariennes dressed in white blouses and skirts of calico and dark blue Amana cloth, which they purchased from this German utopia located one hundred miles to the east. The men wore bib denim overalls and straw hats. All adults worked in wooden shoes called sabots. Breakfast was taken in their homes with their families. At noon they were summoned by a dinner bell to the refectory for the main meal of meat, vegetables, and milk or water. They returned to the building for a modest supper of stew. The first floor of the refectory had nine round tables that each sat eight or ten people. On its walls J. C. Shroeder, a German artist, painted landscapes topped by rows of women's heads with curling locks connected by garlands of vines and flowers. He sketched in huge letters "Equality" over the door and the word "Liberty" above the fireplace. Half of the building's second floor was a recreation hall for dances and plays and had a billiard table. The other half of the floor was used for the library. They had a barn, a slaughterhouse, and workshops for baking, shoemaking, and blacksmithing as well as a laundry and a pharmacy. Women were seamstresses and cooks and did the laundry. As in Cheltenham the children attended a public school located within walking distance of the colony. In this one-room frame structure, seventeen-year-old Icarienne Hortense Montaldo gave them singing lessons and taught courses in reading, spelling, and arithmetic for the younger students and in chemistry, natural philosophy, physiology, hygiene, and geography for the teenagers. From time to time Schroeder gave drawing lessons. Indeed, the Icarians enjoyed the same simple wholesome life as their Amana neighbors. Both utopias were agricultural villages aiming just to produce "enough food for the society's population and, in addition, raw materials for various business enterprises." So, a decade after the end of the Civil War, the Corning Icaria was "based predominantly upon agriculture, reluctant to enlarge the profitable milling operation, and unenthusiastic about hard work in general."[52]

Unfortunately, in this bucolic setting in 1876 there arrived several younger men who had fought in the Paris Commune uprising of 1871 and who were imbued with the enthusiasm of militant communism. They were appalled at what they found. No longer was Icaria, as Cabet had envisioned, a beacon light for the betterment of humanity. Instead, these Icarians were complacent—if not outright dull—farmers largely unconcerned with what was happening in the world. In the fall meeting of the general assembly, these young men demanded basic changes. Women should be given full suffrage. Anyone should be admitted who was of good character. The family homes were a source of individualism and selfishness and should be replaced by communal apartments. They planned to revive the Cours icarien in order to increase discussion of serious moral and social issues.[53]

After a year of debate in which nothing was settled, things came to a head in the fall 1877 meetings of the general assembly when the community, reminiscent of Nauvoo in 1856, split into belligerent camps. On one side were the Conservatives, made up of Marchand and the older Icarians, and on the other side were the young Progressives, led by a thirty-year-old mechanic, Émile Péron, backed by two other young men, Simon Dereure and Alexis Tanguy. On September 26, 1877, Péron harangued the assembly, controlled by the Conservatives, and accused them of intransigence. He threatened that if the Progressives' reforms were not accepted, they would boycott all work assignments and refuse to participate in communal life.

During the first week of October the Progressives drafted two documents, the "Social Program" and the "Reciprocal Engagement," and circulated them for signatures. The "Social Program" argued that an Icarian must commit "his knowledge, energy, and existence to the general interest and the cause of the people and not to the interest of some individual or to a mediocre community." They insisted upon equal rights for women. They believed that rules for communal life should be based upon reason, discussion, and truth—not blind adherence to Cabet's writings. For example, they condemned his rigorous admission policy that required a detailed knowledge of his publications. They wanted to embark on an outreach mission to American cities and distribute Icarian literature to the "suffering and oppressed." They demanded an end to the importance of farming, in order to diversify economically and make the colony "great and prosperous" by selling colony-made products in Corning. They wanted family homes, the "source of inequality, selfishness, and individualism," to be torn down and replaced with communal buildings. The second document was much shorter and simply stated that, after the present "pseudo-community" was dissolved, they would continue to build the real Icaria.[54]

In the assembly meeting on October 6, the Progressives moved to reorganize the community into two "autonomous branches" that would live in separate locations. Marchand wanted no part of such a division. He pulled the old Nauvoo trick on the Progressives. He temporarily locked the warehouse and refused to give the Progressives any food or supplies. They in turn hired lawyers and sued the Conservatives in Adams County Circuit Court, claiming they had a legal right to community goods "proportional to their needs." Marchand acquiesced to the Progressives' demands and unlocked the warehouse. Afterward the two camps took turns using the refectory for meals. Every morning each group went to the warehouse and took out its share of meat, vegetables, and fruit, and its allotment of wine from the refectory kitchen.[55]

In this acrimonious environment, a six-man commission made up of three Conservatives and three Progressives met to see if a reconciliation was possible. It was hopeless. When the Progressives suggested they should keep the existing buildings and the Conservatives should move out, the older Icarians were livid. Charles Levy said that such a proposal was "an insult." He shouted, "You young fellows must leave! You have your youth, enthusiasm, capabilities. You have the work habits to clear the fields. Why, then, do you want to sit still, here on what we have created?"[56]

On January 14, 1878, the nineteen Conservative men appeared before Judge D. D. Gregory of Adams County Circuit Court and submitted a written statement. They offered to work with the Progressives to restore "good disposition" to Icaria if they could get them to cooperate. But if not, then they would give each Progressive a $100 severance subsidy. This sum, when added to the refunds the Progressives were entitled to under the community constitution, would give them a total of over $8,000. The

Progressives responded by having the local weekly newspaper, the *Corning Union,* print on February 21 a statement denouncing the offer as unfair and stating that they were going to petition the judge for a jury trial to settle the standoff.[57]

On March 2, 1878, Sauva, the leader of the Conservatives at the time, convened a meeting in the refectory. They condemned a jury trial as too expensive and time-consuming. Instead, they would ask the judge to appoint an arbitration board of former Icarians living in the county. The Progressives went along with the idea of arbitration but wanted the board to be made up of Americans. The judge took both arguments under advisement. During the next six months, while awaiting his decision, both sides published their respective positions. Sauva wrote the Conservative view in *La crise icarienne, 1877–1878* (The Icarian crisis, 1877–1878). In May the Progressives started a newspaper, *La Jeune Icarie* (The young Icaria), in which they reiterated their demands, the most important of which was giving the franchise to women.

Finally, in June 1878, the judge rejected arbitration and ordered a jury trial for the August session of the court. The trial began on August 9 and lasted nine days. The Conservatives' lawyer Frank M. Davis represented the defendants. He said that the Progressives (he called them "the separatists") were misdirected if not dishonest zealots who wanted to spread communism beyond the community. They were going to open stores in Corning to compete with local businessmen. Inside Icaria these "troublemakers" were asking for changes that went "far beyond that which was outlined in its charter of incorporation." He concluded by asking the judge to end this "menace" by ordering the radicals expelled. The Progressives' attorneys, J. H. Maley and J. D. McDill, spoke for the plaintiffs. They informed the jury that the only way anyone could be expelled from Icaria, according to its constitution, was by a vote of two-thirds of the men in assembly. The actual remedy to the situation, they said, was found in state law. Under Iowa statutes, the community was chartered only as an agricultural corporation. But the community operated a sawmill and sold lumber and also sheep's wool for profit. As a result the articles of incorporation had already been violated, and the judge should dissolve the community and distribute its assets equally among its members. On Friday August 16, the jury deliberated from eleven in the morning until ten that evening. On Saturday morning, the clerk of the court James W. Widner read the sealed verdict: "We the jury find for the plaintiff." The Conservatives were stunned. Davis immediately filed a motion to have the verdict set aside and asked for a new trial. Judge Gregory overruled the motion. He ordered the charter vacated and appointed three American trustees to distribute its assets. He wrote: "It is therefore ordered and adjudged by the court that the defendant—the Icarian Community of Adams County, Iowa—

be and is hereby ousted and altogether excluded from the franchise or privileges of a corporation and that said defendant cease to exercise any of the powers, rights or privileges of a corporation under the laws of the State of Iowa." He named two Icarians, one from each side, to represent its interests to the trustees. The trustees stipulated that the Conservatives would remain on the original site and own the western half of the colony. The Progressive would have to build another community on the eastern half of the property, about 1,204 acres, where they could put up their buildings at least a mile away from the Conservatives.[58]

Complying with this decision the Progressives dragged some of the existing structures on logs to the new location and began to build a refectory. They called themselves "Young Icaria," and for four years they tried to rekindle communal life. But the task proved impossible. As Albert Shaw, who met with these communards, put it: "There were too many clever men, and no one with a gift of leadership sufficient to assimilate and unify the group . . . . there was no real 'solidarity.'" Another problem was the open admissions policy. *La Jeune Icarie* conceded that they took in "all sorts of unfortunates—reformers, disciples of all known schools . . . they had free lovers, Shakers, nihilists, libertarians, socialists of all shades, cranks of all sorts." Within a year there were twenty-five provisional members and thirty-two permanent Icarians. In Corning, they opened a shoe shop, a blacksmith's forge, and a broom factory, but most of the new members, while willing to work in skilled crafts and in the colony stores, had no time for the hot and dirty routine of farming. When it became obvious that they had to do farmwork just to keep the community going, they left. Within four years Young Icaria's debt had risen to over $7,000 and all of their shops in town had closed.[59]

In 1884 they sold their land and moved to Cloverdale, California, about eighty miles north of San Francisco. Naming their community Icaria Speranza (Icaria of Hope), they took out a $15,000 mortgage for an 885-acre ranch and planted a hundred acres of wheat and put in peach trees. They also built a sawmill. The colony was administered by five committees, elected by an assembly in which all adults could vote. They abandoned communism and ran the colony on a profit-sharing plan. Now the community owned the property and income but annually distributed the profits equally among members. The colony also allowed private property, and members could keep up to $50 in cash as a personal fund. However, Icaria Speranza had only ten families and lacked the manpower and the capital to sustain a self-contained community. They compounded the problem and made it practically impossible to recruit new members by insisting that an applicant demonstrate fluency in French and be versed in Cabet's publications. When they were unable to meet their obligations, in June 1886 their creditors filed a suit in the county circuit court. On August 3, the court dissolved the colony and ordered all its land and assets sold to pay its debts.[60]

By that time, back in Iowa, the Conservatives had become just a small group of mostly retired farm families. New Icaria, as they called themselves, consisted of thirty-four people—twelve men, ten women, and twelve teenagers. They were indistinguishable from other farmers in the county except for their French accents and wooden sabots. Like their antagonists in California, they had revised the admission rules to make it difficult to become an Icarian. Now the candidate had to receive a nine-tenths' majority vote to be admitted as a provisional member. Then, after a year's probation, he or she had to pay a fee of $100 for each adult and $20 for each child. Marchand's daughter, Marie Marchand Ross, visited the colony briefly in 1890 and found nine men, six of them between sixty-one and seventy-four years old, and eight elderly women. She was overcome with melancholy. "The community really did not exist any more," she wrote, "since there were only a few people left and most of them very old and not able to do the heavy work of the farm."[61]

The Icarians themselves accepted their situation. On February 16, 1898, they silently gathered at one table in the now nearly vacant refectory. Unanimously they voted to dissolve Icaria. Marchand, eighty-one years old and still in charge, said he would ask the circuit court to appoint him as receiver to supervise the process. On Saturday morning, October 22, Judge Horace M. Towner signed the order dissolving the last Icaria. "The lamp of mystical idealism, lit by Cabet's imagination in the Reading Room of the British Museum some sixty years before, had gone out."[62]

CHAPTER SIX

Hutterite Bruderhofs

The Hutterites created the last nineteenth-century religious utopia in the Heartland and, along with the secular Icarians, formed the longest-lived experiments. According to Donald B. Kraybill and Carl Desportes Bowman, they were originally one of four Anabaptist denominations of sixteenth-century Europe: the other "free" church sects were the Mennonites, the Amish, and the Brethren.[1] However, only the Hutterites lived communally in a *Bruderhof* (or "brother's farmyard"), practiced *Gutergemeinschaft* (community of goods), and *Gelassenheit* (complete submission to God). In Europe they abandoned communalism for seventy years from 1693 to 1763, and again for forty years from 1818 to 1859. Followers of Jakob Hutter, they traced their beginnings to Zurich when, in 1525, Conrad Grebel gave a former Catholic priest, George Blaurock, a "true Christian baptism." After Hutter was executed by torture and a public burning in Innsbruck in March 1536, his followers fled to Moravia, in the eastern Holy Roman Empire. Here they swore complete submission to God and emphasized, as Gertrude E. Huntington put it, that "all material goods, all gifts from God, one's life and limb, must be surrendered to God and the church."[2]

Between 1565 and 1618, called the "golden years of the Hutterite movement," 102 Bruderhofs appeared in Moravia, each with a population of about 450 individuals. The communities usually had about forty thatched-roof structures surrounding a central square. The buildings were family living quarters, workshops, a dining hall and kitchen, and schools. The community was led by a *Vorsteher* (First Preacher), who directed the raising of livestock, planting of corn, cultivation of orchards, and the operation of a flour mill, sawmill, and winery. They prospered from income earned by craftsmen who built carriages for the local nobility or were skilled watchmakers, coppersmiths, and dyers. Hutterites were also renowned for the high quality of their ceramics, roof and wall tiles, and tableware.

In 1618 the Thirty Years War broke out between Catholics and Protestants. Both sides ravaged the Bruderhofs since they "stood out among the poverty-stricken villages of Moravia, attracting the invaders with their full barns." Moreover, their pacifism meant nonresistance and made them easy targets for marauding troops. During the first year of the war alone, over thirty colonies were destroyed, and by 1621 an estimated one-third had been looted and sacked. Ravaged by hunger and disease, the survivors scattered into Hungary, Transylvania, Romania, and eventually southern Russia.[3]

By 1770 most of them had arrived at the estate of Count Peter Alexander Rumiantsev-Zadunaisky, located 120 miles north of Kiev on the Desna River. The count signed a twelve-part contract with them that guaranteed the community of goods, assured protection for religious freedom, and granted them exemptions from taking oaths, serving in the military, and from paying property taxes. Under the count's protection the Hutterites prospered. But when he died in 1796, his two sons tried to rescind the contract and force the Hutterites to work on the farmlands of Tsar Paul I. The Hutterites petitioned the tsar to intervene, because, they claimed, the contract was a binding agreement that could not be arbitrarily broken. The petition was granted, and in 1802, on orders of the tsar, they were relocated to two thousand acres of crown land at Radichev, eight miles from the estate. Here they built a community to house forty-four families. Soon they replicated the communal life with a mill, distillery, and shops for making pottery, leather goods, cabinets, and tailored goods.[4]

Within a decade, however, Jakob Walther led a movement to dissolve the community of goods, stating that he would "rather die" than continue to live in a Bruderhof. Walther and his followers, about thirty families, had grown up in the peaceful environment of Russia and scoffed at the idea of communal life. Also, according to Yaacov Oved, they "lacked a serious approach to duties and work, and their discipline grew slack." Conservatives, led by Johannes Waldner, insisted on continuing the sacred traditions: "I would rather go to the martyr's stake than give up the old practice," Waldner declared.[5]

But in 1819, after a fire destroyed most of the homes in Radichev, they, too, established private farms. Thereafter, the two groups lived noncommunally, physically separated from each other on opposite sides of the Desna River. Waldner was the Vorsteher for both factions, though, while Walther supervised all financial matters. Unfortunately, private farms could not sustain the communities since only seven hundred of the two thousand acres were arable. So, in 1834, they petitioned the tsar to move to crown lands in Molotchna, Crimea, in an area already settled by Mennonites. Their request was denied.

In 1842 a Mennonite government official, Johann Cornies, agreed to sponsor the relocation. With his backing the government permitted sixty-nine families to settle at Hutteral, on condition that they send their children to Mennonite schools and have their adolescents work on Mennonite farms. They were allowed to keep their style of dress and to live in their own village, although it had to be laid out like a Mennonite settlement, with houses on both sides of a main street and barns and shops in the rear. The move was salutary. Now, in contrast to the isolation they had known in Russia, they were in contact with a prosperous community of six thousand Moravians. The Hutterites flourished; and in 1848 the tsar permitted them to build a second village called Johannesruh, then three more at Hutterdorf (1856), Neu-Hutteral (1857), and Scheromet (1868).[6]

The experience of living among the Mennonites fostered a desire to return to communalism, because some Hutterites who lacked the sect's traditional motivation became Mennonites. In 1859 Michael Waldner, a blacksmith, organized a community of goods called the *Schmiedeleut,* or the blacksmith's people. The next year, Darius Walter organized the *Dariusleut,* or Darius's people. Until 1864 the three groups—the noncommunal villages, the Schmiedeleut, and the Dariusleut—lived peacefully alongside each other. But in 1871 the tsar introduced compulsory military service. When this happened their leaders went to St. Petersburg to meet with the Imperial Council to ask for exemptions if they would colonize undeveloped parts of the country. The council rebuffed their request. It did agree, however, to assign them nonmilitary service if drafted.[7]

Under these circumstances, in April 1873, some communal and noncommunal Hutterites sent a delegation to the United States to find a place to colonize. Paul Tschetter and his nephew Lorenz, both noncommunal, arrived in New York City and went by train to Elkhart, Indiana, to visit John Funk, a Mennonite publisher. Hiring him as a guide and interpreter, they traveled by mail coach to Minnesota, South Dakota, and Manitoba. Tschetter's diary recorded his impressions of the "fine orchards and pastures and beautiful fields of grain" of the Indiana Mennonites. South of Grand Forks, he found "very fine level land, black soil, and a good growth of grass . . . [and] excellent hayland." Michael Hiller, a railway agent, arranged a meeting with President Ulysses S. Grant on July 27, 1873, at Long Beach, New York. Tschetter wrote that "the President received us in the most friendly manner and we presented our petition to him personally." The petition requested exemption from military service and jury duty and the right to have their own schools. Grant responded by letter. He informed them that, though he could not act on the request because the second and third items were under state law, he predicted no reinstatement of the draft for "the next fifty years."[8]

After the two men reported their findings, a minority prepared to leave the Ukraine for the New World. "What is often forgotten," Rod Janzen has pointed out, "is that these 425 people represented only one-third of those individuals—all of whom had the same ethnic and historical roots—who in the 1870s referred to themselves as 'Hutterites.'"[9] Families of Schmiedeleuts and Dariusleuts, with an equal number of noncommunal Hutterites, left Hamburg in June 1874 for New York City. They arrived on July 17 and went by train to the Dakota Territory where in August, for $25,000, the Schmiedeleut bought twenty-five hundred acres on the Missouri River west of the town of Yankton. They called the colony Bon Homme. They put down $17,000 and assumed a mortgage for the balance. The Dariusleut purchased a similar parcel of land, located about forty miles north of the Schmiedeleut colony, at Wolf Creek near Silver Lake. A third communal group of thirteen families, known as the *Lehrerleut* (teacher's followers) and led by a teacher, Jacob Wipf, left Russia in 1877 and lived communally on 5,440 acres at Old Elmspring acres near Parkston.[10]

At the time of the 1880 census, 443 Hutterites were living in Bruderhofs along with farmsteads of 822 noncommunal Hutterites (including Paul and Lorenz Tschetter). Known as *Prairieleut* (prairie people), they lived on private farms, "taking advantage of the Homestead Act or buying out previous settlers who had given up on South Dakota for one reason or another." During the first years there was extensive contact between the communal Hutterites and the Prairieleut; and at least nine Prairieleut families joined the communalists and twelve communal families became Prairieleut. There were nine "crossover" families—those who lived first on private farms, then became communal, and finally returned to private property. Considerable intermingling occurred in terms of marriages, trading, and social activities. Even so, for the most part, the communal Hutterites saw the Prairieleut as not fully committed to the gospel because they refused to surrender individualism. Life, they believed, "required daily cooperation, openness, group discipline and an emphasis on simple living," Janzen concluded. Therefore, the "Hutterites felt the *Prairieleut* were selfish and materialistic." As far as their American neighbors were concerned, most Bruderhofs were located in ravines and were so physically removed that people thought they were Mennonites.[11]

The communal Hutterites, while largely isolated from Americans, had contacts with the Amana villages and with the Rappites at Economy. In 1875, just after their arrival in South Dakota, the Rappites loaned them $3,000 to construct a flour mill. In 1879 when the Bon Homme colony ran short of money after battling grasshoppers, locusts, and spring floods and the resulting crop failures, the colony contacted the wealthy Pennsylvania commune for another loan of $3,000. They also invited the Rappites to visit the colony, and the offer was accepted. Jacob Henrici came away impressed with the sincerity of communal life in the "ark" and granted Bon Homme the loan. In 1889 the Rappites negotiated a resettlement of nineteen Hutterite families to Tidoute, Pennsylvania, under the leadership of Michael Waldner. Two years later, however, these Hutterites returned to South Dakota to build a new Bruderhof at Milltown. Still, the two societies proposed to keep in touch because of the similarities of their beliefs and communal life. The only issue that divided them, the Harmonists said, was the Hutterite sanctioning of marital relations. Mutual contact continued for over a decade. In 1878 Bon Homme encountered financial difficulties when it had to split up and start a second Bruderhof, the Tripp colony, because of its increased population. So the Hutterites got in touch with Amana for help, and that community responded by offering a loan. According to John W. Bennett, "several *Prairieleut* Hutterian families intermarried with the Amana people in the late nineteenth century."[12]

In 1898 with the outbreak of the Spanish-American War, the Hutterites feared they could become involved in supporting the war through taxation or conscription. They sent a delegation to Winnipeg, Manitoba, to explore the idea of moving there. This venture resulted in a visit from members of the Canadian Ministry of Interior. They recommended that the Hutterites be allowed to settle under conditions enjoyed by the Mennonites, granted an exemption from military service, and be permitted to have their own educational system. But the U.S. Congress never passed a conscription act, so only one Bruderhof actually moved to Canada, and it returned to South Dakota in 1905.[13]

By 1910 the number of Hutterite colonies had increased significantly, because of their rule that a new community must be started when a Bruderhof reached 110 inhabitants. They believed that each new generation must have the experience of living in a small but growing community. Life was not the same as they had known in the Ukraine. Now they lived in agricultural colonies, except that they also made household utensils and farm tools. They raised livestock, waterfowl, and pigeons. They had water-powered mills that ground flour and cornmeal, which they sold to their American neighbors. Their geese, ducks, and pigeons provided meat to eat and feathers for bedding. They made their own shoes, tanned leather, and spun wool. The largest and most prosperous, Bon Homme, in the 1900 census listed four hundred cattle, twenty-three hundred sheep, two hundred hogs, seven hundred geese, two hundred ducks, and twenty-one horse teams to pull the farm machinery.

In 1917 when the United States entered World War I, seventeen

Bruderhofs housed over two thousand communards in South Dakota, and there were two in Montana. But in just one year the demographic picture changed dramatically: sixteen new colonies were started in Canada. The cause of this exodus was twofold. One aspect was Congress's passing and strict enforcement of the Selective Service Act. This required registration of all males between the ages of twenty-one and thirty-one, with no exemptions. The other aspect was the rabid anti-German hysteria that swept the nation in the months after the war began. The federal Committee on Public Information, headed by George Creel, flooded the country with propaganda that whipped up hatred toward German Americans. Many believed that the country was honeycombed with agents of the Kaiser. Congress reacted in the Espionage Act of June 15, 1917, and the Sedition Act of May 16, 1918, that imposed a fine of $20,000 and twenty years in prison for any citizen interfering with, or even opposing, the war.[14] Congressman Victor L. Berger was expelled by the House, newspaper editors were arrested, and Socialist Party four-time presidential candidate Eugene V. Debs was sentenced to twenty years in prison. Hutterites were among the victims of this paranoia.

Hutterite elders decided to obey the Selective Service Act but told the men not to wear a uniform, obey orders, or assist the war effort. As a result drafted Hutterites were beaten and tortured. Some were pushed naked into a cold shower and dragged outside along the ground. Others were submerged in tanks of water and almost drowned. Some had to stand at attention in freezing weather for hours. Some were chased across open fields by men on motorcycles until they collapsed from exhaustion. After such torments all draftees were confined in stockades on bread and water diets.[15]

One such episode resulted in death. Four inducted men—Jacob Wipf and three Hofer brothers—refused to sign admission papers and wear a uniform. They were sentenced to thirty-seven years in prison and shipped to Alcatraz. There they were locked in the "hole" and slept on wet concrete floors without adequate clothing or food. Insect bites made their skin erupt with sores. Guards beat them with clubs and hanged them for hours from the ceiling with their arms tied behind their backs. After four months at Alcatraz they were sent to Fort Leavenworth, Kansas, chained together two-by-two and guarded by six armed soldiers. Upon arrival at the base they had to stand at attention outside in the chilling cold for hours. Two of the Hofer brothers, Joseph and Michael, collapsed and were hospitalized. David Hofer and Jacob Wipf were put in solitary confinement on a starvation diet. Each day they had to stand nine hours with their hands tied and their feet just touching the floor. They, too, collapsed and were hospitalized. A telegram was sent to their wives permitting them to visit the four men. The women arrived at the hospital at midnight and found their husbands too weak to talk. When they returned the next morning Joseph was dead. Michael died two days later. The elders dispatched a special delegation to meet with President Wilson to protest these atrocities. They only saw Secretary of War Newton D. Baker. He not only refused to help but issued an order to court-martial any soldier who refused to follow orders.[16]

Local newspapers in South Dakota and Montana attacked "these German-speaking people." They alleged that these "Kaiser supporters" profited from the high prices for agricultural products but refused to buy Liberty Bonds. Yankton high school students tossed German textbooks into the Missouri River. A vigilante mob invaded the Jamesville Bruderhof, stole one hundred cattle and one thousand sheep, and sold the animals for $14,000. They used the money to purchase war bonds. Another marauding group raided Bon Homme. In May 1918 the *Sioux Falls Press* praised these actions and concluded that the Hutterites should "pack up what they can carry and return to that part of Europe whence they come. . . . We should ask them to be so good as to leave behind the land this nation practically gave them."[17]

The elders contacted the Canadian government and received assurances that they were welcome and would be granted the same exemptions given them in 1899. They sold their acres at enormous losses and purchased land in Alberta and Manitoba where they constructed fifteen Bruderhofs. Only the Bon Homme community refused to emigrate.[18] By 1940 there were fifty-two communities in Canada. But by then the economic impact of the Great Depression had caused some Schmiedeleuts to contemplate returning to the United States where, they hoped, they might get help through various New Deal programs. Most Dariusleuts and Lehrerleuts wanted no part of going back. The Schmiedeleuts contacted South Dakota politicians and found them anxious to support anything that might increase agricultural production. The Americans told them the government would respect communal ownership of property and exempt them from state taxes. Over the following years fifteen new Bruderhofs were built back in that state. When World War II started, pacifism again became an issue, but the 1942 conscription law allowed for conscientious objectors. So, instead of drafting Hutterites, the War Department had them serve in the Civilian Public Service program. In Canada the government built camps for the Hutterites and put the units under the authority of the Department of Mines and Resources. "Altogether in the United States and Canada," Hostetler observed, "there were 276 Hutterite objectors serving in some type of public service work."[19]

For Hutterites who remained in Canada, relations with their neighbors gradually deteriorated. Many Canadian farmers concluded that the communards were eventually going to own all the best land. The fact was that the Hutterites did pay premium prices, and they were always able to outbid Canadian bidders. Consequently, in 1942, Alberta passed the Land Sales Prohibition Act, which prohibited selling land to them. The law was justified, said its sponsor, Solon Low, "to allay public feelings which had been aroused to the point of threatened violence." In 1947 this was replaced by the Communal Property Act. Now Hutterites were allowed to purchase up to sixty-four hundred acres if the property was forty miles from an existing Bruderhof. Then, in 1960, the Alberta law was changed again in the Communal Property Act, which eliminated the forty-mile requirement but demanded that all land sales to Hutterites be approved by a communal property control board and the Alberta cabinet. In 1972 this law was amended by the *Report on Communal Property*, which encouraged the creation of a liaison office to supervise Hutterite purchases. The report had the Dariusleut and Lehrerleut each choose three elders to serve in the office. But when new colonies were started in Saskatchewan, local opposition persuaded the provincial government to investigate their activities.[20]

Land restriction encouraged the Hutterites to move back to the United States. Between 1945 and 2000, the Dariusleut constructed eleven Bruderhofs along the foothills of the Rocky Mountains as well as one colony at Warden, near Spokane, Washington. During the same time period the Lehrerleut started twenty new colonies in Montana. But, as in Canada, Hutterite expansion led to the charge of land monopoly. In 1953 the South Dakota legislature passed a law halting the purchase of additional acreage for existing Bruderhofs. Even so, the return to the United States continued. By 2000, the *Hutterite Telephone and Address Book* listed the following distribution of Bruderhofs: Washington (6), Montana (46), North Dakota (6), South Dakota (52), and Minnesota (6).[21]

Regardless of where they were located, each Bruderhof was built identically, laid out on a plan that symbolically represented a model of the universe, a "vestibule of heaven" as they were called. One member claimed that it was a "small enclosed porch outside of heaven." Consequently, each colony was orderly and regimented. "A ritualized program," Kraybill and Bowman observed, "of indoctrination, regimentation, and compliance ensures constancy and impedes change."[22] In the center there was an open square surrounded by living quarters, either apartment (called long houses) or three-room homes, on the east, south, and west. The dining hall with a bell and the church were placed at the northern border of the square. The hall also served as a laundry and a bath- and showerhouse. This strict geometry was an expression of Hutterite thought. As one man said: "You don't walk crooked to the earth, you walk straight, that is how buildings should be, straight with the compass and not askew." A long house contained four units, each with three rooms. The homes were all built to the same design. There was a central "entrance room," with a stairway to a second-floor storage area and furnished with a table and chairs, a cupboard with dishes, and a washbasin. On either side was a bedroom with a double bed, a sofa bed, and a crib. One bedroom was for the parents while the other was for children. Boys and girls slept together until the age of twelve when they were segregated with a separate, added room. Regardless of the ages of the children, extra rooms could be added according to the rule that there could be one room for every six children. Behind the dining hall was a two-room *Klein schul,* or kindergarten, for children aged from three to five years old. It had a table and benches, a cupboard, a sleeping section for naps, and a fenced-in play area. The school for children over the age of five was south of the square behind the living quarters. In larger Bruderhofs, there were two such buildings, side by side, for a German and an English school. They always located the barns, stables, chicken pens, grain bins, and feed mill northwest of the living area. A butcher and electrical shop stood to the immediate west of the square. The cemetery was in the southwest corner.[23]

Although the size of a Hutterite community varied, with the newer ones being the smallest, the average was thirty-five hundred acres. The colony was a highly mechanized farm, because Hutterites welcomed machinery so long as it was directly related to production and did not interfere with religious traditions. They refused, for example, to use radios and televisions, and they prohibited private automobiles. "Mechanization," Oved noted, "has continued to be at a high level and technical adaptability has characterized all their farming." A community produced between fifteen and twenty bushels per acre, although the land was not fertile enough to grow commercial crops such as wheat. Instead, as Gertrude Huntingdon put it, their "large-scale diversified agriculture [involved] the growing of wheat, oats, barley, and truck gardens and the raising of hogs, beef cattle, dairy cattle, laying hens, broilers, turkeys, geese, ducks, and bees."[24]

Two typical Bruderhofs were the Lehrerleut Milford, started in 1945 near Augusta, Montana, and the Schmiedeleut Forest River, founded in 1950 near Fordville, North Dakota. In the mid-1970s, Milford owned 4,500 acres and farmed with machinery, electricity, and trucks. It annually produced about 28,000 bushels of barley, 12,000 bushels of wheat, and 9,000 bushels of oats. They marked off 11,500 acres for pasture and gathered 36,000 bales of hay for winter feed. Milford had 40 dairy cows, which provided the community with milk and butter, and 500 beef cattle. Over 2,000 ducks and geese swam in the pond. Inside two buildings they raised pigs for brood sows and for feeding and fattening. Each year they slaughtered 1,000 lambs, whose meat and wool were sold to outsiders. Forest River was representative of Schmiedeleut communities in its extensive mechanization. About the same size as Milford, it raised 1,200 hogs, 44,000 chickens, 20,000 pullets, and 50 dairy cows. These Schmiedeleuts harvested grain for livestock, which they placed in storage elevators and a feed mill. Three truck gardens provided vegetables. They had an electric shop, a carpenter shop, and a blacksmith's shop. And, beginning in 1990, they "ran a grain salvage business that took them throughout the upper Midwest."[25]

Hutterites looked pretty much the same wherever they lived. This fact was not incidental, because, as Paul Conkin pointed out, the "main visible symbol of Hutterite separation from the sinful world is clothing and idiosyncrasies of personal appearance." They were not as plain and inflexible as the Amish, and their rules and ordinances on what was banned, which constituted the largest number of the bylaws, permitted variety and allowed some color and decorations. Men wore dark hats and ready-made jackets and trousers with suspenders. They used work shirts during the week and white shirts on Sunday. Married men were required to grow beards. Women abjured cosmetics and had a common style of dress. All clothing was made in the colony from cloth purchased in bolts. They wore wide, dark, ankle-length skirts and light-colored long-sleeved blouses covered by dark-colored fitted bodices. There was variation in the type of scarf they chose, but usually it was blue with white polka dots. In the summer they wore bonnets for protection from the sun. Children dressed as their parents. The young people spoke a "Hutterish" dialect (akin to that found today in the Carinthia province of Austria) until they were taught High German and English in school. Everyone used High German in religious services.[26]

The daily routine was orderly and regimented. The bell rang at a quarter past six in the morning, to summon the adults to breakfast. At a quarter to seven the children ate, in either the kindergarten or the school. A few adults, however, were awake much earlier. Some women were up at half past three to mix the bun dough, some cowmen were up at half past four to start milking, and new mothers were up at five o'clock to nurse their babies. The bell clanged again at a quarter past seven to start the day's work. Everyone stopped at nine o'clock for a snack. A ten o'clock bell meant that children should take their snack in the kindergarten and the school. At a quarter to twelve the bell summoned adults to their assigned places in the dining room for lunch. There, men and women seated by age sat at tables on opposite sides of the room. With four people to a table, they ate in silence, serving themselves from main dishes placed in the center of the table. At half past two the bell called women to the kitchen to prepare the evening meal. At five o'clock they brought food to the homes so that small children could have supper there. At six o'clock the rest of the children were served in the dining room. At half past six the bell mustered the adults to a brief service in the schoolhouse after which they moved to the dining room for supper, using the same seating arrangements as at lunch. When the meal was over, they socialized until they adjourned for the evening service. Interestingly, in marked contrast to the austerity of their daily routine, the Hutterite diet was varied and wholesome. "The enforced austerity of their life," Conkin pointed out, "does not preclude good but simple food and occasional allotments of beer, homemade wine, and even whiskey." The supper table included pork, fowl, beef, goose grease, starchy vegetables, breads, and sweet syrups.[27]

Women followed a strict daily schedule throughout the week. On Monday they did the washing, mending, and ironing. On Tuesday they turned to housework—usually dusting, cleaning, and polishing floors. Wednesday through Friday they worked in the truck gardens. On Saturday the unmarried women cleaned the schoolhouse for Sunday services. In the afternoon they returned to their homes and prepared for the next day's events. Women also cooked the food according to an exact time pattern. For example, on Monday and Wednesday they baked bread, and on Tuesday and Saturday they baked rolls. On Sunday they selected what would be served each day of the coming week for breakfast, lunch, and supper. A menu for one week of April 1964 for a Dariusleut colony listed exactly what was on the menu. For example, on Monday, breakfast was bacon and eggs with bread and cheese; lunch was hamburger and onions, potatoes, buttered carrots, cherries, and plums; supper was fresh bread with cheese, baked beans, fried potatoes, hamburger, and cold duck. On Thursday, breakfast was fried eggs, bread with cheese and celery; lunch was fresh bread, beef, horseradish, potatoes, buttered beets, and rice pudding; supper was French-fried potatoes, ground carrots, boiled eggs, and fresh bread.[28]

A church service on Saturday evening marked the onset of Sunday's routine. Here women and girls wore a designated Saturday dress and, along with the men, sang hymns and listened to accounts of Hutterite history. Then everyone went to bed early. The day began with a special breakfast where women dressed up in their best dresses, and children wore clean clothes. Then the women changed into "Bible clothes" and joined the men at a nine o'clock service in the schoolhouse. It ended at half past ten. After the noon meal everyone returned to their homes for a rest until half past four. Unbaptized members, however, met with a Sunday school teacher to learn Hutterite history, memorize hymns, and discuss the morning sermon. During this free time families sometimes visited other Bruderhofs. Many colonies permitted no work on Sunday.[29]

The evening service took place in the schoolhouse where, in an undecorated room lined with benches, men sat on one side and women on the other according to age and facing the colony preacher and officers. Children sat between the adults and the preacher. He began the service by leading a "quiet time" after which, still seated, he announced the hymn and sang its first line from a hymnbook, or *Gesangbuchlein*. Only the preacher had this book in which were transcribed songs about the Bible or

Hutterite history. Everyone then imitated him, line by line, through the hymn by singing in a loud high voice to demonstrate their deep feelings about a people freed from sin. Next, in a high-pitched monotone he preached a sermon that included passages from the Bible and Hutterite history. He always conveyed the same simple message: obey God's laws, love your neighbor, and avoid temptation. He closed with a benediction of a memorized prayer as everyone knelt with hands folded and faces uplifted. Then everyone went to the kitchen for a snack. At nine o'clock the women prepared the children for bed and soon afterward the adults retired. At sunrise on Monday the weekly routine began all over again.[30]

Communal cohesiveness was reinforced by singing and taking communion. The first activity was a daily practice, the second was observed just once a year. Hutterites sang everywhere—in the home on long winter evenings, in school, at work, and in church services. No instruments were permitted, and their intonations in loud, shrill, nasal voices were described by one historian as having a "hypnotic, emotional catharsis" as well as an "outlet for emotional expression." Sung from memory, many songs had over a hundred stanzas and went on for hours. They "contain the drama of their lives and their world view—paraphrases of great Bible stories, songs of the martyrs, and touching experiences of the faithful."[31] There were variations, however. Singing in religious services was slower than at school or at home but was just as loud and vigorous. And there were special occasions for singing such as at a wedding or a funeral where intonations might go on for hours.

The annual communion was a time of spiritual renewal. It was observed the day after Easter by all baptized Hutterites. There was no fasting prior to the ceremony nor was there ceremonial foot washing. Bread for communion was baked from a special recipe. At the start of the ceremony the preacher ate a piece of the bread and then the loaf was passed around the congregation hand to hand. Any fragments were returned to the preacher's table. Wine, either made in the colony or purchased, was distributed in simple white pottery pitchers. As with the bread, the preacher first drank it and then distributed it to the congregation. Finally, after the serving of the bread and wine everyone sang loud praises to God.[32]

Hutterites had no other forms of entertainment or social organization other than singing—and, except for needlework, no crafts or arts. They read only on religious topics or on practical matters of running the Bruderhof. They had no newspapers or periodicals. Aside from singing, their main source of diversion was animated conversation. "They are delightful conversationalists," Conkin observed, "although somewhat limited as to topics."[33] Another pleasant pastime for them was to take a Sunday afternoon trip to nearby Bruderhofs and, sometimes, make visits to colonies farther away. Private diversions were hobbies such as crafting leather goods, repairing motors, or embroidering. Hutterite men did not hunt or fish. Their cultural life was so Spartan, if not barren, because Hutterites believed that "living in the ark" allowed for no frivolity, individualism, pride, or sensual pleasure.

Baptism, which took place on the Sunday before Easter or on the Sunday of Pentecost, marked the child's admission to adulthood and occurred for men between the age of nineteen and twenty-six and for women about the age of twenty. It was, Kraybill wrote, "the point of no return in Hutterite life." An individual voluntarily requested baptism and promised to commit his or her entire life to the Bruderhof. After this pledge the person went through six to eight weeks of instruction. They memorized the *Taufspruch,* or baptismal recitations, and were taught three baptismal sermons called the *Taufreden.* These documents dated from the Moravian period and focused on repentance, rebirth, and church discipline. They memorized a baptismal vow that included a pledge "to consecrate, give and sacrifice self with soul and body and all possessions to the Lord in heaven."[34] A two-part ceremony began on Saturday when candidates were examined on their beliefs. On Sunday the preacher delivered a baptismal sermon and placed his hands on the heads of the individuals, praying that they keep strong in faith and piety until death, while an assistant sprinkled them with water. Once their baptism was completed, the young Hutterites were considered adults and allowed to marry, and the men were admitted to the governing body, called the *Gemein.*

The Gemein admitted new members, voted on policy matters, and elected a seven-man executive council. It also chose the preacher and annually evaluated his performance. His duties included transcribing sermons in longhand, leading church services, and performing marriages, funerals, and baptisms. He kept a record of births, deaths, and marriages and an account of all travel outside the Bruderhof. His subsidiary responsibilities were supervising the school, hearing voluntary confessions, and suggesting the appropriate penance for transgressions. In the larger colonies an assistant preacher aided the preacher in his duties and served as the representative to the outside world. A steward, along with some shop managers and farm foremen, oversaw the economy and managed financial matters. Women did not participate in the discussions or vote in the Gemein, but participated in the Gemein by singing hymns, praying, and greeting visitors.[35]

In fact, women were subordinate to men in all aspects of communal life because Hutterites believed God created men in His image to reflect His glory. Not only were the officers all men but only a man could teach in the German school.[36] Men performed all essential farm tasks such as planting and harvesting, herding the cattle, and slopping the pigs. All shop mechanics, shoemakers, carpenters, and other artisans were men.

Every Sunday the steward drew up the week's work plan and wrote job orders. For example, he might assign two men to run a large tractor, and he designated the work hours. He usually appointed the older man as the "boss" with instructions to keep the machine running. During harvest time, the steward appointed the men who would run combines and drive trucks to gather the crops. All assignments were rotated, and individuals performed at least two jobs throughout the year. For example, the shop mechanic became the combine repairman in the fall. A farmer was a carpenter in winter. The preacher concentrated on bookbinding in winter and looked after the geese in summer. If a person finished a job early he went to the steward to find what else remained to be done.

As a result there was no individualized conception of work. Humility was emphasized, and if a person showed any sign of resentment at his job he was brought before the Gemein to apologize for the infraction. However, experimentation and competition were encouraged (the competition was never between individuals but between work units). For example, the overseer of the chicken-raising operation learned all he could in order to increase production. The dairyman tried to learn as much as he could from farm magazines about livestock and disease prevention.[37]

Women performed jobs related to the internal functioning of the community. They were the head tailoress, head cook, and head gardener. Two women ran the kindergarten. The steward assigned duties each Sunday to women between the ages of fifteen and forty-five. They did the cooking, milked the cows, canned fruits and vegetables, butchered chickens and ducks, assisted with slaughtering pigs, plucked feathers from chickens and ducks, and cleaned the communal buildings. In addition to such responsibilities, women were expected to wash their family's clothes, care for their children, and keep their homes in pristine condition. Women also supervised a "sharing of goods" based on formulas found in a rule book. Several times a year the head tailoress determined what clothing would be given to each mother. The mother, in turn, kept a record of what she received and who in the family was given the clothing. The head tailoress also provided each woman with a stipulated amount of yard goods for her to sew her own and her family's clothes. The rule allowed each ten-year-old boy three yards and six inches of jacket material. Men and boys over the age of fourteen were rationed four yards. For each infant the mother received two yards of material for shirts, four yards for dresses, and four yards for diapers. Nine yards of material were permitted for a girl's dress. The head tailoress gave the mother bedding, pillows, comforters, dishes, and eating utensils.[38]

Hutterite equality meant that one person must not have too much while another person suffered. Property "ownership" meant the right to use what the colony provided according to three types of reciprocity:

general, balanced, and negative. The first type, general reciprocity, dealt with allowances without accountability such as a small monthly allotment of cash and a quart of wine and twelve bottles of beer four times a year. General reciprocity included personal belongings such as a wallet or a watch and items purchased in the colony store with the cash allotment. The second type, balanced reciprocity, meant that one had to give something back in return for what was received. For instance, if someone was sick, another person did the work and was paid in goods or food. This kind of reciprocity also took place daily at mealtimes. If a chicken was served at supper, they were supposed to share it equally on a formula of one chicken for each table. But when an individual ate the best slices at one meal, the next time others would take the choicest portions. Sometimes balanced reciprocity meant barter, as when one mother traded part of her allotment of goose feathers for another mother's assignment of cloth. The third, negative reciprocity (trying to get something for nothing or to cheat), was strongly condemned as violating Christian charity. Hutterites also condemned any expression of carnal desire; they proscribed dancing, excessive drinking, instrumental music, skating, and skiing.[39]

The main agency of socialization was the family. Children were seen as gifts of God; the Hutterites prohibited birth control. The average family often included a dozen children, although some colonies eventually relaxed the rule on contraception. Elders supervised all contact between the sexes. However, young men and women met during visits between Bruderhofs, at social time after supper, on Sunday afternoons, and at funerals and weddings. Often this supervision was circumscribed, and a de facto dating system prevailed in some colonies. As one sixteen-year-old girl explained: "If a boy wants a date he goes out with one of our guys and tells him; then he calls out the girl he wants. . . . If she wants, she goes along with him. If not, she says no. . . . In all the colonies, each boy gets a two-week vacation [during winter] and then they can go and visit whenever they please."[40] Open dating, or courtship as it was called, began only after a couple were engaged to marry.

Marriage was the final stage on the road to full adulthood. First, a young man decided on the woman he wished to marry and informed his father of the decision. Then the two of them went to the prospective bride's home and received her parents' permission for the young ones to marry. Next, the young man had to get the approval of the Gemein. This was followed by a visit to the girl's home, where the couple drank wine with her parents. In the afternoon the young couple visited other families, served them wine, and received their blessings for a happy marriage. That evening there was an engagement party called a *Bulba*, in the colony kitchen, that sometimes lasted past midnight.[41]

There were times when marriages could not occur—immediately before

Christmas and from just before Easter until after Pentecost. About half the marriages took place in November and December, and almost none during the spring planting and fall harvest. The wedding took place at a Sunday service where the preacher asked the groom four questions dealing with his responsibilities as a husband and the bride three questions concerning her obedience to God and her husband. After they had answered the interrogatories, the preacher inquired if the couple would be "faithful to each other and to your faith and never leave one another, until death will separate you?" Both parties, with hands joined, responded "yes." Whereupon he blessed them: "We herewith bear witness that you marry each other as godfearing partners according to the order of God and the example of the forefathers."[42]

Finally, he presented the couple to the congregation. After the service, everyone adjourned to the kitchen for a meal served with beer and wine, followed by singing. Throughout the afternoon they enjoyed more snacks and drinks accompanied by still more singing. The celebration ended with evening vespers where everyone was given an allotment of sweets as a departure gift. During the remainder of the evening the bride and groom mingled with the guests and then retired to an apartment, which usually was next to the living quarters of the groom's parents. The husband was now a full member of the Gemein, and the bride lived as an obedient and dependent wife.[43]

In performing the work assignments, Hutterites were governed by a strict protocol. A man must be responsible, kind, and cheerful, and must follow all colony rules. He must suppress jealousy, envy, and competition by open interaction with his "brothers and sisters." A woman must be a diligent worker and attentive to her family. On the job Hutterites always discussed an issue until they reached a consensus. The more prestigious jobs were awarded by seniority (age, in other words) and never because of work performance. The only occasion when talent and ability were considered was in the Gemein vote for officers. If these rules were violated, the individual appeared before the Gemein for censure. If the problem continued, members of the colony would shun—but not banish—the person. The violator would be confined to his or her home for a period of time and could speak to no one but the preacher. In extreme cases, the person would be denied the privilege of attending church services and would have to take meals alone after everyone else had finished.

When adults could no longer perform their work assignments, they became "older persons." There was no arbitrary age for retirement. For a woman it was usually between the ages of forty-five and fifty, or about the time of menopause. For a man it was when he became convinced he could no longer physically keep up with the work. For women the process was more regulated, and some jobs were given up sooner than others. For example, milking was the first task to be turned over to younger women. Next came cooking and baking. After retirement a woman would go to her daughter's home to assist in housekeeping and to look after her young grandchildren. As people became more infirm, they were cared for in their home by their children and came to meals as long as they were able. "No elderly person is forced to choose between the extremes of doing nothing or holding a full-time job," Hostetler concluded, and "loneliness is unknown among the Hutterites." Also, there was considerable contact between the elderly and the young, and the Hutterite emphasis on tradition brought the elderly much respect. The "older people" constituted about 25 percent of a Bruderhof, and life expectancy was the same as in the regular population.[44]

Communal living presented external as well as internal problems. Some outsiders resented the Hutterites' economic success. Others were offended at their aloofness and by the fact that, except for business matters, they "have few personal relationships with even their immediate neighbors" and "take no part in neighborhood events except in times of emergency, such as river floods." There were those who resented the fact that Hutterites allowed visitors only by special appointment, and when these visitors were admitted they complained that the communards were simply not friendly. Hostetler explained this segregation as necessary because "prolonged, intimate, primary relationships with non-Hutterite neighbors can be a serious threat to colony harmony unless properly managed."[45]

This insularity restricted serious contact with other communal societies also. The early contacts with Amana and the Separatists were brief and had no impact on Hutterite life. There was, however, one exception, the interaction with the Society of Brothers. This communal group was founded by Eberhard Arnold (1883–1935) in Germany in 1920. In 1930 and 1931 he and his wife spent time with Hutterite colonies in the United States and Canada and came away impressed with their communal living. In turn, the Hutterites were equally impressed with his knowledge of Scripture. In December 1930 Arnold was "confirmed in the service of the Word with the laying on of hands by the elders" to spread the Hutterite faith in Germany.[46] Backed financially by the Hutterites, Arnold began to preach Hutterite doctrines in the Fatherland and established two Bruderhofs there. His emphasis on pacifism, however, caused the Nazis to dissolve the communities. After Arnold's death in 1935, his followers moved to England and then, in 1940, to Paraguay, where they built three communities with a total membership of over five hundred.

In the 1950s some elders from the American communities went to Paraguay and discovered practices that they found repellant to the Hutterite way. For example, they condemned the Society of Brothers for smoking, dancing, and attending movies. They were shocked that women could deliberate in the communal assembly. On the other hand, Society people, at the time called the "New Hutterites," were dismayed at what they learned was done in the United States, such as donations to the Red Cross and the absence of missionary work. One Society elder concluded: "We are a different people. We have only just now come out of the world and . . . though we should be in agreement on the main issues, in some ways we must differ from you." Speaking for the American delegation, elder Samuel Kleinsasser concluded: "We cannot operate like you here." When they returned to America they reported that the New Hutterites were just too worldly and recommended that all further contact with them be terminated.[47]

The Forest River colony, "which had more than its share of dissident members," continued to keep in touch with the Paraguayans. The colony invited them to visit their Bruderhof, and the New Hutterites accepted. But the result was a fiasco because, as one member of the American community put it, "they invaded . . . like an army, bringing thirty-six people, including nurses, teachers, lawyers, and four ministers, and took command of the place from the first day on." For over two weeks elders from other Schmiedeleut communities visited Forest River and tried to get the Paraguayans to leave and to persuade the Forest River people to break off all contact with them. When they failed to achieve either objective, they placed Forest River on probation.[48]

In the fall of 1956 the Paraguayans relocated to Farmington, Pennsylvania, accompanied by thirty-six sympathetic Hutterites. Soon afterward, the Society of Brothers still in South America moved to join their brethren in Pennsylvania and formed two new settlements, the Evergreen Community (1957) at Norfolk, Connecticut, and the Darvell Community (1972) at Robertsbridge, Sussex, England. Tension between the Hutterites and the Society of Brothers culminated in an effort at reconciliation. In January 1974, a delegation from the Society, led by Heini Arnold, Eberhard's son, went to Manitoba and met with a delegation of seventy-one preachers from the Schmiedeleuts. They apologized for what had happened at Forest River and agreed to accept whatever the Hutterites might decide as punishment. The two groups never reconciled, however, and remained separate from each other as distinct societies.

The strained relationship between the Hutterites and the Society of Brothers led to discord within the Schmiedeleut communities. In the mid-1990s sixty colonies, mostly in Manitoba, swore allegiance to Jacob Kleinsasser and became known as the *Kleinsasserleut.* Another group formed a community known as the "Oilers" because of their investments in oil. Their official name was the Schmiedeleut Conference of the Hutterite Brethren. A third faction of about 110 Bruderhofs was called *Gibbleut* after their leader, an attorney named Donald Gibb. This faction's official name was the Schmiedeleut Committee Group. "This division within the Schmiedeleut," Kraybill and Bowman commented, "has been very painful, acrimonious, and complicated. . . . Hostile feelings have become so strong in some cases that factions have sued each other in courts of law, breaking the historic Anabaptist taboo on litigation."[49]

TODAY TWENTY-FIVE HUNDRED members of the Society of Brothers calling themselves Church Communities International live in eight communities in Pennsylvania, New York, and Connecticut, and in two colonies in England. The Hutterites number about thirty-six thousand and live in 390 Bruderhofs in the United States and Canada. They are committed to communal life, condemn worldly temptation, and live peacefully with their neighbors. Kraybill and Bowman visited ten Schmiedeleut colonies in South Dakota and Manitoba in 1992 and 1994 and came away with a keen sense of why, despite external hostilities and internal divisions, Hutterites have created a communal society that has endured for several centuries. "All know who they are, to whom they belong, and why they were born," they wrote. "There is no unemployment here, and indeed people gladly work without thought of paycheck. . . . There is joy and laughter here, some occasional humor, and of course no worry about retirement or financial security."[50]

CHAPTER SEVEN

Chicago Area Utopias

Zion City, Spirit Fruit Society, and House of David

For reasons never fully understood, by the twentieth century, utopian community life in the Heartland had all but evaporated—except for the continuation of the Amana and Hutterite colonies. Where communitarianism did appear, it was confined geographically to the Chicago area and across the lake from the Windy City in southwest Michigan. In Chicago in the late nineteenth century, John Alexander Dowie laid plans for his theocratic Zion City on sixty-five hundred acres on the shore of Lake Michigan. In 1905 Jacob Beilhart, a Seventh Day Adventist evangelist, moved his small Spirit Fruit Society from Lisbon, Ohio, to a ninety-acre site in Lake County some forty-eight miles northwest of Chicago. And two years earlier Benjamin Purnell and his wife, Mary, both itinerant evangelists, incorporated "The Israelite House of David, the New Eve, the Body of Christ" south of Benton Harbor, Michigan.

Zion City

John Alexander Dowie opened his Zion Tabernacle, called the Little Wooden Hut, in 1893 at Jackson Park near the entrance to the Columbian Exposition. Nearby he established a divine healing home called the Zion Hotel. Then, in February 1897, Dowie dedicated the Central Tabernacle on Michigan Avenue (formerly St. John's Episcopal Church), with a seating capacity for over three thousand. The next year he founded his Christian Catholic Apostolic Church and established its headquarters, called Zion, in the Imperial Hotel on Michigan Avenue and Twelfth Street. In two years 6,246 converts had joined the church. So Zion's birthplace, Chicago ("the great melting pot of the Midwest, the 'City of Sin' to many preachers," in the words of Philip L. Cook), "was fertile soil for a movement which would nurture those dissatisfied with society."[1]

Dowie stood just five feet four inches tall and looked like a two-hundred-pound Moses, with a long flowing beard. This "minister of healing" was born in Edinburgh, Scotland, in 1847 and claimed to have read the Bible at the age of six. In 1860 his father, a tailor and itinerant preacher, moved the family to Adelaide, South Australia, to live next to his brother, Alexander, a shoemaker and businessman. Nine years later, young John Dowie, after rising to a junior partnership in a wholesale dry goods operation, returned to Scotland to enter the University of Edinburgh in order to prepare for the ministry. At the university he became the unofficial chaplain in the school's infirmary, where he attended lectures on medicine, observed patients, and watched surgical operations. As a result of this experience Dowie "developed a lasting skepticism toward the medical profession."[2]

In April 1872 he was ordained a minister and became pastor of the Congregational Church at Alma, Australia, close to Adelaide. His first post was a frustrating one because of the apathy and heavy drinking of the male parishioners. Consequently, in 1874 he moved to Sydney, New South Wales, to assume the ministry of the Newtown Congregational Church. He became a leader of the local temperance society and was active in social reform projects. After traveling as an evangelist for two years, he campaigned unsuccessfully for Parliament and blamed his defeat on the liquor interests he had targeted in his speeches. "Bacchus," he wrote to his parents, was the "supreme ruler" in politics. Disgruntled, he moved to Melbourne and opened the Divine Healing Association and held street meetings. This led to his arrest for violating an ordinance that prohibited such activities.[3]

In 1888 he left Australia for a mission of healing in England and planned to cross the United States en route. He landed in San Francisco in June and used the city as a base from which to conduct faith-healing sessions along the coastal towns of California. The following year he started a periodical, *Leaves of Healing*, that featured testimonials of his followers and his diatribes against the Devil and alcohol. At this time he assumed the title of Doctor. Four years later he moved to Chicago and opened the Zion Tabernacle.[4]

There Dowie, standing on a platform and wearing a clerical robe, preached for hours without notes, quoting long passages of Scripture from memory. He displayed a collection of articles left behind by cured members of his congregation, calling the articles "tools of the Devil" or trophies "captured from the enemy." This collection included medical appliances, revolvers, brass knuckles, tobacco pouches, and of course liquor flasks. His message was consistent: total acceptance of Scripture and of his own power of divine healing. God had not visited illness upon people to "chasteneth" them from sin. Rather, the Devil caused all diseases. Jesus had been sent by the Father to heal the sick. This power had been transferred to his Disciples when he said that they would do "greater works." Dowie went beyond faith healing, however, to attack sweatshops and the exploitation of poor folk by bankers. He denounced the lynching of negroes. He demanded federal support for public education. He opposed capital punishment. He was a pacifist and condemned all wars.[5]

In January 1895 Dowie was arrested for practicing medicine without a license. Infuriated, he launched a crusade against "doctors, drugs, and devils," the editors of the city's newspapers, freemasons, and the major Protestant denominations. All of these enemies allowed the use of alcohol, tobacco, and drugs and totally neglected social reform. In the *Leaves of Healing* issue for September 30, 1899, he announced his "Three Months Holy War Against the Hosts of Hell in Chicago." He urged his readers to oppose sin wherever they found it. In the October 8 issue, he promised to "smash the apostate church" because they "have been the form of godliness and deny the power." The Baptist Church must be "utterly smashed." The Congregationalists were "living on the Pilgrim Fathers' dust; the brains of a dead theology." The Presbyterians were "a miserable people on God Almighty's earth."[6]

After a similar diatribe appeared in the issue of October 18, 1899, over two thousand medical students from the city's colleges and "several thousand more sympathizers" marched on Zion's headquarters at the Imperial Hotel screaming and cursing and throwing "bottles containing filthy-smelling liquids." Police arrived, scattered the rioters, and hauled away in patrol wagons "these young doctors assisted by a number of their professors." Despite the fact that Inspector John D. Shea of the Chicago Police Department had promised Dowie protection for his right of free speech, other incidents followed. On October 27, a streetcar carrying Dowie and his followers to an appearance in Hammond, Indiana, was attacked, and every window in the vehicle was shattered. On November 1, the police invaded a meeting in Oak Park to escort him back to the city "and out of the hands of a mob." Dowie reacted by creating the "Zion Guard," a group of men who wore jackets with the word "patience" braided in gold letters and a cap with a visor portraying a bronze dove with an olive leaf in its beak. They patrolled neighborhoods of their "healing homes" to prevent vandalism and accompany Dowie as an armed guard wherever he went.[7]

In December 1899 he denounced the city's newspapers. The editors, he said, should be sent to the penitentiary. He claimed that "the politics, the religion, the social ethics of the press are entirely dependent upon the directions which are given in the counting-house." Then, on December 14, he asserted: "I do not believe there ever will be a truly honest and God-fearing newspaper in Chicago until Zion prints it." On December 31, 1899, he announced his plans for Zion City.[8]

The announcement came as no surprise to most of his disciples because, as early as February 8, 1895, he had discussed in the *Leaves* the need for a new location for his ministry. In any event, on New Year's Eve 1899, he stated that he had received a gift of land that would allow him "to lay out a town, radiating from the new Zion Tabernacle as a center, so that they may dwell in Zion all the time: for it is proposed to call it by that name." Four years earlier he had projected that the city would be a refuge "from the rum-soaked, tobacco-reeking streets of Chicago." In April 1895, the *Leaves* had described "a Great Plan for a new Zion just outside the borders of Chicago where we may fully establish all our Institutions, found a Church in a location for about 25,000 persons when fully occupied." Dowie believed that people other than those interested in faith healing would come to live in a "pure city" where average middle-class Americans would be able to reconcile the "inconsistencies of life." In the *Leaves* issue appearing on April 25, 1896, he wrote that "the Lord will 'build up' in the little city of Zion, in the vicinity of Chicago, and will rapidly extend throughout the world a Christian catholic apostolic church."[9]

The full story of the acquisition appeared in the spring 1901 issue of *Leaves* when Dowie disclosed the details of the "secret purchase." In the fall of 1898 he had formed the Zion Land and Investment Association, led by deacons H. Worthington Judd and Daniel Sloan and engineer Burton J. Ashley. In December 1898 they had gone to Waukegan, forty miles north of Chicago, and inspected a tract of land north of the town that stretched to the Wisconsin state line. The following day they returned and took photographs. When they reported back, Dowie was convinced that God had chosen the spot for the holy city. In July 1899, when Ashley and Sloan returned to explore the area further, they discovered that the Chicago & Northwestern Railroad traversed the property and saw how the sloping tilt of the terrain toward Lake Michigan was excellent for drainage and sanitary facilities. Real estate agent E. D. Wheelock handled the details of the purchase of 150 parcels from local farmers. "Not one farmer complained of misrepresentation," Cook observed, "and all said that they had received considerate treatment."[10]

On Saturday morning, January 6, 1900, Dowie and ninety devotees, enthusiastically chanting the refrain "We're Marching to Zion," left Union Station to go by train to the Promised Land. Newspaper reporters accompanied the entourage. Arriving at the site, Dowie gathered everyone together at the spot he had picked for the new temple and answered reporters' questions. When one man asked if he had any doubts as to the success of the project, he answered: "No, Sir! Not in Zion. Our people are those who give their all—if necessary—to further their just cause. The plan for Zion City must succeed." In a bid for membership, he said that anybody who "obeys the laws which we will form and which our officers are to administer" would be welcome. He boasted that there would be 20,000 residents in Zion City within a year, and in twenty years "there will be 200,000 people." After Dowie's benediction, the crowd sang the hymn "Go Forward, O Zion," and he led a procession back to the train waiting to return to Chicago.[11]

Throughout the summer of 1900 eleven trains transported ten thousand people from Chicago to Zion. Others arrived on horseback, in wagons, on bicycles, and on foot. Dowie placed a seventy-two-foot observation tower at the spot where the tabernacle would stand and at each corner put a blue, white, and gold flag with a red cross in the center. "As the participants went back to Chicago and their homes," Cook wrote, "they no doubt wondered just how long it would be before the marvelous wonders, heard this day, would come to pass, remembering especially Dowie's confident assurance six months earlier of employment for workers."[12]

Dowie drew up a detailed plat map for a city covering sixty-five hundred acres, ten square miles. The Zion Lace Industries, worth one million dollars, would be the city's main industry. It was to occupy at least fifty acres and employ fifty thousand workers. He placed an enormous tabernacle in the center of the two-hundred-acre Shiloh Park. He located a recreation park at the eastern corner next to Lake Michigan and adjacent to the city's waterworks. On the west end of the park were other manufacturing and business establishments. One- and two-story residential homes were in the south, west, and north quarters. He planned to erect a feed store, a creamery, and a post office. In addition to publishing *Leaves of Healing,* Dowie put out a biweekly newspaper, *The Coming City.* At the south end was a brickyard, a lumber mill, a blacksmith's shop, a freight warehouse, a telegraph office, and a general store. Farms with barns, tool sheds, and fifty teams of horses and wagons were where the holy farmers would grow vegetables and harvest hay.[13]

Dowie called his utopia "a theocracy of the heart," with the Bible as its "supreme law." He declared: "I deny the doctrine of Democracy. . . . It is the incarnation of accursed selfishness, the government of man by himself and for himself . . . the government of a selfish brute. . . . The government of John Alexander Dowie by God Almighty and for God Almighty is the best government for him."[14] Accordingly, in April 1900, residents elected the Council of Overseers to serve under Dowie and to administer the fire and police departments and the offices of city engineer and finance. The council, however, was merely a rubber stamp for whatever Dowie wanted, passing ordinances without discussion and by unanimous approval. In May 1900 the council created the Zion Restoration Host, or Zion's Army, made up of the adult male residents. Those who would not join the Restoration Host had to leave the community. Or, as Dowie put it: "If you are not going to be workers for God, I never invited you to Zion City. I invited people to Zion City who would work for God. . . . Woe to Them that are at ease in Zion." Its mission was to wage war on the devil. Each man swore to recognize Dowie as "the Messenger of the Covenant, the Prophet foretold by Moses, and Elijah the Restorer." He took the title of Elijah III, the third manifestation of prophets Elijah and John the Baptist. In the "Vow of the Restoration Host," the men pledged submission to Dowie's commands, which transcended "all family ties and obligations." Obedience to him superseded "all relations to all human government."[15]

His New Jerusalem flourished. By September 1901 two hundred buildings stood at the site. Expecting a population of two hundred thousand, Dowie planned an extensive streetcar service. He had started a fishing industry on the lake shore that summer. Freight trains carried boards from the lumberyard to Chicago. There was a brick factory and a candy factory, a bakery, and a laundry. The men completed the building of the Tabernacle with a seating capacity for over five thousand worshipers, enlarged by 1903 to hold seventy-three hundred. In March 1903, Dowie created the Zion Building and Manufacturing Association to supervise the construction of all new buildings and private houses. The association sold stock shares for $20 to raise a capital fund of $500,000. All profits were divided: 20 percent as dividends to shareholders and 10 percent as a tithe to Dowie. He ordered the city's retail operations, called the Zion Stores, to use a profit-sharing basis where the customer would share "in proportion to the amount of his purchase." All goods would be bought in "great quantities" and sold only for a profit that would pay for the expenses of handling. There were no "middlemen" and "money-kings" in a city dedicated to the "fatherhood of God and the brotherhood of man."[16]

Religion dominated daily life because "holy living" was paramount, along with the other two Dowie doctrines of "salvation" and "healing." And the rigidity of the religious schedule in the city amazed all visitors. Every morning began with a prayer, with the blowing of a whistle (later the ringing of a bell) at nine o'clock. Everyone paused for two minutes with heads bowed until the whistle sounded again. The same ritual occurred each evening. Before starting one's job (as a worker, city employee, or farmer), a person devoted fifteen minutes to prayer on bended knee. A church official conducted this service at the job site. In every home a "family altar" dominated the living room. A "parish officer" appointed by the Council of Overseers for the thirteen parishes or wards had the responsibility to inspect the home regularly and to supervise the moral condition of family members.

These men also noted the condition of the kitchen, the pantry, and the family finances. As counselors they gave advice on domestic relationships, using information given them in special "officers' meetings."[17]

The weekly routine was as dominated by religion as the daily one. On Tuesday evenings there was a two-hour prayer meeting, divided into three parts for prayer and Scripture reading, for giving testimony, and for socializing. On Wednesday evening, after prayer and Bible reading, they made plans for the future development of the city and discussed social problems. They also listened to lectures on topics such as youthful moral conduct and beautification with landscaping. Sunday services in the Shiloh Tabernacle began at half past six in the morning and continued throughout the day.[18]

Domestic relations centered on Old Testament precepts. In a sermon in the Tabernacle Dowie's wife, Jane, used Scripture to advise wives that "the Body is the Temple of the Holy Spirit" and "must not be despised." Since fathers spend time away from their families at work, mothers had to be both father and mother. In this role they must never "put evil in your children's minds." She admonished, "Don't scold, don't beat, . . . talk lovingly. But . . . there is a time for the rod." In her other discourses, she touched upon topics such as mate selection, the evil of birth control, and divorce. In a January 1904 Tabernacle address, overseer John G. Speicher lectured on "Authority in the Home" and emphasized parental responsibility for the shaping of children's character. Dowie, speaking in the Tabernacle as the general overseer, pointed out that the father must demand absolute obedience to his decisions and, along with the mother, make the home "the most sacred thing outside of the Church of God." Touching on lust, the prophet stated that "I will have Zion pure" and condemned "filthy pictures and bad books." Finally, to assure his control over marriage he required every potential bride and groom to answer questions on their beliefs and personal habits before he would give his permission for them to marry.[19]

Children in school were taught religious perfection by teachers who sincerely believed that the Christian Catholic Apostolic Church was leading a mission to establish the Kingdom of God. Accordingly, they felt they must operate a "sanctified" school system to ensure the supremacy of God, the brotherhood of all, and individual free will. They must prepare their students "for service in the Master's Kingdom." They must "teach [them] how to pray so as to receive answers to their petitions." Overseer H. D. Brasefield developed a curriculum that would prepare the students to "be men and women of God, whose characters are the resultant of a harmonious development of body, soul and spirit." Education must make an individual "fit to commune with God and to so live and work and pray that he may lift his fellowmen up to a higher plane of life."[20]

On January 6, 1902, Dowie laid the cornerstone for the city's central school and began construction of four other smaller frame structures. Within three years seventy-five teachers were hired to train two thousand students from first to twelfth grade. In the central building, each room was assigned just one subject, such as reading, mathematics, art, or science. School athletics were dominated by an acute sense of Christian cooperation. For example, all games started with a prayer, readings from the Bible, and a hymn. Students were told that competition should be discouraged and that instead they should play to elicit one another's love. Zion's sports included four baseball teams and football, cricket, basketball, tennis, and golf. School recreational activities such as band concerts, ice-skating parties, and sleigh rides were chaperoned by parish officers and were opened by prayers.[21]

The Zion city police, under Dowie's direction, enforced a Draconian code of moral propriety. In a series of ordinances they created a catalog of "blue laws" that forbade all recreation on the Sabbath and prohibited smoking, drunkenness, swearing, gambling, spitting, and riding bicycles on the wooden sidewalks. Compliance with these rules was about 100 percent; only one-tenth of 1 percent of Zion's citizens were ever arrested and most times this was for violating the no-smoking ordinance. Perhaps one reason why most residents complied with these laws was Dowie's insidious system of spying. He told his followers that it was their Christian duty to inform the police about "hidden iniquities," because if they did not, they "would imperil the purity and progress of Zion." Moreover, if they failed to tattle they were guilty of sin and would be "so judged."[22]

"Outwardly the Zion movement appeared to be thriving," Cook wrote, "as converts continued to flow into the city." In November 1903 the *Leaves* boasted that "such is the demand for our products that we suffer from want of capital to extend these great and profitable Industries." It printed a letter written by financial manager Charles J. Barnard dated November 12 where he claimed that "the demand for our products [is] so great, that we must . . . have additional capital to enlarge the capacity of our factories."[23] The truth, however, was that by the end of that year the city's economic structure had started to collapse. Dowie did not pay his bills, and in late November 1903 fourteen creditors took him to court. On December 2, the U.S. District Court in Chicago declared Zion City bankrupt and appointed receivers to examine its assets. Dowie reacted by promising to pay "dollar for dollar" all of the obligations within a year's time and pledged that all future business would be on a cash basis. He persuaded workers to accept scrip for wages. This done, the receivers concluded that the general overseer and his officials were competent to continue to conduct the city's affairs.[24]

On New Year's Day 1904, Dowie returned to Australia to recruit more converts. Early on that bleak, damp day, several thousand devoted followers tramped across the flats of the Lake Michigan shore to the railroad depot to bid the prophet farewell. Traveling in style in a private car belonging to the president of the San Antonio & Arkansas Railroad, Dowie was accompanied by several aides. They went to San Antonio and then pushed on to Los Angeles where, on January 17, he addressed a crowd of thirty-five thousand at Hazard's Pavilion. Ending up in San Francisco, Dowie and his retinue embarked for Australia, where he conducted meetings in Sydney, Melbourne, and Adelaide.[25]

Back in Illinois, Overseer Speicher took charge of running Zion City. He faced manifold problems and suffered the absence of Dowie's charismatic personality to rally the residents in order to solve them. Unemployment was perhaps the most pressing problem. Industries had not created enough jobs, and men had to find work in Waukegan, Kenosha, and other towns. In February 1904, Speicher slashed wages 20 percent in all but the lace factory. Supervisors agreed to a 50 percent cut in pay. Nevertheless, the furniture store and the candy factory closed in mid-February. The candy factory had employed eighty people and was the city's most profitable operation. Added to these problems was the fact that debt payments Dowie sent to the creditors drained the city's finances. For example, the June 1904 installment alone was $90,000. By the spring of 1905 most of the remaining factories had reduced wages by 50 percent.[26]

Backed by the other overseers Speicher sent Dowie a letter warning him of dire consequences if events continued as they were going. He advised that "a pronounced retrenchment and assumption of simplicity on the part of the General Overseer and his family" was necessary to "inspire confidence." Dowie, irritated, did not respond. Perhaps his indifference was prompted by other letters that painted a rosier picture of the situation. He was told that a poultry association had been formed to start a new business of raising chickens. The Zion storehouse was functional and still made groceries available for those families in need. The land association had paid the county property taxes, amounting to over $44,000, for all of the citizens.[27]

Dowie returned in July 1904 and received a stupendous welcoming ceremony. As his train arrived at the depot the band played a rousing march. Several thousand followers beamed as the overseer and his wife walked among them, greeting them with "Peace to thee!" Then the couple boarded a carriage and proceeded up Shiloh Boulevard as a solid row of adoring Zionites lined the street on both sides. They passed under a fifty-foot arch with large letters on the top that read "Welcome Home." At Elijah Avenue Dowie stood and offered a prayer. Then he told the throng that his mission abroad had been immensely successful. In the "great cities," he said, it had been always possible "to stir up the rabble." At that point thunder rumbled and rain began to fall. "The artillery of heaven is answering 'Amen,'" he roared to the cheering crowd. As the downpour increased, everyone dispersed. Cook observed that although soaked, "the majority of the people returned home and to their jobs, happy and feeling secure. . . . The Zion colors were flying once more from the giant flagpole, the shepherd of the flock was home."[28]

By this time Dowie, infected by visions of grandeur, searched for more fields to harvest. Between two and three thousand worshipers gathered in the Shiloh Tabernacle to listen to his future plans. His address, "Zion: A Crown of Beauty in the hand of Jehovah," was published in the July 23, 1904, issue of Leaves. Oblivious to the economic situation he announced he was going to build another Zion City in Mexico and spoke of "the many Zion Cities which are to follow this." He described a fifty-square-mile plot of land in that country where property could be bought for fifty cents an acre. The "Mexican Zion" could grow cotton for Zion City's lace industry and provide food for its tables. A reciprocal trade would be developed between the northern and southern Zions. In the winter of 1905 Dowie went to Mexico City and met with President Porfirio Díaz, who was supportive of Dowie's plans but cautioned him to be careful in dealing with Mexican businessmen.[29]

When Dowie returned in April 1905 he was stunned. Under Speicher the economy had imploded. Factory managers did not have enough money to pay for machinery repairs. The First Apostle's initial reaction was to find a scapegoat for the disaster. He picked on Barnard, Zion's financial manager, and announced in a Sunday service that the utopia's financial problems were caused by "the duplicity, treachery, falsehood, and ingratitude of one man, who tricked us, and lied to us" and that his department "has been shamefully mismanaged." Barnard, who by this time had already left the city, told newspaper reporters that he had for some time warned the First Apostle that he would leave unless there was "more business and less religion." Dowie appointed a new manager, Alexander Granger, and predicted that Zion's economy would once more become solvent. More than the defects of one individual were behind the city's economic problems, he said. At the core was the lack of faith on the part of many residents. The inconveniences, he said, were temporary. But they were not.[30]

In August 1905 the building and manufacturing association dissolved. But Dowie persisted in plans for the Mexican "Paradise Plantation." On Sunday, September 24, prior to his leaving for Mexico City, he held a five-hour service where he explained his vision of the future in a sermon "Going Forward." Afterward the fifty-seven-year-old patriarch retired to his dressing room and collapsed, paralyzed on his right side. Unable to walk, but mentally unimpaired, he left for Mexico City and returned just before Thanksgiving. On December 3, he suffered another stroke. Needing rest, he decided to visit Jamaica. Just before he left, he established an administrative triumvirate: V. V. Barnes, general counsel; Alexander

Granger, general financial manager; and John G. Speicher, overseer and chair of the commission. Dowie stated in his "Farewell Letter" that God had told him to decentralize operations. Overseer Speicher responded with his own letter pledging "unswerving loyalty" to the First Apostle and predicting the start of a new era of progress.[31]

Over the ensuing months Dowie replaced this triumvirate, and each new appointee failed to solve the deepening economic crisis. Schoolteachers were paid only part of their salaries. People began to gather on street corners to discuss the problems. One man who organized a meeting was arrested. Malaise spread, now, because of the growing realization that the Lord's Prophet, who had always preached that illness was the work of Satan, was not recovering. Was he, also, in the Devil's clutches? In February 1906 the latest overseer, a thirty-six-year-old former missionary named Wilber Glenn Voliva, led an open revolt against Dowie's leadership. In a sermon entitled "Disease Is the Result of Sin," he assailed the prophet's spiritual purity. "God never raises up a new leader," he said, "until the leader whom He has been using has apostatized." As autocratic as Dowie, Voliva declared that "the officers must obey me and the people themselves must obey." With arms raised high above his head he asked, "Won't you help me?" They hollered back, "We will!"[32]

On April 2, 1906, Voliva sent a telegram to Dowie, then staying in Mexico City. It was signed by himself and five other officers. "You are hereby suspended from office and membership for polygamous teaching and other grave charges," it read. "Quietly retire," it commanded. Thousands had suffered "through your shameful mismanagement."[33] Back at Zion City Voliva published an exposé of these charges and of Dowie's alleged plan to collect a harem at the southern Zion.

On April 5, 1906, Dowie left Mexico City determined to defend his life's work. Arriving in Chicago on April 10, he announced that he would reside there while exonerating himself. He told reporters from the *Chicago Tribune* that Voliva's charges were ridiculous. He retained a lawyer who petitioned the Lake County Circuit Court to revoke the power of attorney Dowie had given Voliva on his appointment as overseer the previous January. The attorney also obtained a court order that authorized Dowie to enter Zion City and hold services in the Tabernacle. When he arrived in the building on April 29 he was met by only a small gathering of about two hundred people.[34]

The fate of Zion City was decided in bankruptcy court in July 1906. Judge Kenesaw M. Landis heard arguments from attorneys representing Voliva and Dowie, who sat in a wheelchair. He ruled that Dowie was only a trustee and not, as his lawyers claimed, the owner of Zion property. The judge further ordered the appointment of a receiver for the estate, a Chicago businessman named John C. Hately, until Zion's economic problems were resolved and its debts paid. Finally, he directed that an election should take place in September to choose new city officers. Of the 1,918 ballots cast, Voliva received 1,900 votes. Dowie's name was not even on the ballot. The prophet spent his last days at Shiloh House, his Zion City home, where he developed heart disease and dropsy. He became delirious, and on March 9, 1907, he died. Judge Visscher V. Barnes, a Yale Law School graduate who had joined the community in the spring of 1902 and was the judge of Zion's court of arbitration, preached at his funeral.[35]

By 1911 over fifteen hundred people had left Zion City, and those who stayed accepted Voliva's authority. He led the community until his death in 1942 and made substantial changes. For example, he sold the lace factory to Marshall Field and Company of Chicago. He organized the remaining factories into Zion Industries, which he directed until this organization collapsed in bankruptcy during the Great Depression. Voliva, "though not in Dowie's class as a showman," as Timothy Miller observed, "nevertheless had one eccentric doctrine that was widely publicized: he taught that the earth was flat." By the twenty-first century, Dowie's Christian Catholic Apostolic Church is still a strong force in the community, although the blue laws are gone, and physically it looks like any other midwestern town. Cook was no doubt correct when he concluded in 1996 that Zion (its shortened name) is mainly a "tourist oddity for history buffs and students of religious and utopian history."[36]

Spirit Fruit Society

Jacob Beilhart, founder of what H. Roger Grant called the "gentle utopia," was born on March 4, 1867, one of ten children of John Beilhart (Beilhartz), a German immigrant, and Barbara Schlotter, an Ohio native. Their homestead, a farm nestled in the rolling hill country of Ohio next to the Pennsylvania border, was prosperous until his father's sudden death in 1873. Even so Barbara (who "possessed an acquiescent personality"), aided by the hard work of the older children, kept the family together.[37]

Young Jacob's life centered on the drudgery of agriculture, and he attended the local school only during the winter months. He later lamented that "work was about all I received as an education." In 1884 he went to live with a brother-in-law in southern Ohio as an apprentice harness maker. When this family moved to eastern Kansas the following year, Jacob went with them. Soon afterward he converted to Seventh Day Adventism. This fundamentalist sect, led by Ellen Gould White (1827–1915), believed in the imminent Second Coming of Christ—or as one member put it, "Get right with God for the end of the world can come at any moment!" In addition, they forbade the use of meat, alcohol, tobacco, coffee, and tea. His conversion in 1884 was a sad experience, however, because, he later remembered, it "cost me every friend I had, even my mother, for to all of them I was lost."[38]

For a while he earned a living as a harness maker, but at the age of twenty he became a full-time evangelist and traveled door-to-door in western Kansas selling Adventist books and pamphlets. Being "glib and tenacious," he was a remarkable success proselytizing among the two thousand Adventists living in that part of the state. Grant described him as a "somewhat diminutive man (about 5'9") with sparkling blue eyes and a neatly trimmed black mustache," who spoke with a "loud and firm" voice. That same year, in 1887, he married an Adventist girl named Loruma (Lou) who bore him two children, Harvey and Edith. In May 1887 they moved to Colorado where, he bragged, "I broke all the records of all the canvassers which they ever had selling the books."[39]

In the summer of 1887, the newlyweds relocated to Healdsburg, California, a village sixty-five miles north of San Francisco, where Jacob entered the Adventist Healdsburg College. He failed to finish the academic year, probably because of homesickness and a lack of money, and returned to the Midwest. He enrolled in the nursing program at the Adventist Sanitarium in Battle Creek, Michigan. Its two-year course in the Training School for Nurses, directed by Dr. John Harvey Kellogg, was one of the earliest in the country.

Beilhart thrived at the school. He learned from Kellogg the technique of "hydropathy," or therapeutic uses of water to improve the nervous system. Kellogg's other practices included daily enemas and drinking large amounts of water to stimulate the "colonic flush." Beilhart also became convinced that healing had more to do with prayer than with medical procedures. "One day," he later remembered, "I was called to see a sick girl who had heard me tell of my faith in healing by prayer." She was close to death from typhoid fever, he anointed her, and "she was healed immediately; the temperature going from 104.5 to about normal in a few minutes." But soon afterward, when he rejected the Adventist doctrine of vegetarianism, Kellogg asked him to leave the school.[40]

Before he departed, he nursed and became a close friend of Charles W. Post, a wealthy land salesman who had entered the sanitarium because of acute stomach problems, which physicians then called neurasthenia. In June 1892 Beilhart and his wife joined Post and his wife to open the La Vita Inn Company, in a large house located on ten acres on the east side of Battle Creek. There, with Post as president and Jacob as vice president, they treated sick individuals, many of them discouraged Kellogg patients, with "mental therapeutics"—or healing through the powers of Christian Science by mental suggestion. For two years Beilhart stayed at the La Vita Inn studying the "mind-cure," certain that disease was an error of the mind.

In 1894 he left the La Vita Inn, purchased a lot in Battle Creek, built a small house, and started a harness business. Over the next four years he developed the central ideas of his worldview—later called True Life, Natural Life, Universal Life, and finally Spirit Fruit or Spirit of Christ. These doctrines were at the basis of the communal utopia that he founded in 1898 in Lisbon, Ohio (which he moved to Ingleside, Illinois, seven years later). The essence of Spirit Fruit is quite simple: unselfishness. Beilhart wrote that one "can never receive the Spirit of Christ [or Spirit Fruit] until you take the position of giving first and last thought for others." All selfish acts must be renounced. He pointed to the words of "Sweet Jesus" in the Sermon on the Mount: "Do unto others as ye would have others do unto you." There was no joy in receiving. From the Theosophists he borrowed the idea of a universal oneness. In his monthly publication, *Spirit Voice,* he wrote often of the "one Spirit," which was "indescribable and always present." A person could reach this "holy state of being" and the Spirit that "rules all" through unselfishness.[41]

Beilhart's Spirit Fruit was also based on bisexuality. He thought that he was androgynous because after his father's death he became deeply attached to his mother. He believed that she instilled in him a feminine sensitivity, a special gentleness, and noncompetitive tendencies. His masculine side developed as he grew older. This side, however, was dramatically different from the feminine and expressed itself in crudeness, materialism, and competition.

Beilhart had radical ideas about marriage and sexual relationships. Relying on Edward Carpenter's book *Love's Coming-of-Age: A Series of Papers on the Relations of Sexes,* published in 1896, Beilhart advocated free love. The prevailing marriage arrangement, he said, allowed husbands to treat wives as property, an outrageously selfish practice akin almost to slavery. Contemporary wives, in performing their "duty" to their husbands, impaired their health. He called this male domination the "penis trust." Outside of marriage, he believed, a woman through her lover and spiritual guide could find her "spirit voice." Sexual freedom, with men and women living together communally, meant "sexual laissez faire." However, as Grant observed, the "free love that the Spirit Fruiters espoused does not actually fit the category of 'varietism,' the desire for intercourse with a variety of partners." Beilhart expected that couples would stay together for a considerable amount of time.[42]

Lisbon in the late 1890s was a town of 68,590 residents located about twenty miles south of Youngstown, Ohio. The Beilharts rented a two-story brick house at 157 North Jefferson Street. From this location in March 1899 Beilhart put out the first issue of *Spirit Fruit,* a four-page pamphlet printed monthly at a Lisbon newspaper building and sent free to recipients, without advertising. He embarked on a series of speaking engagements, first in the Lisbon area and later in Chicago and Boston, where he spoke about his Spirit Fruit. Because of the responses to the pamphlet and from those who heard him speak, Beilhart expected that some individuals would want to live with him communally. So he moved to a larger brick house on Pine Street and rented a farm east of town. In the June 1899 issue of the *Spirit Fruit,* he wrote, "The Home . . . contains five acres of good ground with plenty of fruit trees, a fine spring of water, and a large fifteen room brick house, in need of repairs."[43] In June 1900, according to the census marshall, Beilhart and his wife were living at the farm with four "boarders"—two men and two women.

Since more people had told him they wished to join the community (over a dozen would soon arrive), he decided to establish "a true home" located "up the hill" from the Pine Street house. Known as the Holmes Seminary, this was a parcel of 5.2 acres with a spacious three-story brick house and several buildings. The house had a first floor that was used for communal purposes such as the kitchen, dining room, and living room. The second and third floors had ten private sleeping rooms, and even overnight visitors had separate accommodations. He took out a mortgage for $2,500 from the Lisbon Firestone Brothers Banking Company with the intention of paying it off from local sales of dairy and poultry products.[44] On April 1, 1901, Beilhart filed articles of incorporation for his society in the office of the secretary of state in Columbus. He listed seven adults and three children as residents. The document stated that all property was held communally, and its purpose was not to make a profit but, rather, "to unite as one and assist others in eliminating [selfishness] from their nature by practicing unselfishness in our own lives and by helping others."[45]

The society grew slowly for the next four years. Beilhart actually did not want the colony to expand, because, as he wrote to William Alfred Hinds, the author of *American Communities and Co-operative Colonies,* "I think large community life is not a success." There were no admission requirements, except that the person agree with Beilhart's ideas, and no membership list. Four communards who joined after 1901 were from Chicago; the others came from Lisbon, Boston, and the state of South Carolina. They formed a diverse group, which included a farmer, a plumber, a teacher, and a physician. All, however, "seemed to have experienced some dramatic personal loss or to lack a sense of belonging in life."[46]

Daily life focused on growing vegetables, tending a flock of chickens and a few dairy cows, and performing domestic chores. The men "hired out" to do odd jobs in Lisbon. They bought a small hand-operated press to print the *Spirit Fruit,* usually five hundred copies a month. Although the pamphlet did not earn any significant income it did generate donations, which covered printing costs and helped with expenses. It was not until Irvin Elmer Rockwell, a wealthy Chicago businessman known as "Rock," joined the colony in 1904 that it found a permanent benefactor. Beer was kept in a barrel in a cool springhouse and whiskey was permitted. There were no dietary restrictions. Sundays were reserved for rest and relaxation and for discussions of Spirit Fruit. Everyone kept personal property and their own money, although they voluntarily contributed to a common treasury to cover food supplies, the mortgage, and taxes.

They practiced free love. Only one resident was celibate. The others used the private bedrooms for sexual relations. Or, as child member Robert "Buster" Knowdell later put it, "There was a lot of prowling around at night." But no one had more than one partner at a time, with the exception of Beilhart, who had relationships with Lou, his wife, and Virginia Moore, a young woman who had lived in Lisbon with her mother before becoming a member of the group. Lou tolerated the liaison for a while but eventually left the colony and returned with the two children to her parents' home in Kansas. She never legally divorced him. Beilhart's sister Mary had two children with two different fathers.[47]

Newspapers sensationalized the free love aspect. The first case involved the wife of a Dr. Bailey, a well-known Chicago physician. Mrs. Bailey arrived at the colony after telling her husband she was going to travel east to visit some relatives. When she failed to return to Chicago, her husband hired a private detective, who located her at the colony. Dr. Bailey tried unsuccessfully to persuade her to leave. He even sought, also unsuccessfully, to obtain a writ of habeas corpus to gain her release. Failing in these measures, he hired a lawyer to draw up papers to have a judge declare her to be of "unsound mind." When Mrs. Bailey found out that this might happen, she agreed to come back to Chicago. The final episode in this tale of "alleged abduction" was reported in the Chicago press. It described how, as the couple were getting ready to depart from the railroad station in early June 1901, "Beilhart made his appearance to bid the woman good-bye." When the husband slapped him in the face several times, "Beilhart offered no resistance but rather extended the other cheek. The incident ended without further violence and the Doctor and his wife left on the train."[48]

The second episode involved Katherine Herbeson, a seventeen-year-old Chicago girl. She had heard Beilhart speak in that city and found his message a solace during her divorced parents' custody battle over her. After she came to Spirit Fruit in 1904, her father, a lawyer, informed William Randolph Hearst's daily paper, the *Chicago Evening American*, that his daughter had been forced to become an "inmate" of an "awful free-love nest." They had even given her the nickname of "Blessed." On June 1, 1904, the father and Charles L. Grise, his son-in-law, arrived in Lisbon. Accompanied by the sheriff they went to the colony, gathered up Katherine and her belongings, and took the three o'clock train back to Chicago. According to Grant, this story "rocked the Lisbon community and contributed to the Spirit Fruiters' eventual decision to leave Ohio."[49]

In 1904 Beilhart established a Chicago branch of the society in rented rooms in the Leiter Building, at 81 South Clark Street. City newspapers found out about the group and described it as a "fantastic" religious sect, saying that Beilhart claimed to be the "Messiah" who had absolute contempt for marriage as an institution that "man has established." The *Buckeye State,* the local newspaper, picked up on the story. Its headline announced: "'SPIRIT FRUIT' SOCIETY HAS TAKEN CHICAGO BY STORM." The Reverend Mr. James P. Anderson, pastor of Lisbon's First Presbyterian Church, emerged as the leader of the attack on the Spirit Fruit community. In remarks published in the *Buckeye State* on June 9, 1904, he wrote that the society was a "plague on our hometown." He went on to reveal that he and a "brother minister" had been spying on "their doings" from the roof of stables next to the property. He was convinced "that the Spirit Fruit [Society] is rotten to the core." The editor of the newspaper joined the crusade to get rid of them. He claimed that Beilhart "either 'abducted' innocent females or was at least guilty of brainwashing them." On June 16, 1904, the editor printed a warning that had been circulated in town on placards by Reverend Anderson. It read: "Wanted—Fifty good women, over twenty and under fifty years of age; also fifty good honest-hearted men with families, to meet upon the Square when called upon, and go to the Spirit Fruit farm and tell them to take their departure at once or take the consequences, as tar is cheap and feathers plentiful."[50]

In a letter printed in the *Buckeye State* on June 23, 1904, Beilhart wrote that if "fifty heads of families" signed a petition requesting them to leave "we will comply with the request." He announced that he would hold a public meeting "at our home in Lisbon next Sunday" to which he invited any "who care to come and hear me." Lemonade would be served. That afternoon several hundred Lisbon residents gathered on the lawn in front of the house to hear Beilhart's views on marriage, the family, and sex. After the speech Spirit Fruit women conducted house tours and chatted with some of the crowd. The event lessened tensions between the colony and the town considerably. "Even the Reverend Mr. Anderson," Grant wrote, "seemed resigned to the utopia's presence."[51]

Historians are uncertain about what influence this event had on Beilhart's decision to relocate. What is known is that in early October 1904, he discussed how Chicago would be a "better environment for our work." It seems that Rock was an important influence in persuading the Spirit Fruiters to make a new home near his business activities. The first announcement of the impending move appeared in the *Buckeye State* on November 3, 1904, stating, "he has about decided to sell the community home here and buy another location." It took over a year to liquidate the

Ohio property. One must keep in mind that, as Robert Fogarty has pointed out, the "Spirit Fruit did not dissolve; it merely relocated."[52]

The new utopia was in Ingleside, in Lake County, Illinois, twenty miles from Lake Michigan with access to the mainline of the Chicago, Milwaukee, & St. Paul Railroad. This rail connection was important, because it enabled Beilhart to keep in touch easily with the Chicago branch. With money from the sale of the Lisbon property and subsidies from Rock, he initially purchased ninety acres and rented a farm; by 1908 he had leased or purchased three hundred more acres of cultivated land. Beilhart told Hinds in a letter written in March 1907 that they had built a thirty-five-room house "made of cement" with all modern conveniences. The structure, worth $18,000, was constructed entirely by the residents. They did everything "from hauling the sand and gravel to making the block-molds and tamping them by hand." He further informed Hinds that the thirteen residents "have all things in common, and no one owns anything."[53]

The Chicago branch lasted only a year before some of its members moved to Lake County. Despite its brevity, Grant thinks that its members "unquestionably created utopia within an urban context."[54] The Chicago branch included Dora Greenlee, a Chicago divorcée; Evelyn Arthur See, who in 1906 would found a cult called the Church of the Absolute Life to purify neighborhood children by indoctrination; Richard "Dick" Fischer, a salesman, and his wife, Mary; and Belle Norris, a single woman in her late twenties. Their lives centered on Beilhart's frequent lectures, which often attracted over two hundred curious visitors wanting to learn about the details of Spirit Fruit.

Giving dignified talks, Beilhart was no street-corner evangelist. He focused on "loving individualism," as he called it. "Love," he said, "not force or power should control living." On marriage, he declared, "The marriage arrangement by law, as we know it today, is a terrible mistake." He argued, "If two people fall in love, nothing in the world should keep them apart." When he condemned police violence against workers, as in the Haymarket Riot and the Pullman strike, Chicago newspapers claimed that "the cult has caught the fancy of the city's anarchists, especially the women."[55] When the colorful well-known anarchist Will Jackson and his wife, Aimée Montfont, joined the group, the owner of the Clark Street building, Joseph Leiter, ordered them to leave. Fortunately, Jackson was able to lease a large room over a vinegar factory at 681 West Lake Street. They stayed there for the next nine months, listened to Beilhart's speeches, and discussed the principles of Spirit Fruit.

In February 1905 the police disrupted one of these meetings and served a warrant listing violations of Chicago building codes. The officers escorted about twenty-five people, including Beilhart and Jackson, onto the street. Jackson, whose name was on the lease for the room, was arrested and taken to the West Lake Street station. He was interrogated, released on bail, and later fined. According to newspaper accounts a police sergeant felt that the raid was not only about building codes. They quoted him as saying, "We want that bunch out of this city. . . . I know that I speak for many others, including those who work and reside in this neighborhood." Following the episode Beilhart found new quarters in an office building at 363 West Dearborn Street. However, this space was seldom used. On the urban experience Kate Waters, who was born and raised in that city and joined the Lisbon community, later recalled that it "was so much better than Lisbon," since Chicago at its worst "exuded only skepticism and not enmity."[56]

Meanwhile, at Ingleside, construction of the stone mansion, called the Temple House, gave them what sociologist Rosabeth Moss Kanter called a commitment to community. Or, as Grant put it, "no other activity during the colonists' years at Ingleside . . . produced greater satisfaction than the building of the massive mansion house." It was a Herculean task, observed a reporter from the *Cleveland Leader*. Men in brown overalls and women in bloomers worked "like beavers" from dawn to dusk. While the mansion was being built they slept in the farmhouse—men in the loft and women in the upstairs bedrooms. Everyone ate meals communally in the kitchen.[57]

Their most important economic activity was dairy farming. They owned thirty Holstein cows, which grazed on colony property and on 143 rented acres nearby. The cows were milked twice daily, and the cans of milk were hauled to the railroad depot for shipment to Chicago. In 1906 crops included fifteen hundred bushels of oats, a thousand bushels of corn, and a hundred tons of clover hay. Each year the yields increased. They had a large flock of chickens and a vegetable garden, which by 1907 covered several acres near the mansion. Beilhart handed out no work assignments. As he reflected early on, "We have no leaders, when one excels in a line of work we follow him."[58]

Many visitors came to open house picnics held in the summer. The *Lake County Independent* and the *Waukegan Weekly Sun* gave full coverage to these events, complete with photographs. As in Ohio, reporters focused on the community members' views on marriage. One account in the *Independent* had a headline about Beilhart that read: "Insists He Will End Marriage Vow." Daily aspects of life, however, were described in the newspaper. A reporter wrote about the noon meal, saying that he found the Spirit Fruiters "an unusually courteous and polite people" exuding an attitude of cheer and innocence. Sometimes at these meals they engaged in unstructured mutual criticism where they analyzed an individual's shortcomings or irritating mannerisms. Not always negative, these discussions sometimes were reassuring and supportive.[59]

The *Grayslake Times* previewed a June 17, 1907, gathering where the mansion would be open from ten o'clock until five. At two o'clock in the afternoon, Beilhart would deliver a "free lecture" on the "Gospel of Work, the Business and Relation of Man." The paper stated that "From all indications Spirit Fruiters found these open houses pleasant experiences." Unlike before, their neighbors were impressed with their deportment and never threatened violence. Many who came to Ingleside were famous. Clarence Darrow, the renowned Chicago lawyer and author, went there frequently. Elbert Hubbard, the "Master of Roycroft," arrived after Beilhart and three women visited him in East Aurora, New York, in 1904. In the February 1905 issue of his publication the *Philistine*, Hubbard gave a glowing account of Beilhart and his ideas.[60]

On the evening of Thursday, November 19, 1908, Beilhart began to suffer severe abdominal pain. By Sunday his condition had deteriorated so much that a Waukegan surgeon, Dr. J. B. Foley, was reached by telephone. He diagnosed appendicitis and, when doing an appendectomy, discovered peritonitis from the ruptured organ. The infection was so widespread that nothing could be done. After intense suffering, Beilhart died on the morning of November 24 at the age of forty-one. On November 28, about thirty people—members of the colony and friends from Chicago—attended the funeral. After a simple service of eulogies, he was buried in a metal and glass coffin in an unmarked grave on the property.[61]

Spirit Fruiters found solace in spiritualism. They believed they had daily communications from Beilhart through Charlena "Ma" Young. The day after his death, she said he had sent her a message that Virginia Moore, her daughter, should lead the society. In the ensuing months, following the noon meal, Ma sat at the dining table surrounded by colony members. With eyes closed she entered a trance. Knowdell remembered in 1981, "There is no question in my mind that they all believed that the spirit never dies, and Ma's daily writings . . . were accepted as their link between the present and the hereafter." Ma transcribed these revelations, called the Message of the Day, on a tablet and then Virginia read them to the group. Such séances revealed "that although Jacob was beyond their physical reach, he was not beyond their love."[62]

Nevertheless, adjustments had to be made. For example, no one could replace Beilhart to conduct seminars and hold speaking engagements. Consequently, ties with friends in Chicago were gradually severed, and the communards went to the city only to shop or for entertainment. The *Spirit Fruit* ceased publication. Fewer visitors came to the colony and donations to it dried up. Newspapers now ignored the Spirit Fruit Society, and the *Chicago Record-Herald* alone published an article about it on January 15, 1911. Despite these changes its economy remained solid, and it continued to prosper as an agricultural commune.[63]

In late 1913 the eleven remaining members of the society decided to relocate to California. Grant speculated on the reasons for this decision.

Beilhart had always talked "glowingly" about the West and of his experiences at the Healdsburg College. They knew about Katherine Tingley's thriving Theosophical Society utopia at Point Loma. And, no doubt, they were aware of the Salvation Army's "back-to-the-land" experiment at Fort Romie in Monterey County. Finally there was the psychological element involved in relocation. "The simple desire to start afresh," Grant suggested, "with a site that was affordable, manageable, and devoid of the memories of Jacob's tragic death surely had appeal."[64]

In the winter of 1914 two men from the society went by train to San Francisco and reconnoitered an olive tree farm and cannery near the village of Los Gatos, located at the eastern slope of the Santa Cruz Mountains. They leased this as a temporary base from which they could find a better location. In midsummer, back at Ingleside, they loaded personal belongings and household goods into a boxcar at the railroad station and shipped them to California. They auctioned the remaining possessions—livestock, agricultural tools, and equipment. Then they boarded a passenger train for the four-day trip to the Pacific Coast. They spent the next ten months at the Los Gatos farm picking olives and canning them in fifty-gallon oak barrels.

In the spring of 1915 they found a permanent site, soon to be known as Hilltop Ranch, about eighty acres less than a mile north of the city of Soquel in Santa Cruz County. The price was $7,965, payable over five years. They packed up all of their belongings, Knowdell remembered, and moved there by train. They first lived in large tents put up at the top of a hill that rose two hundred feet above the surrounding countryside. Gradually, a large ranch house was built that included both private and common areas. They ran a profitable dairy operation and a poultry business with White Leghorn hens and a rooster. By 1917 they began to grow vegetables commercially and hauled them by truck to a farmers' market in Santa Cruz. They remained together for fourteen years until, as Miller put it, "only the aging of the members and the death of Virginia Moore, the group's later-day leader, ended one of America's longest lived yet oddly obscure communal experiments."[65]

The House of David

Miller considers the House of David "one of the most fascinating communal groups to emerge in the twentieth century." Its founder, Benjamin Franklin Purnell, was a follower of Joanna Southcott (b. 1750) who, in England, proclaimed that she was "Lamb's Bride," who would vanquish Satan and lead the Lost Tribes of Israel back to Jerusalem. She predicted that an elect of 144,000 adherents would have eternal life. In 1814, the year of her death, she announced that she was pregnant and would bring forth the Messiah, called Shiloh, in a virgin birth. One of her many followers, James Jezreel, a former British soldier, moved to the United States and carried Southcott's message to gather together the ancient Hebrew tribes. Before he died in 1885 his disciple Michael Mills organized a group of Jezreelites in Detroit.[66]

Purnell was born in 1861 into a poor farm family in Greenup City, Kentucky. At the age of sixteen he married a local girl named Angeline Brown, fathered a daughter, and became an itinerant preacher. He ended up in Richmond, Indiana, working as a broom maker. Here he converted to the Jezreelite creed and met Mary Stollard. He married her on August 3, 1880. Three years later he divorced Angeline. For the next twelve years the couple traveled throughout the Midwest in a two-horse covered wagon as Jezreelite ministers. In January 1892 they joined the Mills Detroit colony.

But in March 1895 Purnell had a revelation that Mills was a false prophet and that he, as the seventh messenger calling himself Shiloh, would lead the gathering of the Israelites. The Mills group rejected his claim, and so, back in the wagon between 1895 and 1901, he wandered about the Heartland "as a rejected prophet in search of mission and congregation."[67] Benjamin and Mary Purnell stayed for a while in Fostoria, Ohio, at the homes of Silas Mooney and John Pelton until, in 1902, he and Mrs. Mooney were discovered copulating in a berry patch. In the meantime, with $400 donated by Pelton, Purnell wrote and published *The Star of Bethlehem*, the first statement of what would become the beliefs of the House of David.

After this sexual exposé, the Purnells moved to Grand Rapids, Michigan, where Benjamin attracted a small group of believers and some well-to-do sponsors. From there, in 1903, he relocated his disciples (the exact numbers are unknown) to a site just south of Benton Harbor, Michigan. At the time it had summer resorts and hotels that attracted visitors from Chicago and Milwaukee. Here, in a print shop, he published pamphlets, tracts, and manifestoes on the Second Coming. Three kinds of believers joined the communal utopia. First were the original members who were personally converted by the Purnells. The second contingent were recruited by Benjamin and Mary Purnell in 1905 when they went to Melbourne, Australia. This group donated over $100,000 to the community. Native-born Americans, the third group, joined the gathering between 1905 and 1917.

Purnell preached vegetarianism, the rejection of alcohol, and the need for men to grow long hair and beards. He promised immortality of the body, a doctrine that Robert Fogarty claimed laid the basis for Purnell's "plan for religious and sexual seduction."[68] Purnell explained that Adam and Eve originally were without sin, but that evil was done when Eve had sexual intercourse with the black devil serpent called Gadreal. Consequently, only total continence would purify the blood of this evil and when that occurred the body would reap life everlasting. Members of the House of David, he said, achieved this immortal perfection in four stages. In the first stage, when they joined the community, the person had evil in his or her blood inherited from the Fall. The second stage came when, living in the society, they had their blood slowly cleansed. In the third stage, they were "without blood" and lived by a life-giving spirit. The fourth stage, the "ingathering" of 144,000 descendants of the ancient Hebrew tribes, arrived when everyone became "God-men" at the beginning of the millennium. Purnell claimed that he was at the third stage getting ready for the fourth.

The community's "Articles of Association and By-Laws" named Benjamin and Mary as absolute rulers, or "anointed heads," of the House of David. They in turn chose twelve trustees for four-year terms of office. They also appointed the other officers—a president, vice president, secretary, treasurer, four male "pillars," and four "head female officers" called "sweepers."[69]

In 1905 the first residence building, the "Ark," was completed. It was a three-story frame structure joined to another residence, "Bethlehem," by a stone arch with the inscription "House of David." In 1909 a two-story stone residence and administrative building called "Shiloh" was put up for the Purnells and other colony officers. Another building, "Jerusalem," housed single men and women, the men on the second floor and the women on the top floor. Usually, two or three individuals slept in the same room. Celibate husbands and wives also shared a room. Other structures soon were built. In a large communal dining hall, simple vegetarian meals were served three times each day. Breakfast consisted of oatmeal, toast, and coffee or tea. At lunch and dinner they ate vegetables and pies. The population of the House of David had grown to 385 by 1907 and steadily increased over the next two decades to about 800 residents. By then the community looked like a small town. It had a theater, an amusement park (called Eden Spring) with a miniature railroad, a zoo, baseball and basketball teams, a marching band, and two orchestras. It operated a lumberyard and a sawmill on an island in Lake Michigan as well as a cement factory and flourishing tailor shops. Nearby, they cultivated five farms.

Education of the children—who lived with their parents until the age of twelve, after which they were housed in "Jerusalem"—was unimportant. Purnell said it was less useful than dung because at least dung "can be put on the ground and do something."[70] In the Ark 175 children were taught by two teachers, but there were only eight grades, the minimum required by state law. It was a religious school and emphasized moral training, mainly instruction in Purnell's writings and how to work for the good of the community and the ingathering. For adults the Purnells opened a "School of Prophets" for further training in his doctrines.

Life in the House of David was regimented. The "sweepers" daily inspected the conduct of the residents. No one could leave the compound without permission from the Purnells. Also prohibited were room visitations, "unseemly letter writing," and walking alone. A Rule Book had to be strictly followed. For example, everyone went to bed at ten o'clock and rose at five in the morning. The Rule Book forbade playing cards, arguing, wearing black, and fraternizing with outsiders. It condemned "pleasure seeking" and forming close friendships. Those who failed to comply with the regulations were called "scorpions" and were eventually expelled. Benjamin wore fine white dress suits and expensive jewelry; Mary changed her elaborate gowns up to six times a day; everyone else dressed in simple clothing made out of flour sacks in the tailor shops.

Beginning in 1907 complaints of sexual and financial misconduct "threatened to destroy the gathering, and these charges served as the impetus for the House of David to turn inward and further secret itself from the world at large that it hoped to convert."[71] In that year one of the Melbourne group, William Cleveland, sent a letter to the British consulate in Philadelphia. He confessed that, after he lived in the community for two years, his faith had weakened because of Purnell's relations with colony women. He had tried to leave and get back the $150 he had given the colony, but Purnell returned only $55. He asked the consulate to help him regain all of his money.

The consulate then contacted the Michigan deputy attorney general in Lansing, Henry E. Chase, who launched an investigation into the House of David under the prosecuting attorney for Berrien County, Charles E. White. White reported that, although it was hard to learn "about the inner workings of this society," it was "a somewhat immoral organization." Their conduct was "secretive," he wrote, but he had heard "little things" that convinced him they were "extremely immoral." He recommended further probing to get to the truth of what was going on. Acting on this advice, on May 11, 1907, Chase sent a letter to Benton Harbor Presbyterian minister Elisha Hoffman in which he asked for more information and stated that "their morals are not good . . . they deceive the people and get their property away from them." A month later Hoffman replied, describing "discrimination in the treatment of members" most of whom are "very low in intelligence and education." She also reinforced White's charge of immorality but focused on Benjamin. "He seems to be," she alleged, "very free, from the statements made to me, taking improper liberties with the women who have faith and comeliness." Mildred Giles, a former member of the House, wrote to Chase that Benjamin continually sexually harassed her and "lots of times at headquarters he would meet me on the walks and slap me on the breasts." She went on to recount an episode between Purnell and Josie Lewis, where he "grabbed her in a room and closed the door after her and felt of her teats and another time she said he pinched her in the privates."[72]

Cleveland broadened the immorality charge to include Mary, in a letter dated July 1908. He described "undue familiarity with the brothers on Mary's part . . . and when not well, which is very often, has two of the brothers viz. Francis Thorpe and Wm. Hannaford to bath her and won't have females to do it." The allegations kept coming. Chase found out that in 1909 during an outing in a sailboat with twenty young women on board, Purnell reportedly had sex with some of them. On a trip to Chicago, he allegedly slept with several women. A series of group marriages took place in 1910, 1914, 1917, and 1923. According to Clare Adkin, "Benjamin's fear of an investigation purportedly stimulated him to make sure that each girl with whom he could be accused of having carnal experiences with was married off. Therefore, if one of these girls was examined, her lack of virginity could easily be attributed to her husband." In the first ceremony, in December 1910, under Mary's direction twenty couples were married in Benton Harbor before a justice of the peace.[73]

In 1914 Lena Fortney, after defecting from the colony, charged Purnell with what amounted to rape. She stated that she had joined the House of David in 1908 at the age of fourteen and lived with three other girls in the Ark. She explained in an affidavit dated June 30, 1914:

> I have seen Benjamin come into the room a great number of times. . . . [He] told us he was just like Jesus and had the right to have intercourse with us girls. He then took me into another room and there were two girls in another bed. I protested but he told me he could come into my room where other girls were. . . . I have had intercourse with him and have seen him have intercourse with other girls many times in the same room. The fact is well known among the women of the colony.

Edith Clark signed an affidavit the same day that explained Benjamin's prerogatives. He told her that "he was the son of Man and it was our duty to have sexual intercourse with him in order to be in the inner court—that every woman must be passed by the king." In other words, he promised the women immortality. Two other women described Purnell walking naked in front of some of the women telling prurient stories. Older women told new arrivals to obey him, the Shiloh, in his sexual commands.[74]

Did other members of the House of David know what was going on? Fogarty believes that as early as 1909 at least an inner circle was aware of the Purnells' activities. Rumors about sexual malfeasance spread throughout Benton Harbor. This was no incidental matter since such conduct was a violation of Michigan's "virgin law." Still, the attorney general's office allowed them to continue religious activities, such as missionary work outside the colony, and to conduct business. By 1919 Purnell, then fifty-eight, was "still an impressive figure particularly when in the company of the handsome Mary. In their forty years together they had accomplished a great deal, achieving wealth, power, and some dubious fame." But two years later an event occurred that ended up in the courts at Grand Rapids and signaled the eventual collapse of the colony.[75]

It involved John Hansel. He had joined the House in 1912 along with his wife, two daughters, and four sons. At the time they donated all their property and money to the community. But he became disillusioned with, as he put it, "a humdrum life of labor . . . with no compensation except such food, clothing or sleeping accommodations as the colony afforded." He decided to leave and sue for back wages. In December 1920 he found out about Purnell's dalliances with women from a future daughter-in-law and became more determined than ever to sue the prophet. In reaction to this threat, on November 7, 1921, 444 members of the colony signed an affidavit expressing their confidence in Benjamin and Mary Purnell and claiming that charges of immorality against them were "absolutely false."[76]

At this time Myron Walker, the federal attorney for Grand Rapids, announced that he was contemplating a grand jury investigation into the colony. Then two more defectors, the sisters Gladys and Ruth Bamford, filed a suit against Benjamin. "Their defection and lawsuits were serious threats," noted Fogarty, "and their eventual testimony, coupled with that of the Hansels, made prosecution of Purnell a certainty."[77] Benjamin Purnell went into hiding just before Christmas 1922 and did not reappear until he was discovered by the police in 1926. Thereafter leadership of the community was assumed by Harry Thomas Dewhirst.

In April 1923 the attorney general served papers on the colony officers. A grand jury was called, and the presiding circuit judge Harry J. Dingeman opened an inquiry. Twice the police raided the property searching unsuccessfully for Purnell. Failing in this effort, they launched a nationwide dragnet for him, advertising that a "suitable reward will be paid for his arrest, delivery to an officer of the Michigan State Police."[78] Meanwhile, he became critically ill with tuberculosis and diabetes. On November 16, 1926, Bessie Daniels Woodworth, who had had sexual relations with Purnell but had left the colony in 1925, led the police, along with photographers, to his hiding place. They found him in a nightgown and slippers with women attendants running around all over the place. He was arrested and then released the following day on bond.

Between January and May 1927 the prosecution, led by the special assistant prosecuting attorney George E. Nichols, "geared up for what was billed the biggest trial in the history of the state." The House of David had three attorneys, including Dewhirst. Purnell himself, so ill that he lay on a stretcher, testified in August. He admitted to no immorality except the charge of bigamy. He then told a startled courtroom that Mary had a liaison with Francis Thorpe, a colony officer, and was a "wicked person" who was undermining the House of David.[79]

The case of *People v. Purnell* began on May 16 and lasted until August 17, 1927. More than two hundred witnesses were called, over five hundred exhibits presented, seventy-five depositions introduced, and a fourteen-thousand-page transcript compiled. On November 10, 1927, Judge Louis Fead filed his decision at the Berrien County Courthouse in St. Joseph. He found for the plaintiffs and declared "the existence of a public nuisance."[80] He determined that the Purnells were guilty of teaching and practicing perjury. The judge ordered Benjamin to vacate the colony and announced he would name a receiver to replace him. But before a receivership could be appointed, Purnell died of tuberculosis on December 16. After he failed to come back to life, miraculously, as he had claimed he would, Purnell's body was embalmed for later resurrection and interred in the colony chapel, where it remains today.

After Benjamin's death a bitter feud developed between Dewhirst and Mary. He tried to get her removed as a trustee. She petitioned the court to dissolve the community, sell its property, and distribute the funds among the members. "As two wild animals locked in a death struggle, the only avenue of survival for either was to back down together." So, on February 18, 1930, they signed a division agreement. Mary and 217 followers received $60,000 in cash, the unfinished House of David Hotel, and some other small buildings. She called her community the City of David. Dewhirst and 214 followers kept control of the original buildings and three farms and maintained the right to call themselves the Israelite House of David. In 2009 the two groups, numbering about fifty individuals in total, live at their respective sites.[81]

CHAPTER EIGHT

Contemporary Heartland Utopias

The five intentional communities described here still exist and were all religious utopias. Indeed, the three in Chicago (Reba Place Fellowship, Olive Branch Mission, and Jesus People USA) were different forms of evangelical outreach to the poor. The other two (Padanaram Settlement and Stelle Community), while not so much missionary societies, also endeavored to build God-centered communities in preparation for a future life after the millennium.

Reba Place Fellowship

Reba Place Fellowship began in the fall of 1954 when John Miller returned to teach at Goshen College, Indiana. He was a Mennonite Old Testament scholar who had earned a doctorate in theology at the University of Basel, Switzerland. He had become inspired by the history of the Bruderhof (the Society of Brothers) and wanted the Mennonites everywhere to live as an intentional community. He and six other adults, called the "group of seven," started to take communion in a "house church context," without an assigned minister, but the outrage of the Mennonite college officials "so frightened some participants that the group largely floundered." What they wanted to do was serious, because Mennonites believed that the bishops' and ministers' control over communion was the basis of church discipline. So, for a small group of men and women to take communion on their own "was tantamount to declaring themselves independent from the authority of the church."[1]

They nevertheless continued their interest in communalism, and in the fall of 1956 Miller and his wife went to the Bruderhof colony in Woodcrest, New York. On the way they visited Paul Peachey, then on the faculty of Eastern Mennonite College, and several married students who were considering founding an intentional community. Miller returned to Goshen College with a "burning interest" in the idea and, with a group of students, organized a Fellowship House. This was enough for Harold Bender, the dean of the college, and Paul Mininger, Goshen's president. They placed Miller on a leave of absence.

By this time the Fellowship had begun to consider a new direction for an intentional community, not retreating in rural isolation like the Hutterites and Bruderhof but, rather, living in a metropolitan area where they could confront the evils of society. An undated Reba House pamphlet later explained:

> Our cities are beginning more and more to resemble vast ant heaps, lacking within them the vital smaller communities that alone make a truly human life possible. . . . When possible we want to live within easy walking distance of one another. Scattered as many of us are during the working days across the sprawling network of the city, we want to come home at evening time to one neighborhood where we are readily available to one another in times of need. We want to be able to meet daily if necessary without climbing into our cars and going half a city away. We want our children to grow up experiencing more than the lonely crowd. We want them to know in their daily life the reality of a closely knit circle of families and friends.[2]

Miller got in touch with Ray Blair, head of the Chicago Mennonite Ministers' Fellowship, and initially received a welcoming reply. But when President Mininger found out what was going on, he expressed to Blair his concern about Miller's "offensive idea" of building a communal congregation. Further assistance from Blair's organization disappeared. At this point, in the winter of 1957, several Mennonite families living in the North Side of Chicago suggested that Miller consider locating his fellowship in south Evanston. There were three reasons. First, the city's General Hospital would provide opportunities for voluntary service. Second, the sizable number of black families living there desperately needed personal service. Third, Evanston's Mennonite church was "very weak" and without a center in that part of the city.[3]

Miller communicated these points to his father, Orie Miller, who was the executive secretary of the Mennonite Central Committee (MCC). On July 6, 1957, the MCC executive committee met in Chicago's Hotel Atlantic and approved the "Evanston Voluntary Service" project under John's leadership. The committee sent money for furniture, rugs, and a

kitchen stove, and $350 for "operating expenses." Also in July the son
purchased a house at 727 Reba Place, and by September he and his wife
and two children, plus two other couples, were living there. Within a year
thirteen residents as well as several visitors had moved in, and a second
house was purchased across the street. "Reba Place Fellowship," Timothy
Miller observed, "was soon a thriving community of individuals whose
commitment to Christian service dominated their lives."[4]

Members of Reba Place took outside service jobs or taught in local schools
and deposited their wages in a common treasury.[5] The community's main
goal was to provide service programs to individuals in need. These included
setting up a halfway house, called Hospitality House, on the third floor of
the Monroe Street building, for people leaving mental hospitals and for
the mentally handicapped; operating a day-care center to assist Central
American refugees; providing help to refugees from Cambodia; and
converting a warehouse into a meetinghouse with seating for community
meals for the poor. Some members went beyond service to social-justice
issues and became activists for civil rights and, later, for peace during the
Vietnam War.

In June 1958 they started publishing a newsletter called the *Reba Place
Circular* that continued to appear monthly until March 1961. About one
hundred copies were mailed to friends and acquaintances intending to
"draw closer to . . . those everywhere whose hearts and minds have been
awakened to a similar vision of life under the rule of God." Reba Place
Fellowship sponsored a "Summer Seminar on the Church in the Inner
City" that enrolled fifteen college and seminary students. "The streets
[around the seminar location]," one participant wrote, "are frequented
by human derelicts, sitting on the steps of numerous taverns, or walking
listlessly down the sidewalk."[6]

Reba Place Fellowship developed close ties with other Christian
intentional communities. It had extensive contacts with the Bruderhof
and even explored, unsuccessfully, the possibility of uniting with them.
Over the years it kept in touch with Koinonia Farm in Americus, Georgia,
and in September 1967 Koinonia's leader, Clarence Jordan, offered to give
them the farm, "since the Fellowship represented the closest thing to his
own vision."[7] Jordan died of heart failure in November 1969 before any
action was taken on the offer. Reba Place at various times communicated
with the Sojourners Community of Washington, D.C., and the Forest River
Hutterite colony in North Dakota.

Some members felt their children needed a better environment than the
congested streets around Reba Place, and in 1971 they proposed starting
a rural community, Plow Creek Fellowship, as a separate intentional
community. After almost a year of discussion they reached a consensus
to purchase, with money loaned from the Bruderhof and other sources,

a 190-acre farm near Tiskilwa, Illinois. Four families moved there and, with the help of some single men who came on weekends as a volunteer working crew, they built houses on the property. In 2006, according to Plow Creek's Web site, "about 45 folks . . . actively participate in our life together. Half of those are children, so we have lively times."[8]

David and Neta Jackson considered that the years between 1972 and 1978 marked the zenith of Reba Place Fellowship, "a time when community life was all absorbing." As they explained:

> Here was a church that lived as life together seven days a week, 24 hours a day. If you were lonely and had no family, you were given a family. If you had nothing, a place to live, a car, furniture, clothing, and food were made available or shared. If you were dependent on alcohol or drugs or if your marriage was falling apart, Christian brothers and sisters would surround you and support you and help you try to put the pieces of your life back together. If you were disillusioned by "church," and wondered how stained glass, sitting in pews, taking up collections, and coffee fellowships had anything to do with the church of Acts, here was a modern day group of Christians where "all the believers were together and had everything in common."[9]

Membership peaked in 1978, with 152 adults living in fifteen extended-family households located within three blocks of 727 Reba Place.

About this time, however, internal conflicts began to appear. Differences arose over the role of women in a patriarchal fellowship. For years after John Miller left the community in 1968 to join the faculty at Conrad Grebel College (affiliated with the University of Waterloo in Ontario, Canada), the community was led by elected male officers and the highest office, the eldership, was held by a man. In 1980 the community established a church that noncommunal members could join. A document called the "Clarification of Membership—Ways of Participating in the Church" was adopted, stipulating three types of members:[10]

1. Full Communal Members.

2. Congregational Members. A noncommunal status where individuals agree to uphold the same principles found in the community.

3. Affiliate Members. Individuals committed to Christianity without much definition of structure.

Forty congregational members were admitted in August 1980, and the ensuing months were chaotic. Some communards left Reba Place Fellowship and lived elsewhere, and by 1987 just half of the 120 residents were fully communal. As a result, only this segment continued "living in common facilities and with common finances, and the community [moved] to a model in which religious activity centered in small, intense fellowship groups." In 1987 ten adults from Reba Place Church moved to rented apartments in the "target community" of Rogers Park in north Chicago, and eight years later they began having public worship services there.[11]

In 1995 after a visit Rich Foss wrote: "Now, after nearly forty years, Reba Place Fellowship owns a dozen houses and over a hundred apartment units, which it manages for its members, for Reba Place Church members, and for lower-income people. . . . This arrangement makes possible common work on the buildings, and it puts members within walking distance of each other, creating an intimate village hidden within the urban scene." In 2000 Reba Place Fellowship advertised in the *Communities Directory* that only "forty-some members and children" lived in multifamily communal homes and apartments. Their ministries included "a shelter for the homeless, care of refugees from . . . Central America, low-income housing, personal counseling, and a peace witness program." In 2006 the Reba Place Web site declared: "Today, Reba Place Fellowship is a group of about three dozen people living in Evanston, Illinois, and the Rogers Park neighborhood of Chicago. We still pool our incomes in a common purse and seek to live simply. . . . And we still live as a close-knit community, sharing our daily walk with Christ with each other and with many friends and neighbors."[12]

Padanaram Settlement

In September 1966 Daniel Wright led a contingent of his fundamentalist congregation—five men, three women, and several young children—to an eighty-six-acre farm near the town of Williams in southern Indiana. With only "a tractor and an old mule," as one member recalled, they started to cultivate the marginal land. He named it Padanaram, from the Book of Genesis, to show its religious identification. From this inauspicious start, according to Rachel E. Wright-Summerton, Wright's daughter, the community had grown by the year 2000 to two hundred members, united "for the purpose of building a microcosm city of kingdomism, the future religious and political (polit theo) style of living to be practiced in the millennium."[13]

Wright was born in 1917 into a working-class family living in a small town near Des Moines, Iowa. In an August 1973 interview, he told sociologist Jon Wagner that as a child he had developed "a capacity for extrasensory perception and an abiding interest in religious questions."[14] Although his family belonged to the Church of the Brethren, in 1933 he converted to fundamentalist Christianity. His religious convictions made him a conscientious objector during World War II. After the war he traveled about the Midwest holding revivals. He wrote several religious tracts and, at the age of thirty, became pastor of a small congregation in Indianapolis. Wright confided to Timothy Miller that he had experienced a profound religious experience that year. "I saw [that] the end community," he said, "was the salvation of the human family and it took teamwork and loving their neighbor as themselves and I realized that it had to be upon a religious base also."[15]

Wright felt called by the Lord to a remote valley of Martin County, Indiana, where the congregation "pooled our money," Wright-Summerton recalled, and purchased a rundown farmhouse without toilet facilities. "The first twelve years," Wright's daughter wrote, "were virtually years of silence" since the group had little contact with outsiders except for occasional interviews that Wright gave to local newspaper reporters.[16] Only in 1976 did the first document about the community appear as a mimeographed pamphlet entitled *Padanaram*.

Much of what has been written about this early period comes from Wagner, who lived there from June to December 1972, conducted regular visits afterward, and wrote a Ph.D. dissertation on the community at Indiana University in 1975. They constructed a log-cabin community, beginning with a lodge for married couples with sections, called dorms, for single men and women. Later they put up log houses for the couples. Meals were served in a communal dining hall where everyone, including children, ate together. Three women, certified teachers, taught in a log schoolhouse for first through sixth grades and ran a preschool and kindergarten. Padanaram had cattle, hogs, and a vegetable garden. Most important, as an economic base, they opened a hardwood logging operation and a sawmill and acquired twenty-seven hundred acres of forestland. By 1972 the business had grossed over $100,000 from selling the finished lumber to area lumberyards.[17]

Four years later, Wright told Miller, they moved the sawmill to Bloomington "and have been there ever since with that particular economic venture." By then, they had "expanded into composting and other commercial activities[, and] the commune had revived and strengthened its subsistence activities including farming and meat production." Over the years, Wright-Summerton said, their main income has been "from our renewable forest products business: sawmilling, selective timber buying, veneer sales and land improvement."[18]

Work assignments were rotated frequently, and "a lot of the women [did] all kinds of jobs, not just one job," in order "to grow." They practiced "cooperative equality," which Wright-Summerton remembered meant doing "whatever I can do best, let me do it . . . as a woman. . . . And if a man, let a man do what he can do best." There was no competition between the sexes.

"We just sort of found our cooperative places together." Besides, there was "only a limited number of jobs available," she pointed out. Wright confided to Miller that this cooperation was possible because the members were "spiritual realists." Everyone worked together "like a football team to make a touchdown." Discipline for lazy individuals was through group pressure. Member Steven Fuson told Miller that "they feel that 'discontentedness' with how their behavior is, and pretty soon they just leave."[19]

Padanaram received a charter of incorporation from the state to be a "village trust" with a board of seven men who served as managers. Members paid no rent, but since it was not a church, the community did have to pay taxes. It "was not exempt in any way," recalled Wright-Summerton. Fuson said that there was no effort to recruit new followers. "We don't proselytize or recruit members," he pointed out, "so whatever has come down the road and joined was the way new recruits were selected. We take in anyone willing to work. . . . We view that as divine procedure." Such a casual process did, however, cause trouble. Wright remarked that when they brought a black preacher into "a hotbed of the old Ku Klux Klan," the neighbors "were hostile about that thinking that he would be marrying some white woman. . . . They threatened to burn a cross in our yard."[20]

According to Wagner, Wright believed life was a battle between Carnality and Wisdom—that most humans lose this struggle and indulge in sexual gratification, aggression, competition, and war. Wright preached, however, that Wisdom, or the "path to God," could overcome Carnality for a select number of individuals. They would receive Wisdom and then would live communally in a continual quest for moral improvement. He conceived of communal living as a "school" where each member, although sometimes succumbing to Carnality, gained the path of Wisdom with the ongoing toleration and assistance of other communards. Women were unable to gain as much Wisdom as men because, he said, "man is the head, woman is a [sic] heart," and "they are not alike mentally, emotionally, or physically." He had a printed list of gender characteristics such as "No woman can hear or tell the truth . . . no two women can be friends . . . no man can be equal with a woman . . . no man can trust a woman and trust God."[21]

Padanaram members resented Wagner's assertion that the community was an oppressive patriarchy. Rather, they saw themselves, as Wright-Summerton put it, as "men and women living under a Godly order." Fuson conceded that it was, perhaps, just "mildly patriarchal. . . . We're patriarchal so that in every area Wisdom surfaces." All decisions, however, were by consensus, Fuson pointed out. They meet "one night each week for input on menus and to discuss future plans." In this assembly, men and women decide both political and economic questions. Padanaram women saw their role as one of "cooperative equality" with the men. Wright-Summerton, for example, believed that there was a lack of competition between the sexes because "we just sort of found our cooperative places together." In fact, she believed that their women were "much more liberated than the so-called 'liberated women' [on the outside] because in the communal atmosphere the women have everything they could want. . . . You can have a family and you can go over to the nursery and nurse your baby, and you can have as many children as you and your husband want to and yet, you still have your work area."[22]

Still, there is no doubt that daily tasks were gender based. Men did the logging and the milling, ran all the equipment, butchered the cattle and hogs, drove the trucks, and kept the business records. They conducted the community's diverse businesses, such as a painting and wallpaper enterprise, window washing, woodworking, food services, landscaping, and a colony print shop. Women did the cooking, washing, canning, and cleaning. The sexes worked together only in harvesting the vegetable garden.[23]

Communal marriage, Wright said, was different from marriage in mainstream America. Conventional marriage allowed women to control and manipulate men through "romantic love," because husbands had a destructive worship of the flesh. The wife used this compulsion to make her husband do whatever she wanted. In Padanaram the partners had different yet loving responsibilities. The "hussyband" restrained any "hussy" or unruly wife by teaching and taking care of her, but he never abused or exploited her. The wife was obedient, faithful, and supportive of her husband at all times. Children were "treated with affection and responsibility; that is their due as human beings and as members of the community."[24] They lived with the parents until they were thirteen, at which time they moved to the single men's or women's quarters. While in the nuclear family, though, they could be disciplined by the community, or "Superma and Superpa," which meant that any adult could correct any child.[25]

In 1986 Padanaram started to invite visitors in for a few hours each year, on a Sunday in mid-October. The open house was advertised in local newspapers, and a few hundred people came the first year. In 1993 four thousand outsiders attended, and the open house "has served as a very positive force within the local area and has created many friends along with the curiosity seekers." In 1990, the settlement sent mailings to other communities and former visitors inviting them to attend "conventions" held the first weekend in June and in mid-October. These events have been "the main contact with other communities, which have sent their literature and announcements of their special events."[26]

Its 1998 publication, *Padanaram Settlement,* called it "a twentieth-century communitarian settlement" with "villagers" who "live in many wood lodges and have their own apartment dwellings." Wright informed Miller in 1997 that the lumber business was "a several million dollar investment," and Fuson boasted, "Everything is paid! We owe nothing!"

As Wright-Summerton glowingly described the settlement in the 2000 edition of *Communities Directory,* Padanaram (also by then known as God's Valley), was a bucolic community living on three thousand acres of "woods, streams, organically certified farmland for produce and herbs." They had orchards and cattle. They practiced five communal principles: the Golden Rule, holding all things in common, distribution to each according to need, "from he that has much, much is required," and "he that won't work, neither shall he eat."[27]

The year before Wright's death in 2001, according to his daughter, he "started changing things," anticipating the impact that the passing of a charismatic leader almost always has on a utopian community. Some individuals saw fundamental alterations taking place after Wright's death. For example, Warrior LaMar, a graduate student at Indiana University and sometime resident of Padanaram, emailed this author in September 2006 that "Padanaram is definitely no longer an intentional community. . . . Very few things are still considered communal in the settlement." In 2005 an ex-member, Gloria Lewis, commented in the Intentional Community Database on the "sad state of affairs" she found there. The "communal kitchen is gone, [and] most people work outside of [the] community. . . . Not many people [are] there," she complained, "founding family members [mostly]."[28]

On the other hand, Nicole Brooks, a reporter for the *Bloomington Hoosier Times,* called Padanaram a "remarkable experiment." In a feature story on June 11, 2006, she described a vibrant community with a population of 150 residents ranging in age from children to senior citizens. Wright-Summerton told Brooks that many adults living there own their businesses such as window-washing or house-painting enterprises, and running the Good Earth Compost Company, which she called "a well-known name in the Bloomington area." Some adults have jobs in towns like Bloomington, Bedford, and Shoals. Only vestiges of communalism endure, however. For example, residents of the apartment buildings share electric and heating bills. Although families buy their own groceries, "folks still get together for an occasional meal, for celebrations and for coffee in the mornings." Spiritual meetings, mainly meditation and discussion, are held every Wednesday evening and Sunday morning in a large building called the Barn. Wright-Summerton believes that Padanaram survived problems in leadership after Wright's death because the community was not built on "a personality cult" but, rather, on his teachings, which were kept alive in conversations, "particularly his adage that 'Wisdom is our leader, truth our guide.'" Donald Pitzer, professor emeritus of history and former director of the Center of Communal Studies at Southern Indiana University, has visited Padanaram many times and agrees with Wright-Summerton. "Those who really want to be there," he told Brooks, "are still there. . . . If anything, they seem stronger than ever."[29]

In a summary of conditions called "Padanaram Today (2007)" that Wright-Summerton emailed this author on March 29, 2007, she highlighted its activities. In the "Ecovillage," the communal kitchen is closed and people eat in their homes. The communal school also has been shut down and children attend the county school. Over a dozen young men and women are currently enrolled in universities and colleges. Every morning and on Sundays coffee is served in the Barn, where they also hold potluck dinners and dances and celebrate weddings. Answering a rhetorical question "What is Padanaram?" she wrote, "To us it is a small city, a village . . . a small community of friends. It is a core group of families and single persons who have been here for many years. . . . It has large rent-free wooden lodges, individual cabins, two-family buildings, trailers and many small structures. Its basic values have not changed. It continues to be a village of trust."[30]

Stelle Community

"The first impression of Stelle Community," wrote Corinne McLaughlin and Gordon Davidson in 1985, "is of a typical American suburban development with nicely mowed lawns and neat sidewalks and curbs. Along its streets, men in business suits hurry off to work, and conservatively dressed women take their freckled children to school. Surrounded by miles of corn fields and small towns in the middle of Illinois, Stelle . . . hardly seems to fit the typical image of a new age community." But it was. Or, as Cris and Oliver Popenoe put it, "A closer look at Stelle reveals that it is very different from a typical suburban community." Stelle is an intentional community founded in 1973 by Chicago businessman Richard Kieninger, to prepare for a Doomsday in the year 2000 that was expected to devastate 90 percent of the world's population. The survivors, who would include the Stelle Community, would then build a perfect society. Though the predicted catastrophe never hapened, in October 2006 Stelle's webmaster, Mark Hoffman, described it as a community of forty-four households "located amid the cornfields of northeast Illinois," where values of "sustainability" and the "shared focus on human development creates the sense of family."[31]

Kieninger was born in 1927 and raised in a typical middle-class family in the Chicago suburbs. To his parents and friends he seemed a normal boy. He attended college and majored in chemistry but left during his senior year to take a job as an assistant office manager. Over the following decade he worked as a life insurance representative, a hardware salesman, an aircraft die maker, a cabinetmaker, and a small-business entrepreneur. In the 1950s, while operating his business in Chicago, he became interested in the Lemurian Fellowship in Romona, California, and soon was a believer in the "Lemurian Philosophy." He detailed the main tenets of this philosophy and teachings in *The Ultimate Frontier*, published in 1963 under the pen name Eklai Kueshana. In the book he recounts how, at the age of twelve, he was approached by an elderly gentleman called Dr. White, who "seemed to know a lot about him." Dr. White went on to describe communal groups called the "invisible Brotherhoods," which Christ had established to prepare and guide the peoples of the world for the millennium. Dr. White told him that the Kingdom of God was imminent: "It's you, Richard, who have been appointed to begin that nation." Afterward, Kieninger wrote, although he had only infrequent contacts with White, several "guides" visited him and provided further instructions about the secrets of the Brotherhoods.[32]

After the publication of the book, Kieninger, with his second wife, Gail, organized meetings in his Chicago home to study the principles of the Brotherhoods. They called the meetings the Stelle Group after Robert Stelle, author of books on communal living. A member of the community, Susan Fisher, in an interview with Deborah Altus of the University of Kansas faculty, also pointed out that *Stelle* in German means "the place." Having started with only three adults, by 1967 the Stelle Group had thirty members. The new recruits lived nearby in the Rogers Park neighborhood. In 1968, when the group had increased to eighty, they opened an elementary school, taught by Gail, in Kieninger's basement. The next year they established the Stelle Woodworking Corporation with money donated by several members of the group.[33]

Fisher recalled that in 1970 they "pooled money and resources to buy land to build the community." They purchased 240 acres, an old farmhouse, and a few outbuildings located about seventy-five miles south of Chicago. Over the next three years, the men volunteered long hours to construct frame homes and a modern factory measuring twenty thousand square feet. Kieninger required all members to tithe to cover the cost of materials. In April 1973, back in Chicago, according to Fisher, they celebrated the completion of the town and "people started moving in." She said that by 1996 they had forty-five homes, "some of them duplexes, some of them single family structures."[34]

Stelle grew rapidly. Streets were constructed, and sidewalks installed. New homes were put up. A water purification plant and pumping station was built that used a reverse osmosis method of purification to supply water to 450 residents. It was the "first municipal plant of its kind in North America." They moved the woodworking business from Chicago and called it the Stellewood Company. New enterprises were started: a plastics company, an automatic screw-machine company, and a print shop. All these profit-making ventures were under the control of Stelle Industries Inc., made up of community residents and directed by Kieninger. All nonprofit functions were governed by the Kieninger-controlled Stelle Group. "Morale was high, and growth was rapid," the Popenoes wrote, and "money flowed in as needed, experts joined as required, and people worked long hours with a great sense of satisfaction." By the end of 1974, membership had reached 216 people.[35]

That year, however, Kieninger had an adulterous affair and was forced to leave. He moved to Texas, where he organized a small community twenty-five miles east of Dallas called Adelphi. "Many of Stelle's residents followed him there, and Adelphi grew to a peak of thirty before declining to its present size of sixteen," reported the online encyclopedia Wikipedia in 2006. "The fact that [a] new community could emerge from communal disillusionment," Miller observed, "is strong testimony to the commitment to their ideals of many who walked the communal path." Then Keininger's "wife and her male companion departed for Wisconsin along with forty-two members and tried to start another community [but] nothing more was ever heard from them."[36]

After the Kieningers' exodus, Stelle focused more on personal development and communal cooperation than on physical growth. Members believed that appearance was a reflection of moral values. Fisher remembered that "when you stepped into Stelle in the seventies it was like almost being in the fifties."[37] Men dressed in coats and neckties and the women wore skirts and blouses. Following the rules put down in *The Ultimate Frontier,* they prohibited alcohol, tobacco, and drugs. Because of such restrictions very few new members joined the community.

Family values were a reflection of Kieninger's ideas. Couples lived together for three years before they were married and only after marriage could they have children. As laid out in the book, a woman's role was as mother and homemaker, and if she had children under the age of six she could not work outside the home. During this time she acted as the "Mother-school" and taught her progeny a five-point program. The units included the birth program, the Mother's Individual Staff Person at Home (MISPAH) program, mothers' classes, Montessori classes, and recreation. The first unit involved exercise and nutrition. MISPAH used teachers from the community school, called the Learning Center, who came to the home and gave instruction on music (especially in the Suzuki method of the violin or cello), hygiene, and physical development. In the mothers' classes the preschool mothers shared experiences with one another. The Montessori unit showed the child that education involved interaction with each other and the development of self-discipline. Children from the ages of six to eighteen attended the Learning Center twelve months of the year. Here they were instructed with the "mastery concept" approach to learning, where they mastered one concept at a time. Consequently, every child progressed at his or her own pace without being graded by the teachers. However, regardless of where they were in the "mastery" program, at the age of nine they were taught the "earth children" program of camping, hiking, and boating.[38]

After 1974 the community expanded the Stellewood Company and developed both new methods of house construction and alternative fuel sources. All three projects were based on the prediction in *The Ultimate Frontier* of a two-week cataclysm of earthquakes, volcanic eruptions, and catastrophic shifts in the earth's land masses that would happen in May 2000. Stelle homes were made earthquake resistant by using reinforced concrete and half-inch plywood. Wood stoves and roof solar collectors were installed in homes so that they would be energy self-sufficient. Solar-mass floors absorbed heat. Spaces between the inner and outer walls allowed the circulation of warm air in winter. They had a plant that made ethanol from corn funded with a grant of $52,000 from the Federal Department of Energy. Another grant from the Illinois Department of Energy allowed them to construct a commercial greenhouse measuring thirty by one hundred feet, with growing beds supported on water drums to retain heat diverted to the building from the adjacent ethanol plant. They raised bedding plants and organic vegetables for sale in the Stelle Cooperative Food Mart. Residents, however, came to the food mart and took whatever they needed, recording the items in a counter register. The Continuum Center had a physician and a health practitioner who used holistic medicine. The center's psychologist used a therapy called "Radix," which claimed to release negative emotions and energy blocks from the body. The center tested all food served at the Friday evening communal meal for harmful chemicals.[39]

Stelle Community had three types of residents: full members, associates, and nonresident associates. The Stelle Group members, the first category, included those who had embraced the ideas of *The Ultimate Frontier* and were fully committed to its principles. Associates were new arrivals preparing to become full members. The nonresident associates had read *The Ultimate Frontier,* donated money to the community, and attended "guest week" experiences where they lived with a resident family.[40]

Community matters in 2009, however, are decided by the Stelle Community Association, open to all property owners, which Fisher said is "a homeowners' association that takes care of water and streets." Stelle Telephone operates as a separate corporation. In early 2005 the small number of residents in the Stelle Group "decided to disband and liquidate the organization's assets—the school, the community center, an orchard, a community garden, a pond, a greenhouse, a storage building and about 100 acres of farmland adjoining the village. . . . In late 2005, the Center for Sustainable Community (CSC), an educational organization that maintains its headquarters in Stelle, purchased the orchard, the community garden, the pond, the greenhouse and the storage building. . . . The remaining farmland was purchased by a local organic farmer."[41]

Despite the fact that Dr. White's predicted cataclysm never happened, some aspects of communal life survive. Between twelve and twenty families share a garden co-op, a tool co-op, and a learning co-op for children. "Once every twelve weeks," Debra Levy Larson wrote, on a Monday, "one family cooks a meal for everyone else and they share it together in the community center. On the other eleven Mondays they just come and enjoy dinner cooked for them." The CSC annually hosts permaculture workshops taught by resident Mark Hoffman and outside professionals. The CSC also holds an annual Earth Day open house in the spring and a solar tour in October. Mark W. Wilkerson, in the magazine *Home Power,* called Stelle the "Solar Capital of the Midwest." In the fall of 2005, Larson wrote that Stelle is "not a commune, but a community." Hoffman agreed. Writing on the Stelle's home Web page, he pointed out that "Today no single organization oversees all activities; instead, different groups play various roles. . . . Cooperative living rather than communal living describes the community essence and this approach has birthed a unique set of community traditions." Another current member, identified as "goodrebill," commented that "Living in the community . . . for 25 years has been, on the whole, a wonderful experience for me and my family. Stelle is not exactly 'intentional' as is commonly understood but if one wants to live intentionally and authentically this is a great place to do so."[42]

Olive Branch Mission

Chicago's Olive Branch Mission traces its history back to 1876 when Rachel Bradley founded the Bradley Mission, though the community's modern outreach missionary activity began in 1979. Bradley offered sewing classes to prostitutes with the hope of stopping the growth of prostitution houses that were using girls as young as twelve. She and her women companions held classes in a room of the Morgan Street Free Methodist Church. Six years later Bradley opened the Wells Street Mission to assist needy residents of the neighborhood. "Records indicate that the [Mission]," noted an article in the Olive Branch Mission home page, "successfully closed taverns, saloons and prostitute houses through their street meetings and community activism. . . . It wasn't long before the ministry grew to include homeless men, women and children, further expanding to include the dire needs of alcoholic and addicted men and women who existed on the fringes of society."[43] Bradley and her companions soon were visiting the Cook County Jail and the Cook County Hospital.

In 1891 the Wells Street Mission renamed itself the Olive Branch Mission and relocated to 95 South Des Plaines Avenue. (In 1995 it moved to its present location in a large four-story brick building at the corner of

South Claremont and Sixty-third Street.) In its years at the heart of Skid Row, wrote William Lawrence Smith, it served the needs of "thousands of homeless, alcoholic, mentally disturbed, distraught, and just plain down-on-their-luck segments of American society."[44]

Under Bradley's successors Mary Everhart, Clara Spencer, and Katie Hall, the Olive Branch developed five distinct ministries: the Mission, Operations, Family Ministries, Wesleyan Urban Coalition, and Community Alcohol Rehabilitation Endeavor (CARE). The mission also opened the Skid Row Community Chapel, which offered a free meal followed by a worship service, daily providing up to ninety-five men with breakfast, clothing, work-study programs, and nightly movies. The Operations unit took care of housekeeping, janitorial work, food services, building security, and transportation needs. Family Ministries focused on women and children and offered temporary housing for families as well as food, clothing, and religious services. Women went to a Tuesday afternoon worship service that included Bible studies and educational workshops. Children attended summer day-camp programs. The Wesleyan Urban Coalition collaborated with ten colleges to offer seminars, lectures, and service programs. CARE had both short- and long-term residential treatment facilities. Members had meals, clothing, and sleeping quarters for six people per unit. Participants received individual counseling and attended AA meetings after that organization was founded in the mid-1930s.[45]

Since 1979, under the leadership of Reverend Charles D. Cooper, most of the staff members have been living communally. More than before, Smith wrote, "Cooper and others believe it is necessary to share the Spirit with others in all aspects of life, not necessarily just during religious services. . . . The Mission is based on teamwork, and the directors believe shared life enhances the day-to-day ongoings of the community." The mission's "Statement of Commitment" pledges each member to a ten-part program of action. The first article reads: "I commit myself to the building of community. . . . That I will use my gifts and talents to the girding up of the community gathered here." Beyond the "Statement" there was no formal constitution, and the community saw itself functioning as a family.[46]

A typical day includes lively discussions, shared meals, and communal tasks. Members "visit with [each other] and share both personal and community problems[, which] contributes to the quality of daily life experienced by the communalists." A tolerant atmosphere pervades the mission, and members are not required to abstain from certain foods. They cannot smoke tobacco or drink alcohol, however, and sexual abstinence is expected of single members. An individual's personal property "does not become the common property of the community," and members are paid a salary from a community treasury made up of voluntary gifts and donations. Everyone goes to communal meals each evening from Monday through Thursday. There are weekly meetings to discuss issues and share ideas. Olive Branch has special celebrations at birthdays, Christmas, and Thanksgiving, and a Fall Festival on the first weekend in November. Prospective members are not required to go through a probation to learn a set of rules. Each one simply signs the "Statement of Commitment," and then he or she can vote in staff meetings and express opinions on communal issues. Smith discovered that by 1984 only fifteen applicants had been denied admission, and most of these rejections were primarily the result of a lack of space.[47]

On March 1, 1996, David E. Bates became the eleventh president of the Olive Branch Mission, and he expanded its programs to include nine comprehensive ministries. In his "Message from the President" of October 30, 2006, displayed on the mission's website, he commented on the variety of men, women, and children who "come to the mission every day. . . . Every person comes with their own hurt and need, and with their unique story to tell, into which love is applied in very tangible ways." This love provides hope, which "is literally birthed into the ugliest of circumstances."[48] In 2006 the mission provided year-round shelter, meals, and opportunities for participation in one or more of the following nine areas:

1. *Emergency and Transitional Services.* Homeless services for single men, women, and families with children include shelter and housing, employment linkages, food, clothing, and assessments for additional levels of care.

2. *Life Transformation Opportunities Program.* This operation stresses personal and professional development for individuals addicted to alcohol, heroin, cocaine, marijuana, and nicotine. They are provided residential recovery services, after care, employment training, and referrals to full-time employers.

3. *Community Resource Center.* The CRC is open to needy individuals or families and offers access to services and resources, referral contacts, and networks. It has job-training, job-readiness, and mental health services; courses leading to a General Education Diploma; literacy training; and English as a Second Language classes (ESL).

4. *Daybreak Counseling Services.* This program gives confidential biblical counseling to men, women, and adolescents with emotional and spiritual problems.

5. *Plant Operations / Employment Training.* The mission lists a variety of opportunities for employment training and skill development for men and women.

6. *Youth Services.* The mission provides ten weeks of summer school for up to 150 children, which ends in a Back-to-School Fair where free school supplies and over one thousand free book bags are distributed. Another program offers school-age homeless children living in the mission's family shelter a tutorial evening school program.

7. *Higher Education and Urban Studies.* Each year undergraduate and graduate students from fifteen colleges, universities, and seminaries live for varying lengths of time at the mission's Christian Center for Urban Studies. They participate in programs in missionary training and pastoral training.

8. *Volunteer Outreach.* This department provides opportunities for individuals and groups not affiliated with the Olive Branch Mission. Each year it has over five hundred volunteers to help in after-school programs, mentoring programs, and family shelters. Outreach advertises on the Web site for volunteers with skills in carpentry, construction, plumbing, and other specialties.

9. *The Chapel.* Since opening in 2002, the chapel has offered cross-cultural and community-relevant worship experiences. On Sundays there is a morning Bible study with refreshments, followed by a service at half past ten and another one at seven o'clock in the evening. There is a Wednesday prayer meeting at six o'clock in the evening.

Under Bates's leadership the Olive Branch Mission has established satellite missions in Jamaica, Kenya, and Burundi. Bates has helped to develop Hope Africa University, which began offering classes in February 2000. Its goal is to provide African American students from the United States the chance to study in an "African context." Currently there are three hundred students enrolled in the freshman class. "Service to others is often a goal of communities," Miller concluded, "but few have achieved it as well or as long as the members of the Olive Branch."[49]

Jesus People USA (JPUSA)

David Di Sabatino, in his annotated bibliography of the Jesus People movement, commented that the "emergence of the Jesus People—the offspring born of the peculiar marriage of Christianity and counterculture [of the 1960s]—was the most unexpected social development of the time." Miller called Jesus People USA "one of the largest single-site communes in the United States . . . with around 450 members plus other residents."

John M. Bozeman, in his 1990 master's thesis, found that the "communal aspect of the Jesus People was considered by some to be one of the more impressive characteristics of the entire movement."[50]

The Chicago community was established in June 1972, but the movement began as a fundamentalist youth ministry in Milwaukee. There, in 1969, Jim and Sue Palosaari, who had connections with an evangelical outreach to the counterculture in southern California, assisted by Linda Meissner, who had founded the Seattle-based Jesus People Army, started a community of about twenty-five members called "Jesus People Milwaukee." According to Lindsay Prorock, "The group attracted members of the counter-culture: young persons who were on drugs, outcasts, runaways, and gays—all people who 'needed Jesus.'" For a time they ran a coffee house in the Brady Street neighborhood of Milwaukee known as the Jesus Christ Power House. By November 1971 the commune had grown to sixty individuals. Then within four months it jumped to two hundred. They organized two rock bands, "The Sheep" and "Charity" (later called the "Resurrection Band"), that played in parks, churches, and school gymnasiums. Most significant, in the spring of 1972 they started publishing what would become the main outreach vehicle of the movement, the magazine called *Cornerstone*. Over the rest of the year the communards ministered as "Jesus People USA Traveling Teams" in Wisconsin, Michigan, Illinois, and Florida. "Traveling in an old bus and a few cars . . . they became one foci of media attention—long-haired, hippy evangelists who had set out to 'evangelize the United States.'"[51]

In 1973 they looked for a permanent base and decided on the Windy City. "The decision to locate in Chicago was made out of a sense of obedience to God rather than out of any personal desire to live in the area [because] most of the group was composed of 'nature lovers . . . and hippies that wanted to live out in the woods,'" Bozeman observed. Jon Trott, later editor of *Cornerstone*, wrote, "They were a diverse, heterogeneous community, . . . made up of people from all backgrounds, from college students to high-school drop-outs . . . [from] straight kids who went to church all their lives, and the 'heavies' who have smoked, and dropped shot their way out of reality." The *Cornerstone* pointed out that the "forty-one long-haired, blue-jeaned Christians who hit Chicago's sidewalks in May have stayed to set up a discipleship training ministry under the leadership of Rev. John Herrin." A Full Gospel businessman named Henry Carlson gave them permission to live in the basement of the Faith Tabernacle located at the corner of Grace and Broadway streets.[52]

In the building, married couples slept in temporary rooms created by plywood walls called "Barcelonas," and single individuals used cots in the main room. They soon numbered about two hundred people. For two years this "band of disciples" went out on the streets spreading the gospel. In 1974 John Wiley (J.W.) Herrin, who was married, became sexually involved with a young female member of the community, divorced his wife, left JPUSA, and moved to California. Afterward a council of elders, eventually consisting of nine men and one woman, took charge and helped "prevent the possibility of leadership abuses which take place when one person is in complete control and not answerable to anyone."[53] This body was assisted by twenty elected deacons and fifteen deaconesses.

In 1975 the community moved to an apartment building at 4431–33 Paulina Street that contained six four-bedroom units. They converted the rooms into dormitories for men and women, some housing twenty people, and apartments for married couples and their children. To provide more stable housing than charity or pooling of money could muster, they started several businesses in home repair, painting, roofing, and carpentry.[54] In 1978, after merging with an eighteen-member black Christian Bible study communal group called the New Life Fellowship, they began a program of providing shelter to the homeless. Expansion continued with the purchase in 1979 of "Malden," an old hotel that contained an industrial kitchen and an apartment house. Then they subdivided the Paulina Street house and sold the units as condominiums. Bozeman suggests that "the move from Paulina to Malden marked one of the most significant events in the history of the community," because they relocated from "a middle-class neighborhood to a much poorer, racially mixed area of 'uptown,' a region riddled with gang violence and a variety of social problems." Tommy Tucker recalled in March 1990, "No longer were we going to just pass out tracts. JPUSA would also "integrate ourselves more into society and show people Christianity through our lives on a day-to-day basis."[55]

During the early years, religious services were held in the basement of the Paulina Street building, where water dripped from exposed ceiling pipes. But in 1977 they found an old Methodist church located about a mile from the Pauline Street address, which they used until they sold the property two years later and moved to Malden. In the church they shared "mildly charismatic" services such as one described by Trott.

> Many hands and arms [were] upraised as we sang together to our Lord. Most music (though not all) was composed by members of JPUSA, and lyrics often came straight from the scripture or personal experience. Our drama group, the Holy Ghost Players, made their appearances somewhere between the various worship songs and hymns. . . . Resurrection Band played nearly every Sunday for Radical Christian Worship, though they'd often had a late concert somewhere Saturday night.[56]

Jesus People's beliefs are best summarized in a tract called *Meet Our Family*. It includes ten articles of faith. Jesus People recognize that after being reborn, a person can "backslide" because Satan constantly tempts one to sin. In this case, "only through 'dying to self,' where a person abandons his or her selfish personal desires and comes to care only for the things of God, can a person be truly resistant to such demonic attacks."[57] Bozeman's investigation of JPUSA found that most members were from backgrounds that had one or more of the following characteristics:

1. involvement with drugs and alcohol with a libertine lifestyle and feelings of alienation and despair;

2. a recent religious conversion experience with an acute sense of needing to do something vital with their new Christianity;

3. having a prior interest in communal living, especially among the older members of the community;

4. a "wandering, searching nature";

5. an artistic nature—hence the high number of artists, craftspersons, and musicians in JPUSA;

6. a commitment to make an active Christian faith the center of one's life by serving the poor: "This sentiment," Bozeman wrote, "appears to be much more common to new arrivals than to the older members";

7. a desire to change harmful behavior patterns such as excessive anger.[58]

Communal life involves continued commitment. Full members are prohibited from smoking tobacco, consuming alcohol, and using drugs. Single members must be sexually abstinent, and extramarital sex by married couples is condemned. New members go through a novice period where they learn and practice the ten articles of faith. First, they are assigned to a "buddy" who helps them adjust and teaches them the rules and regulations. The new arrival is also placed in the buddy's "family" to facilitate communal socialization. There are two kinds of rules: one kind called "duty," encompassing chores and responsibilities, the other called "lifestyle," encompassing learning how to do everything in groups—eating, daily living, and work. Any prospective member does not have to make a financial contribution, however, and his or her personal property is not surrendered to the community. Real estate is donated only if the person wishes to do so, and usually such a gift is not accepted until the individual has been in JPUSA for several years. A common treasury is made up of gifts and income from communal businesses. Money from this pool, according to Smith, "is given to members . . . to meet their needs as well as for entertainment, etc., as the supply of money budgeted allows." Nuclear families as well as individuals share meals in the communal dining hall three times a day. Communal meetings are held there three times weekly. Household chores are assigned by the deacons and deaconesses and are rotated regularly. The council of elders governs the community. But "since more than half of adult members are female, it is apparent that here, as elsewhere in our society, women are underrepresented in leadership roles."[59]

During the day, members in groups perform jobs in the fifteen JPUSA ministries. Listed in 2006 under "Jesus People USA—Meet our Family" on JPUSA's Web site were: Belly Acres Design, Brothas and Sistas United, Cornerstone Music and Arts Festival (which attracts over twenty thousand young Christians for camping, concerts, and seminars at a 575-acre site in western Illinois), *Cornerstone* magazine, Cornerstone Press, Cornerstone Community Outreach, The Crossing, Friendly Towers Senior Program, Friars Printing, Grrrecords, Headnoise, Lakefront Supply, Resurrection Band, Riverview Self Storage, and Seeds.[60] There is a structured schedule of evening activities. At seven o'clock on Sunday, chairs are placed in the dining room for "Sunday Night Videos." Usually three movies are shown on televisions through VCR units—one movie for children, another for teenagers, and the third for the adults. Monday is unscheduled except for kitchen duties, a feeding program for the needy, shelter work, and staffing the central desk in the lobby, which is open continuously as a telephone switchboard and crisis hotline. Tuesday has two classes (to which the public is invited) for six-week courses taught by deacons and individuals with special skills. Courses cover topics such as introduction to worship, the Bible, books on the Bible, New Age religions, and cults. The commune's gospel choir, Grace and Glory, practices this evening. Finally there is a community gathering for singing, after which they split into smaller discussion groups. Wednesday is for families, where they sing, pray, and celebrate birthdays. Thursday is free except for the evening classes. On Friday only one class is offered, for engaged couples. Saturday stresses street witnessing, especially for new members, and meetings of mutual-support groups to deal with problems such as anger, overeating, sexual fixations, and other personal difficulties.[61]

Children play a prominent role in JPUSA life. Bozeman found that most of them were born before their parents entered the community, because "couples who married after joining generally abstained from having children at first." Except for infants, who sleep in the parents' rooms, the children have their own bedrooms, usually on the same floor as their parents. These quarters are primarily for sleeping, however, since for most of the day children are with their parents, at school, or playing with each other. As

Snyder Harrar, a resident, related in March 1990, it was "a neat thing for the kids. . . . Our kids can grow up and be together . . . like staying overnight with your friends every night."[62]

JPUSA organized its Uptown Christian School a year after the community was founded because the public schools were unacceptable for moral reasons. The first senior class of five individuals graduated in 1983 from this institution, which is accredited by the state of Illinois. The school is open half days all year and has "gradually expanded its curriculum, partially through use of videotaped Abeka classes in Spanish, world history, science, and English."[63] A few noncommunal students are enrolled, mainly children whose parents find them too unruly to deal with at home, and some temporary students who attend while parents solve marital problems. Regardless of where they come from, all students, under adult supervision, play with neighborhood children on the community's basketball court and skateboard ramp.

As the community enters the twenty-first century its future remains bright. J. Gordon Melton, in *Encyclopedic Handbook of Cults in America*, identified seven characteristics that he considers essential for communal success, and JPUSA features all of them. First of all, the community was able to replace its initial charismatic leader with a "strong system of social control and behavior." Second, it has developed economic self-sufficiency. Third, it has removed itself from outside influences despite living in the midst of the uptown neighborhood of Chicago. At the same time JPUSA has avoided the main reasons for communes' failure that Melton recognized, such as forming for "shallow reasons" with people "wanting to escape their lives." Poor planning, another cause for failure, was eliminated from the start. A fifth reason for communal decline, lack of order, was avoided by the group's hierarchy of deacons, deaconesses, and council of elders. The sixth cause of lack of success, hostility from the surrounding environment, was eliminated by the missionary services JPUSA offers Chicago residents. Seventh, it has so far escaped the effect of financial success, the "malady" that hurt Amana, the Rappites at Economy, and Oneida.[64]

In 1990 Bozeman predicted "it would appear that the group is likely to continue its lifestyle and ministry for some time to come." In 2000 the entry for "Jesus People USA Evangelical Covenant Church" in *Communities Directory* stated, "We have been privileged to function as a resource to the church, a haven for people in need, a learning experience for many whose journey has taken them in our doors and out to serve elsewhere." And in July 2006 Lindsay Prorock wrote, "Three decades after the Jesus People Movement emerged from the youth counterculture of the 1960s, Jesus People USA is one of only a few communal groups to survive intact. After twenty-five years JPUSA is currently still located at the same address and . . . they remain steadfast in their commitment to spread the gospel and extend human services to those in need." In a summary statement of the community's current situation, Tim Bock, manager of its Lakefront Roofing Supply business, wrote:

> As of January 2006, JPUSA numbers 420 people composed of 90 couples, 130 kids, 110 singles as well as 20–40 people from overseas who are visiting us. We live in a renovated hotel in a multicultural, diverse, needy, rapidly gentrifying neighborhood on the north side of Chicago called Uptown (about four blocks from Lake Michigan). [Our] common thread is that we all obeyed a call to serve Jesus and to live a simple communal life in the inner city of Chicago.[65]

Conclusion

I first became aware of the utopian phenomenon while researching for a previous work, *Communal Utopias*. I envisioned dots on a map of the United States indicating the location of all the utopias during this time period, such as Alice Felt Tyler included for the antebellum years in her pioneering study, *Freedom's Ferment*. By far the densest cluster of these dots on a map was found in the Heartland.[1] Despite the depth and riches of this region's communalism, no comprehensive examination has yet been undertaken, and as a consequence its story is fragmented. For example, Arthur Bestor, Jr., in *Backwoods Utopias*, dealt only with New Harmony and the small Owenite colonies founded after its demise. There have been a few state-focused studies, the most recent by Catherine M. Rokicky, in *Creating a Perfect World*. And Heartland utopias have been touched upon (but only touched upon) by Yaacov Oved, in *Two Hundred Years of American Communes;* Robert S. Fogarty, in *All Things New;* Timothy Miller, in *The Quest for Utopia in Twentieth-Century Communes* and *The 60s Communes;* and Donald E. Pitzer in *America's Communal Utopias*.

Some historians, however, have provided an analytical perspective of the American communitarian experience, and the most important of these deserve mention. One of the first scholars of American social history, Tyler, wrote at the time of the epic struggle between democracy and totalitarianism during World War II. She saw utopian communalism as an expression of the democratic faith of the young republic. Either imported from Europe or native-born, each community was an expression of

America's democratic ideas and institutions, a reassurance that the process seen at the genesis of the republic would continue "this vigorous, dynamic democracy."[2] The frontier, with its economic and social openness and its "faith in democracy and freedom," was the stimulus for creating utopian communities. Jacksonian democracy was emblematic of the frontier's political expression in many ways, and it gave rise to an "essential faith of the young republic" to fully encourage and accept (with the exception of intolerance toward the Latter Day Saints) experiments in pure democracy and an exuberant confidence in an egalitarian future. Religion, either evangelical or theological rationalism, reinforced the emphasis democratic faith put on individual expression and salvation for all. It "gave to the Americans . . . their conviction that their institutions could be perfected and their national destiny fulfilled."[3]

A generation after Tyler's analysis, a quite different interpretation of American communalism came from a sociologist, Rosabeth Moss Kanter, in 1972, with *Commitment and Community.* Reacting to the appearance of the "hippie" commune movement in the 1960s, she explored the underlying ideas, values, and dynamics of nineteenth-century utopias and saw many connections between them and the 1960s communes. Her main focus, however, was on the dynamics of how the communities were built and what sustained them in their success or failure. Communities were not expressions of a democratic ideology but, rather, alternatives to American culture. They represented "new ways of being and doing."[4] They were "imaginary societies" that embodied the members' "deepest yearnings, noblest dreams, and highest aspirations." Therefore, cooperation created a self-selective social order based on the idea that what was good for the individual was likewise good for the community. It was a "mutuality of interests" that debunked exploitation, competition, and conflict. The utopias stood as contrasts to the imagined evils of American society, providing both a refuge and a hope for a better life. A utopian experiment, in her analysis, was a success or failure to the degree that it promoted and sustained commitment to community and reduced commitments to outside opinions and opportunities.[5]

Kanter identified a number of essential mechanisms for success. One was the commitment to ongoing participation in the communal relationship. To achieve this "positive cognition," as she termed it, communities organized to make participation rewarding. There was a personal psychological reward for continued involvement and a penalty associated with rejecting it. The essential dynamics were sacrifice and investment: the first to surrender something of value in order to belong and the second to give up control of one's individual possessions. Another cause for success was a strong emphasis on collectivity, for "brotherhood and sharing." Utopia, therefore, was a place where individual emotional needs were met through a communal life that withstood outside threats and internal tensions. Another vital dynamic of group cohesion was primary loyalty and allegiance to the community. Such involvement "makes members more willing to work out whatever conflicts and tensions may arise among them."[6] Another commitment involved seeing one's individual self as an integral part of the whole system, where one's identity is connected to meeting community ideals. Of the utopias Kanter examined, the most successful developed and sustained these mechanisms. Those that did not (twenty-one out of thirty) were unsuccessful communes that "tended to have fewer such commitment mechanisms and in weakened form."[7]

Most critics of Kanter's analysis rejected her emphasis on success or failure and her deemphasis on internal mechanisms accounting for longevity. One such revisionist was Brian Berry, author of *America's Utopian Experiments*. A geographer and student of American urban development in the twentieth century, Berry used Kondratiev's long-wave economic theory to account for periods of communal development. Drawing upon Michael Barkun's 1984 paper "Communal Societies as Cyclical Phenomena," Berry saw the period of intense communal activity coinciding with times of economic depression. His "speculative essay" demonstrated this connection between economic development and the "upwellings of millenarian excitation" as triggered by long-wave crises affecting the nation's economy.[8] Put simply, economic prosperity or depression stimulated millenarian expectations and communal living. In hard times people tend to flock to utopian communities and try heterodox social and economic ideas. Examining American utopianism from the seventeenth century to the wave of intentional communities of the 1990s, Berry concluded that it was not an American democratic ethos nor internal commitment dynamics that accounted for their appearance or demise but, rather, economic downward and upward cycles. Such a transcendent force impacted all utopias, whether religious or secular. Aided by maps, Berry showed a spatial pattern of community development. One such illustration, interestingly, showed the heaviest concentration of nineteenth-century utopias in the Heartland.[9]

Donald E. Pitzer believed that scholars from Tyler to Berry had wrongly seen utopias as successes or failures, whatever the explanation of the causes might be. He labeled his new theoretical framework "developmental communalism," which, he acknowledged, was inspired by Madeline Roemig of Amana during a 1981 conference of the National Historic Communal Studies Association (now called the Communal Studies Association) at the Amana Colonies. She challenged Pitzer in the common belief that after 1932, when Amana abandoned communal ownership of goods, they were no longer a community. Rather, the Amanites were still a religious movement in a postcommunal phase of living together. Amana had not failed as a commune, Roemig maintained, but still functioned as a religious movement. Pitzer came to see not just the Amana Colonies but most utopian experiments as moving beyond their original organizational principles (mainly common property) to new phases of development. His concept was based on three assumptions. One, that communal living was a "generic social mechanism," or phase of growth. Second, that this phase was most often a part of the first stage of growth of a community. And, third, that communities must adjust to changing realities and either discard such principles as community of goods or dissolve, or at best stagnate.[10]

This book is not intended to be a new theoretical analysis of utopian communalism in the tradition of some of these influential works. Instead, it seeks to summarize the importance of communal societies to the history of the Heartland in light of the overwhelming evidence that the prevalence of this lifestyle is largely nationally and regionally past.

Notes

Introduction

1. Robert S. Fogarty, *All Things New: American Communes and Utopian Movements, 1860–1914* (Chicago: University of Chicago Press, 1990), 19.

2. Yaacov Oved, *Two Hundred Years of American Communes* (New Brunswick, N.J.: Transaction Books, 1988), 369.

3. Greeley from Robert P. Sutton, *Communal Utopias and the American Experience: Secular Communities, 1824–2004* (London: Praeger, 2004), x.

4. Timothy Miller, *The 60s Communes: Hippies and Beyond* (Syracuse, N.Y.: Syracuse University Press, 1999), xxi–xxiii.

5. George Kozeny, "In Community Intentionally," in *Communities Directory: A Guide to Intentional Communities and Cooperative Living* (Rutledge, Mo.: Fellowship for Intentional Community, 2000), 16.

6. *Communities Directory: A Comprehensive Guide to Intentional Communities and Cooperative Living*, 4th ed. (Rutledge, Mo.: Fellowship for Intentional Community, 2005); Miller, *The 60s Communes*, xiii, 249–85 (appendix). For a recent discussion of the essential attributes of communitarianism in the United States, see David J. Connell, "Philosophical Reflections on 'The Communitarian Vision,'" *Communal Societies* 27 (2007): 71–81.

7. Eugene Edmund Snyder, *Aurora, Their Last Utopia: Oregon's Christian Commune, 1845–1883* (Portland, Ore.: Binford & Mort, 1993), 34.

8. Jon Wagner, "Eric Jansson and the Bishop Hill Colony," in Donald E. Pitzer, ed., *America's Communal Utopias* (Chapel Hill: University of North Carolina Press, 1997), 313. See also the special issue on Bishop Hill in *Western Illinois Regional Studies* 12 (Spring 1989), especially Wagner's article, "Living in Community: Daily Life in the Bishop Hill Colony," 61–81.

9. Conversation with the author, March 5, 2007.

1 — Shaker Villages

1. Priscilla J. Brewer, *Shaker Communities, Shaker Lives* (Hanover: University Press of New England, 1986), 39. See also Stephen J. Stein, *The Shaker Experience in America: A History of the United Society of Believers* (New Haven: Yale University Press, 1992), 3–4; Robert Sutton, *Communal Utopias and the American Experience: Religious Communities, 1732–2000* (Westport, Conn., and London: Praeger, 2003), 31n3.

2. Seth Y. Wells and Calvin Green, *Testimonies Concerning the Character and Ministry of Mother Ann Lee and the First Witnesses of the Gospel of Christ's Second Appearing; Given by Some of the Agent Brethren and Sisters of the United Society* (Albany, N.Y.: Packard & Van Benthuysen, 1827), 1–18; Edward Deming Andrews, *The People Called Shakers: A Search for the Perfect Society* (New York: Oxford University Press, 1953), 7–8; Priscilla J. Brewer, "The Shakers of Mother Ann Lee," in Pitzer, *America's Communal Utopias*, 40.

3. Andrews, *People Called Shakers*, 8. Stein, in *Shaker Experience*, discounts the importance of the vision in bringing the Shaking Quakers to America. He considers the emigration largely the result of their deteriorating situation in England, because of growing hostility to their activities there.

4. Stein, *Shaker Experience*, 7.

5. Valentine Rathbun, *An Account of the Matter, Form, and Manner of a New and Strange Religion, Taught and Propagated by a Number of Europeans, Living in a Place Called Nisqueunia, in the State of New-York* (Providence, R.I.: Bennett Wheeler, 1781), 4.

6. Sutton, *Religious Communities,* 19; Stein, *Shaker Experience,* 10–11; Stephen A. Marini, *Radical Sects of Revolutionary New England* (Cambridge, Mass.: Harvard University Press, 1982), 76. For a discussion of the religious revival in the Niskeyuna area, see Nathan O. Hatch, *The Sacred Cause of Liberty: Republican Thought and the Millennium in Revolutionary New England* (New Haven: Yale University Press, 1977). Oved, *Two Hundred Years,* 69n8, has a discussion of millennialism and revivalism at the time of the arrival of the Shakers.

7. Rathbun, *Account,* 4–12; Margot Mayo, "The Incredible Journey of Mother Ann," *Shaker Quarterly* 2 (1962): 42–52. Ann Lee's ministry and mission are covered in detail in Stein, *Shaker Experience,* 18–20.

8. Brewer, "Shakers of Mother Ann," 42; Catherine M. Rokicky, *Creating a Perfect World: Religious and Secular Utopias in Nineteenth-Century Ohio* (Athens: Ohio University Press, 2002), 13. Quotes from Stein, *Shaker Experience,* 35–37.

9. Stein, *Shaker Experience,* 43; Rokicky, *Perfect World,* 13. See also "Some Account of the Tenets and Practice of the Religious Society called Shakers," *American Museum, or Repository* 1 (1787): 148–50; Joseph Meacham, *A Concise Statement of the Principles of the Only True Church . . .* (Bennington, Vt.: Haswell and Russell, 1790).

10. Lawrence Foster, *Women, Family, and Utopia: Communal Experiments of the Shakers, the Oneida Community, and the Mormons* (Syracuse, N.Y.: Syracuse University Press, 1991), 30. See also Sutton, *Religious Communities,* 20–21; Stephen Paterwic, "From Individual to Community: Becoming a Shaker at New Lebanon," *Communal Societies* 11 (1991): 18–33; Rosemary D. Gooden, "A Preliminary Examination of Shaker Attitudes toward Work," *Communal Societies* 3 (1983): 1–15.

11. Sutton, *Religious Communities,* 21.

12. John E. Murray, "Determinants of Membership Levels and Duration in a Shaker Commune, 1790–1880," *Journal for the Scientific Study of Religion* 34, no. 1 (1995): 35–48; Metin M. Cosgel, Thomas J. Micelli, and John E. Murray, "Organization and Distributional Equality in a Network of Communes: The Shakers," *American Journal of Economics and Sociology* 56, no. 2 (April 1997): 129–44.

13. Sutton, *Religious Communities,* 21–22; Daniel W. Patterson, "Shaker Music," *Communal Societies* 2 (1982): 53–64.

14. Stein, *Shaker Experience,* 48.

15. Ibid., 53, 454n37; Jean McMahon, "'Weary of Petticoat Government': The Specter of Female Rule in Early Nineteenth-Century Shaker Politics," *Communal Societies* 11 (1991): 1–17; Sutton, *Religious Communities,* 22.

16. Sutton, *Religious Communities,* 23. See also Reuben Rathbun, *Reasons Offered for Leaving the Shakers* (Pittsfield, Mass.: Chester Smith, 1800); Elizabeth A. DeWolfe, "'So Much They Have Got for Their Folly': Shaker Apostates and the Tale of Woe," *Communal Societies* 18 (1998): 21–35; Mary Ann Haagen, "The Truth, the Whole Truth? A Re-examination of James Hervey Elkins' Fifteen Years in the Senior Order of Shakers," *Communal Societies* 24 (2004): 47–64; Ilyon Woo, "From 'Sensual Attraction' to 'A Malady of the Mind': How Hervey Elkins Loved and Left the Shakers," *Communal Societies* 24 (2004): 65–94.

17. For the exact locations of the western communities, see the map in Stephen J. Stein, ed., *Letters from a Young Shaker: William S. Byrd at Pleasant Hill* (Lexington: University Press of Kentucky, 1985), 30.

18. Edward D. Andrews, *The Community Industries of the Shakers* (Albany: University of the State of New York, 1932; reprint, Philadelphia: Porcupine Press, 1972), 60–111, 118–21, 139–42, 229–48; Brewer, *Shaker Communities,* 100; Flo Morse, *The Shakers and the World's People* (New York: Dodd, Mead, 1980), 133; John E. Murray and Metin M. Cosgel, "Regional Specialization in Communal Agriculture: The Shakers, 1800–1890,"

Communal Societies 19 (1989): 73–84.

19. Sutton, *Religious Communities,* 26–27.

20. Stein, *Shaker Experience,* 65, 457n68.

21. Ibid., 61.

22. J. P. MacLean, *Shakers of Ohio: Fugitive Papers Concerning the Shakers of Ohio, with Unpublished Manuscripts* (Philadelphia: Porcupine Press, 1975), 362–87.

23. Andrews, *People Called Shakers,* 84.

24. See the notes by Richard W. Pelham in *The Testimony of Christ's Second Appearing,* Shaker Manuscript Collection, Western Reserve Historical Society, Cleveland, Ohio (hereafter Shaker MSS, WRHS); Rokicky, *Perfect World,* 14.

25. Grace I. LeMaster, "A Study of the North Union, Ohio, Society of Believers" (master's thesis, University of Akron, 1950), 13–14, 17; James S. Prescott, "The History of North Union," 2nd ed., Shaker MSS, WRHS; Rokicky, *Perfect World,* 16.

26. MacLean, *Shakers of Ohio,* 230–31.

27. Stein, *Shaker Experience,* 63–64, 121.

28. *Millennial Praises, Containing a Collection of Gospel Hymns, in Four Parts; Adopted to the Day of Christ's Second Appearing Composed for the Use of His People* (Hancock, Mass.: Josiah Tallcott, Jr., 1813); Daniel W. Patterson, "Millennial Praises: Tune Location and Authorial Attributions of the First Shaker Hymnal," *Shaker Quarterly* 18 (1990): 77–94.

29. LeMaster, "Society of Believers," 10–11, 27; Marjorie Proctor-Smith, *Women in Shaker Community and Worship: A Feminist Analysis of the Uses of Religious Symbolism* (Lewiston, Maine: Edwin Mellen Press, 1985), 69; Priscilla J. Brewer, "'Tho' of the Weaker Sex': A Reassessment of Gender Equality among the Shakers," in Wendy E. Chmielewski, Louis J. Kern, and Marylyn Klee-Hartzell, eds., *Women in Spiritual and Communitarian Societies in the United States* (Syracuse, N.Y.: Syracuse University Press, 1993), 135.

30. Robert S. Fogarty, *Dictionary of American Communal and Utopian History* (Westport, Conn., and London: Greenwood Press, 1980), 93.

31. Rokicky, *Perfect World,* 19.

32. Fogarty, *Dictionary,* 93–94; Michael Barkun, *Crucible of the Millennium: The Burned-Over District of New York in the 1840's* (Syracuse, N.Y.: Syracuse University Press, 1986), 86–87.

33. LeMaster, "Society of Believers," 24.

34. Rokicky, *Perfect World,* 20.

35. Brewer, "Shakers of Mother Ann," 45–46.

36. MacLean, *Shakers of Ohio,* 378–79, 382–84.

37. Stein, *Shaker Experience,* 101 (quotes); Sutton, *Religious Communities,* 25.

38. Rokicky, *Perfect World,* 22.

39. Prescott, "History of North Union"; Rokicky, *Perfect World,* 23; Prescott, "History of North Union."

40. Rokicky, *Perfect World,* 23–24.

41. James McBride, "The Shakers of Ohio: An Early Nineteenth-Century Account," *Cincinnati Historical Society Bulletin* 29 (1971): 126–37; MacLean, *Shakers of Ohio,* 367–79.

42. Rokicky, *Perfect World,* 26–27.

43. Ibid., 28.

44. Ibid., 29; also Proctor-Smith, *Women in Shaker Community,* 40.

45. LeMaster, "Society of Believers," 17–21.

46. Rokicky, *Perfect World,* 41.

47. Ibid., 41–42.

48. MacLean, *Shakers of Ohio,* 93–94; Jean M. Humez, ed., *Mother's First-Born Daughters: Early Shaker Writings on Women and Religion* (Bloomington: Indiana University Press, 1993), 210–11.

49. Rokicky, *Perfect World,* 48–49.

50. Ibid., 49; Brewer, *Shaker Communities*, 131–32.
51. Rokicky, *Perfect World*, 40.
52. MacLean, *Shakers of Ohio*, 66, 97, 237; LeMaster, "Society of Believers," 35, 43–44.
53. Sutton, *Religious Communities*, 28.
54. Rokicky, *Perfect World*, 51.
55. Sutton, *Religious Communities*, 30.
56. Ibid., 29, 30–31.
57. Ibid., 31.

2—New Harmony

1. Karl J. R. Arndt, "George Rapp's Harmony Society," in Pitzer, *America's Communal Utopias*, 57–88. Arndt, the foremost authority on the Harmonists, published ten monographs on their history. For a full listing of his works and other authorities on the Harmonists see Sutton, *Religious Communities*, 60n1.
2. Arndt, "George Rapp's Harmony Society," 60. Rapp made celibacy a requirement in 1807, however, after they left Germany.
3. The earliest published account of Harmony's first years is John Melish, *Travels in the United States of America, in the years 1806 & 1807, and 1809, 1810, & 1811* (Philadelphia: Thomas & George Palmer, 1812), ch. 9. See also Sutton, *Religious Communities*, 38.
4. Karl J. R. Arndt, *George Rapp's Harmony Society, 1785–1847* (Rutherford, N.J.: Farleigh Dickinson University Press, 1972), 62–66; Aaron Williams, *Harmony Society at Economy, Pennsylvania, Founded by George Rapp, A.D. 1804* (Pittsburgh: W. S. Haven, 1866; reprint, New York: AMS Press, 1971); Christiana F. Knoedler, *The Harmony Society: A Nineteenth-Century American Utopia* (New York: Vantage Press, 1954), 6–18; Donald E. Pitzer and Josephine M. Elliott, "New Harmony's First Utopians," *Indiana Magazine of History* 75, no. 3 (September 1979): 225–300.
5. Knoedler, *Harmony Society*, 16; Sutton, *Religious Communities*, 39. See Arndt, *George Rapp's Harmony Society*, 133–40; on the purchase of the site.
6. Knoedler, *Harmony Society*, 16; John Larner, Jr., "Nails and Sundrie Medicines: Town Planning and Public Health in the Harmony Society, 1805–1840," *Western Pennsylvania Historical Magazine* 45 (1962): 225. The sixty-square-foot mansion is described in Elias Fordham, *Personal Narrative of Travels in Virginia, Maryland, Pennsylvania, Ohio, Indiana, Kentucky; and of a Residence in the Illinois Territory, 1817–1818*, ed. F. A. Ogg (Cleveland: Arthur H. Clark, 1906), 207.
7. Arndt, "George Rapp's Harmony Society," 68, 68n9.
8. Sutton, *Religious Communities*, 40.
9. George Rapp, *Thoughts on the Destiny of Man, Particularly with Reference to the Present Times* (New Harmony, Ind.: Harmonie Society Press, 1824), 66. See also Sutton, *Religious Communities*, 39.
10. Donald E. Pitzer, "Education in Utopia: The New Harmony Experience," in *Indiana Historical Society Lectures, 1976–1977: The History of Education in the Middle West*, ed. Donald E. Pitzer and Timothy L. Smith (Indianapolis: Indiana Historical Society, 1978), 77–78, 82–90; Arndt, "George Rapp's Harmony Society," 70–71. As adults, the Harmonists had access to the books in the colony store as well as its several newspapers. Within ten years the community had 340 volumes in the library.
11. George Rapp, *Fiery Coals in the Ascending Flames of Lust for the Elusive Sophia* (Economy, Pa.: Harmonie Society Press, 1826), 229.
12. Arndt, "George Rapp's Harmony Society," 72; Richard D. Wetzel, *Frontier Musicians on the Connoquenessing, Wabash, and Ohio: A History of Music and Musicians in George Rapp's Harmony Society, 1804–1906* (Athens: Ohio University Press, 1976).
13. Arndt, "George Rapp's Harmony Society," 72.

14. Ibid., 68–69; Sutton, *Religious Communities*, 40.

15. Arndt, *Harmony Society*, 205; Sutton, *Religious Communities*, 41.

16. Alice Felt Tyler, *Freedom's Ferment: Phases of American Social History from the Colonial Period to the Outbreak of the Civil War* (New York: Harper & Row, 1944), 123.

17. Lucy Jayne Botscharow-Kamau, "Neighbors: Harmony and Conflict on the Indiana Frontier," *Journal of the Early Republic* 11 (Winter 1991): 507–29. Quote from Karl J. R. Arndt, *A Documentary History of the Indiana Decade of the Harmony Society, 1814–1824* (Indianapolis: Indiana Historical Society, 1975), 1:578. Arndt, "George Rapp's Harmony Society," 68.

18. Arndt, "George Rapp's Harmony Society," 69.

19. Sutton, *Religious Communities*, 41; Arndt, "George Rapp's Harmony Society," 74–76 (74).

20. Sutton, *Religious Communities*, 42.

21. Rapp from Arndt, George Rapp's *Harmony Society*, 308, 309; see also Sutton, *Religious Communities*, 42.

22. One of the most complete treatments of Owen and New Harmony is found in Arthur Bestor Jr., *Backwoods Utopias: The Sectarian Origins and the Owenite Phase of Communitarian Socialism in America, 1663–1829* (Philadelphia: University of Pennsylvania Press, 1970). The most recent treatments of New Harmony are Donald E. Pitzer, "The New Moral World of Robert Owen and New Harmony," in Pitzer, *America's Communal Utopias*, 88–134, and Sutton, *Secular Communities*, 1–16. A fuller history of Owen in Great Britain is John F. C. Harrison, *Quest for the New Moral World: Robert Owen and the Owenites in Britain and America* (New York: Charles Scribner's Sons, 1969). Useful articles include Lucy Jayne Botscharow-Kamau, "Disharmony in Utopia: Social Categories in Robert Owen's New Harmony," *Communal Societies* 9 (1989): 76–90, and "The Anthropology of Space in Harmonist and Owenite New Harmony," *Communal Societies* 12 (1992): 68–89. In 1984 the journal *Communal Societies* published three articles on Owen's communalism: Josephine Mirabella Elliott, "Madame Marie Fretageot: Communitarian Educator," 167–82; Celia Eckhardt, "Fanny Wright: Rebel & Communitarian Reformer," 183–93; and John F. C. Harrison, "Owenite Communitarianism in Britain and America," 234–48. See also Robert Owen, *The Life of Robert Owen, Written by Himself, with Selections From His Writings and Correspondence*, 2 vols. (London: Effingham Wilson, 1857–1858; reprint, New York: Augustus M. Kelley, 1967). The comprehensive edition of Owen's writings is Gregory Claeys, ed., *The Works of Robert Owen*, 4 vols. (London: Pickering and Chatto, 1993).

23. Bestor, *Backwoods Utopias*, 62. See also Rowland Hill Harvey, *Robert Owen: Social Idealist* (Berkeley and Los Angeles: University of California Press, 1959), 1–7; Harrison, *Quest*, 151–54; Harvey, *Robert Owen*, 12–19.

24. Pitzer, "New Moral World," 92–95, 99–100; Harrison, *Quest*, 154–63; Harvey, *Robert Owen*, 36–49.

25. Harrison, *Quest*, 12, 22–23, 28, 33, 48, 79; Brian J. L. Berry, *America's Utopian Experiments: Communal Havens from Long-Wave Crises* (Hanover and London: University Press of New England, 1992), 56–57.

26. Robert Owen, *Report to the County of Lanark (1820)*, in Owen, *Life* 1:301–3; Harvey, *Robert Owen*, 85–89.

27. Berry, *America's Utopian Experiments*, 58–59; Oved, *Two Hundred Years*, 109–10.

28. Pitzer, "New Moral World," 105; Harrison, *Quest*, 163; Anne Taylor, *Visions of Harmony: A Study in Nineteenth-Century Millenarianism* (New York: Oxford University Press, 1987), 74–75.

29. Pitzer, "New Moral World," 106; Bestor, *Backwoods Utopias*, 109–10; Harvey, *Robert Owen*, 92–93.

30. Bestor, *Backwoods Utopias*, 109n59; Harvey, *Robert Owen*, 93–97; George B. Lockwood, *The New Harmony Movement* (New York: Appleton, 1905; New York: AMS Press, 1971), 69–81.

31. Owen's optimism about the prospects are in a manuscript letter to William Allen, April 21, 1825, in the Owen Papers, Manchester Co-operative Union, Manchester, England, a microfilm copy of which is available in the University of Illinois, Champaign, Library.

32. Pitzer, "New Moral World," 113–14; Oved, *Two Hundred Years,* 111–12; Lockwood, *New Harmony Movement,* 83–91; Harvey, *Robert Owen,* 105–7.

33. Oved, *Two Hundred Years,* 112–13; Harvey, *Robert Owen,* 234–44; Berry, *America's Utopian Experiments,* 62–63.

34. *New York Advertiser,* December 3, 1825. The essay was entitled "At Sea, . . . October, 1825," and Owen gave it to the New York newspapers on November 7, 1825. It appeared in the *National Intelligencer,* November 12; *Niles' Weekly Register,* November 12; the *New-Harmony Gazette,* December 14; and the *Shawnee-Town Illinois Gazette,* December 14. Harvey, *Robert Owen,* 134–44.

35. Oved, *Two Hundred Years,* 13–16.

36. Maclure from Sutton, *Secular Communities,* 8; R. D. Owen, *An Outline of the System of Education at New Lanark* (Glasgow, 1824), 34. This was reprinted in the *New-Harmony Gazette,* November 12–December 7, 1825.

37. Bestor, *Backwoods Utopias,* 118–21, 162–63, 175, 181, 186–87, 190; Frank Podmore, *Robert Owen: A Biography* (New York: D. Appleton, 1924), 291–92.

38. Pitzer, "New Moral World," 119–20. See also Lockwood, *New Harmony Movement,* 186–208.

39. Sutton, *Secular Communities,* 9.

40. *New-Harmony Gazette,* February 15, 1826.

41. Ibid.

42. *New-Harmony Gazette,* April 12, 1826–November 7, 1827; March 19, April 16, 1828.

43. Thomas Clinton Pears, Jr., ed., *New Harmony, an Adventure in Happiness: Papers of Thomas and Sarah Pears* (Indianapolis: Indiana Historical Society, 1933), 72; Paul Brown, *Twelve Months in New Harmony* (Cincinnati, 1827; Philadelphia: Porcupine Press, 1972), 14, 18.

44. Pears, *New Harmony,* 77. The Pears family left the community that spring.

45. *New-Harmony Gazette,* May 17, 1826.

46. Brown, *Twelve Months,* 25, 18–19, 223–25; *New-Harmony Gazette,* June 7, 1826.

47. Sutton, *Secular Utopias,* 11; Arthur E. Bestor, Jr., ed., *Education and Reform at New Harmony: Correspondence of William Maclure and Marie Duclos Fretageot, 1820–1833* (Clifton, N.J.: A. M. Kelley, 1973), 346, 377. See also William Owen to Robert Owen, Vincennes, February 7, 1825, Owen Papers;

48. Brown, *Twelve Months,* 94, 119–28; Lockwood, *New Harmony Movement,* 149.

49. Maclure from Bestor, *Education and Reform,* 339, 388. See also Sutton, *Secular Communities,* 12.

50. Brown, *Twelve Months,* 140–41; *New-Harmony Gazette,* August 9–30, 1826; Sutton, *Secular Communities,* 12; Pitzer, "New Moral World," 121.

51. Pitzer, "New Moral World," 115.

52. Maclure from W. H. G. Armytage, *Heavens Below: Utopian Experiments in England, 1560–1960* (London: Routledge and Kegan Paul, 1961), 125; Josephine Mirabella Elliott, "Madame Marie Fretageot: Communitarian Educator," *Communal Societies* 4 (1984): 176–78; Pitzer, "New Moral World," 115; Harrison, *Quest,* 139–47; Bestor, *Backwoods Utopias,* 198.

53. Bestor, *Backwoods Utopias,* 194; *New-Harmony Gazette,* March 14, 21, 28, 1827.

54. Bestor, *Backwoods Utopias,* 195; *New-Harmony Gazette,* March 28, 1827; Brown, *Twelve Months,* 88, 122.

55. *New-Harmony Gazette,* July 12, 1826; *Indiana Journal,* November 14, 1826; also

Lockwood, *New Harmony Movement,* 190–91; *Shawnee-Town Illinois Gazette,* May 13, July 15, August 19, September 30, December 2, 1826.
    56. *New-Harmony Gazette,* May 9, 1827.
    57. Sutton, *Secular Communities,* 15.
    58. Rosabeth Moss Kanter, *Commitment and Community: Communes and Utopias in Sociological Perspective* (Cambridge, Mass.: Harvard University Press, 1972), 123; Owen from Sutton, *Secular Communities,* 15–16; Brown, *Twelve Months,* 98–128.
    59. *New-Harmony Gazette,* March 28, 1827; Richard William Leopold, *Robert Dale Owen: A Biography* (New York: Octagon Books, 1969), 41. For a more recent appraisal of the reasons for the failure of New Harmony, see Pitzer, "New Moral Order," 107–12.

3—Other Separatist Communities

    1. Saxe-Weimar quoted in Arndt, *George Rapp's Harmony Society,* 340, and Knoedler, *Harmony Society,* 25.
    2. Oved, *Two Hundred Years,* 75.
    3. Sutton, *Religious Communities,* 43.
    4. Ibid.; Arndt, "George Rapp's Harmony Society," 78. When Father Rapp died in 1847 at the age of eighty-nine, just 288 communards were living at Economy. For the subsequent history of the community until its demise in 1916, see Sutton, *Religious Communities,* 44–46.
    5. Arndt, *George Rapp's Harmony Society,* 499–546.
    6. Charles Nordhoff, *The Communistic Societies of the United States: From Personal Visit and Observation* (London: John Murray, Albemarle Street, 1875), 318; H. Roger Grant, "Missouri's Utopian Communities," *Missouri Historical Review* (1972): 22; Adolf E. Schroeder, *Bethel German Colony, 1844–1879: Religious Beliefs and Practices* (n.p.: Missouri Humanities Council, 1990), 14.
    7. Schroeder, *Bethel German Colony,* 15. See also Eugene Edmund Snyder, *Aurora, Their Last Utopia: Oregon's Christian Commune, 1845–1883* (Portland, Ore.: Binford & Mort, 1993), 34.
    8. Schroeder, *Bethel German Colony,* 16. The custom of sexual segregation at worship is practiced today at the Amana villages.
    9. Snyder, *Aurora,* 34; Nordhoff, *Communistic Societies,* 315.
    10. Schroeder, *The Musical Life of Bethel German Colony, 1844–1879* (n.p.: Missouri Humanities Council, 1990), 6.
    11. Snyder, *Aurora,* 37; Schroeder, *Bethel German Colony,* 8, 12; William G. Beck, "A German Communistic Society in Missouri," *Missouri Historical Review* (October 1908–January 1909), 64; David Nelson Duke, "The Evolution of Religion in Wilhelm Keil's Community: A New Reading of Old Testimony," *Communal Societies* 13 (1993): 45–70; Grant, "Missouri's Utopian Communities," 25–28.
    12. Snyder, *Aurora,* 50; Keil from Sutton, *Religious Communities,* 47.
    13. Grant, "Missouri's Utopian Communities," 28–29.
    14. Nordhoff, *Communistic Societies,* 329; Sutton, *Religious Communities,* 48.
    15. Sutton, *Religious Communities,* 49. The most recent scholarly treatments of Zoar are Rokicky, *Perfect World* (2002); Hilda Deschinger Morhart, *Zoar: An Ohio Experiment in Communalism* (Columbus: Ohio Historical Society, 1997); Kathleen Fernandez, "The Separatists Society of Zoar," *Communities: Journal of Cooperation,* no. 68 (Winter 1985); Ebhard Fritz, "Roots of Zoar, Ohio, in Early Nineteenth-Century Württemberg: The Separatist Group in Rottenacker and Its Circle, Part II," *Communal Societies* 23 (2003): 29–44. Earlier studies are Catherine R. Dobbs, *Freedom's Will: The Society of the Separatists of Zoar—An Historical Adventure of Religious Communism in Early Ohio* (New York: William-Frederick Press, 1947); Emilius O. Randall, *History of the Zoar Society* (Columbus, Ohio: Press of Fred J. Heer, 1904). A useful dissertation is Edgar B.

Nixon, "The Society of Separatists of Zoar" (Ph.D. diss., Ohio State University, 1933).

16. Morhart, *Zoar,* 14; Randall, *History of the Zoar,* 14; Nixon, "Society of Separatists," 20–21; Sutton, *Religious Communities,* 49.

17. Randall, *History of Zoar,* 5; Neva Jean Specht, "Constrained to Afford Them Countenance and Protection: The Role of the Philadelphia Friends in the Settlement of the Society of Separatists of Zoar," *Communal Societies* 24 (2004): 95–108.

18. Rokicky, *Perfect World,* 59–60; Nixon, "Society of Separatists," 24.

19. Fisher from Rokicky, *Perfect World,* 59; Nixon, "Society of Separatists," 24; Philip E. Webber, "Jakob Sylvan's Preface to the Zoarite Anthology *Die Wahre Separation oder die Widergeburt* as an Introduction to Un(der)studied Separatist Principles," *Communal Societies* 19 (1999): 107–8; Sutton, *Religious Communities,* 49.

20. Sutton, *Religious Communities,* 49.

21. Randall, *History of Zoar,* 84–85; Rokicky, *Perfect World,* 62.

22. Randall, *History of Zoar,* 11–12; Nordhoff, *Communistic Societies,* 103.

23. Rokicky, *Perfect World,* 63–64; Nordhoff, *Communistic Societies,* 106.

24. Nordhoff, *Communistic Societies,* 103–4.

25. Ibid., 109; Rokicky, *Perfect World,* 63–64.

26. Morhart, *Zoar,* 21–25.

27. The twelve floral beds represented the twelve apostles of Christ. William Alfred Hinds, *American Communities and Co-operative Colonies* (1878; Philadelphia: Porcupine Press, 1975), 25; Sutton, *Religious Communities,* 50–51.

28. Nordhoff, *Communistic Societies,* 109–10; Sutton, *Religious Communities,* 51.

29. Levi Bimeler in Oved, *Two Hundred Years,* 85.

30. Sutton, *Religious Communities,* 51; Rokicky, *Perfect World,* 81–82; Alexander Gunn, *The Hermitage-Zoar Notebook and Journal of Travel* (New York: n.p., 1902), 51.

31. Sutton, *Religious Communities,* 51–52.

32. Jonathan G. Andelson, "The Community of True Inspiration from Germany to the Amana Colonies," in Pitzer, *America's Communal Utopias,* 185. Andelson's other publications include *Communal Societies* articles "The Gift to Be Single: Celibacy and Religious Enthusiasm in the Community of True Inspiration," vol. 5 (1985): 1–32, "Introduction: Boundaries in Communal Amana," and "What the Amana Inspirationists Were Reading," vol. 14 (1994): 1–19; also "Postcharismatic Authority in the Amana Colonies: The Legacy of Christian Metz," in Timothy Miller, ed., *When Prophets Die: The Fate of the New Religious Movements* (Albany: SUNY Press, 1991), 29–45; "Tradition, Innovation, and Assimilation in Iowa's Amana Colonies," *Palimpsest* 69 (Spring 1988): 2–5; "Lining the Mean: The Ethos, Practice, and Genius of Amana," *Communities: Journal of Cooperation* 68 (Winter 1985): 32–38; "The Double-Bind and Social Change in Communal Amana," *Human Relations* 34 (1980); "Routinization of Behavior in a Charismatic Leader," *American Ethnologist* 7 (1980): 716–33. Other important articles on Amana are Lanny Haldy, "In All Papers: Newspaper Accounts of Communal Amana, 1867–1924," *Communal Societies* 14 (1994): 20–35; Metin M. Cosgel, "Market Integration and Agricultural Efficiency of Communal Amana," *Communal Societies* 14 (1994): 36–48; Peter Hoehnle, "With Malice toward None: The Inspirationist Response to the Civil War, 1860–1865," *Communal Societies* 18 (1998): 62–80; Peter Hoehnle, "Michael Hofer: A Communitarian in Two Worlds," *Communal Societies* 22 (2002): 83–86; Philip E. Webber, "The Dreams of Christian Metz, Amana's Charismatic Founding Leader," *Communal Societies* 22 (2002): 9–26; Barnett Richling, "The Amana Society: A History of Change," *Palimpsest* 58 (1977): 34–47; Gary D. Carman, "The Amana Colonies: Change from Communalism to Capitalism in 1932," *Social Science Journal* 24 (1987): 157–67. Standard monographs include Bertha Shambough, *Amana That Was and Amana That Is* (New York: Benjamin Blom, 1932); Diane L. Bartel, *Amana: From Pietist Sect to American Community* (Lincoln: University of Nebraska Press, 1984); Philip E. Webber, *Kolinie-Deutsch: Life and Language in Amana* (Ames: Iowa State University Press, 1993).

33. Sutton, *Religious Communities,* 52.

34. Bartel, *Amana: From Pietist Sect,* 8–16.

35. Andelson, "Community of True Inspiration," 187.

36. Nordhoff, *Communistic Societies,* 29; Andelson, "Community of True Inspiration," 187; Nordhoff, *Communistic Societies,* 29.

37. Andelson, "Community of True Inspiration," 189.

38. Ibid., 191–92.

39. Nordhoff, *Communistic Societies,* 32, 33, 34; Sutton, *Religious Communities,* 54.

40. Nordhoff, *Communistic Societies,* 34–35, 36–37.

41. Sutton, *Religious Communities,* 55.

42. Andelson, "Community of True Inspiration," 194.

43. Sutton, *Religious Communities,* 55–56.

44. See Andelson, "Community of True Inspiration," 196–201, on the discrepancies among the seven villages on the vote. Oved, *Two Hundred Years,* 94; Carman, "Amana Colonies," 160–67. For the history of Amana since the Great Change see Andelson, "Community of True Inspiration," 199–201, and Robert Edwin Clark, "A Cultural and Historical Geography of the Amana Colony, Iowa" (Ph.D. diss., University of Nebraska–Lincoln, 1974), 167–269; Henry Schiff, "Before and After 1932: A Memoir," *Communal Societies* 4 (1984): 161–64.

45. The most recent study of the Janssonists is Wagner, "Eric Jansson." Other works include George M. Stephenson, *The Religious Aspects of the Swedish Immigration* (Minneapolis: University of Minnesota Press, 1932); Paul Elmen, *Wheat Flour Messiah: Eric Jansson of Bishop Hill* (Carbondale: Southern Illinois University Press, 1976); Olov Isaksson, *Bishop Hill: A Utopia on the Prairie* (Stockholm: L. T. Publishing House, 1969). *Western Illinois Regional Studies* 12 (Fall 1989) was a special issue on Bishop Hill, which included the following articles: Wayne Wheeler, "Eric Janssonism: Community and Freedom in Nineteenth-Century Sweden and America"; H. Arnold Barton, "The Eric-Janssonists and the Shifting Contours of Community"; Ronald E. Nelson, "The Bishop Hill Colony: What They Found"; Ronald E. Nelson, "The Building of Bishop Hill"; Wagner, "Living in Community"; Elise Schebler Dawson, "The Folk Genre Paintings of Olof Krans as Historical Documents." The issue also includes a bibliography of English-language publications on the colony.

46. Nordhoff, *Communistic Societies,* 343; Tyler, *Freedom's Ferment,* 133–34; Wagner, "Eric Jansson," 298.

47. Isaksson, *Bishop Hill,* 344; Elmen, *Wheat Flour Messiah,* 41 (one woman); Wheeler, "Eric Janssonism," 7–10; Nordhoff, *Communistic Societies,* 344.

48. Philip J. Stoneberg, "The Bishop Hill Colony," in *History of Henry County, Illinois,* ed. Henry L. Kiner (Chicago: Pioneer, 1910), 630.

49. Wagner, "Eric Jansson," 300–302; Nordhoff, *Communistic Societies,* 344–45; Michael A. Mikkelson, *The Bishop Hill Colony: A Religious Communistic Settlement in Henry County, Illinois* (Baltimore: Johns Hopkins University Press, 1892), 30; Barton, "Eric Janssonists," 16–19.

50. Wagner, "Eric Jansson," 302.

51. Wagner, "Living in Community," 71 (quote); Sutton, *Religious Communities,* 57; Lilly Setterdahl, "Emigrant Letters by Bishop Hill Colonists from Noma Parish," *Western Illinois Regional Studies* 1 (Fall 1978): 121–75; Wagner, "Eric Jansson," 310–13.

52. Schebler Dawson, "Folk Genre Paintings of Olof Krans," 92–93; Minnie C. Norlin, *Karin* (publisher unknown, 1936; in Bishop Hill Archive and Research Collection), 27.

53. Adelsward from Ronald E. Nelson, "Bishop Hill: Swedish Development of the Western Illinois Frontier," *Western Illinois Regional Studies* 1 (Fall 1978): 118; Wagner, "Eric Jansson," 306. See also Nordhoff, *Communistic Societies,* 344–45.

54. Sutton, *Religious Communities,* 59; Wagner, "Eric Jansson," 306–7. Root was never arrested for the murder and soon afterward left Henry County.

55. Nelson, "Building of Bishop Hill," 59–60; Setterdahl, "Emigrant Letters," 121–75.

56. Wagner, "Eric Jansson," 301; investments from Sutton, *Religious Communities,* 59; one visitor from Elmen, *Wheat Flour Messiah,* 126–27; Wagner, "Eric Jansson," 313.

57. Nordhoff, *Communistic Societies,* 348–49; Sutton, *Religious Communities,* 59–60.

4—*Fourierist Phalanxes*

1. Carl J. Guarneri, *The Utopian Alternative: Fourierism in Nineteenth-Century America* (Ithaca and London: Cornell University Press, 1991), 2. See also Guarneri, "Who Were the Utopian Socialists? Pattern of Membership in American Fourierist Communities," *Communal Societies* 5 (Fall 1985): 65–81, and "Brook Farm and the Fourierist Phalanxes: Immediatism, Gradualism, and American Utopian Socialism," in Pitzer, *America's Communal Utopias,* 159–80. Jonathan F. Beecher, *Charles Fourier: The Visionary and His World* (Berkeley and Los Angeles: University of California Press, 1986), is the standard biography. Beecher, along with Richard Bienvenue, edited the English-language edition of Fourier's works, entitled *The Vision of Charles Fourier: Selected Texts on Work, Love, and Passionate Attraction* (Boston: Beacon Press, 1971).

2. Sutton, *Secular Communities,* 23–24.

3. Ibid., 24.

4. Guarneri, *Utopian Alternative,* 32.

5. Sutton, *Secular Communities,* 25–26.

6. Berry, *America's Utopian Experiments,* 156; John Humphrey Noyes, *History of American Socialisms* (New York: Dover, 1966), 313.

7. Guarneri, *Utopian Alternative,* 156, 159–60; *Phalanx,* December 5, 1843; also Noyes, *American Socialisms,* 356.

8. *Phalanx,* March 1, May 18, 1844.

9. Ibid., July 27, 1844.

10. Guarneri, *Utopian Alternative,* 156; also Sutton, *Secular Communities,* 29.

11. Guarneri, *Utopian Alternative,* 155, 159.

12. Noyes, *American Socialisms,* 366–67.

13. Ibid. 369; *Phalanx,* May 3, 1845; Rokicky, *Perfect World,* 130.

14. *Phalanx,* June 1, 1844; *Harbinger,* October 2, 1847.

15. Macdonald from Guarneri, *Utopian Alternative,* 179; *Phalanx,* June 1, 1844; Guarneri, *Utopian Alternative,* 158, 163. See also Noyes, *American Socialisms,* 317.

16. Noyes, *American Socialisms,* 364.

17. *Phalanx,* October 1, 1844.

18. *Harbinger,* May 27, 1849.

19. Guarneri, *Utopian Alternative,* 213.

20. Noyes, *American Socialisms,* 331–33.

21. Ibid., 335–36.

22. Ibid., 349, 352.

23. Rokicky, *Perfect World,* 134; Noyes, *American Socialisms,* 351–52.

24. Guarneri, *Utopian Alternative,* 161–62 (ague); Noyes, *American Socialisms,* 351 (sorrow); Guarneri, *Utopian Alternative,* 390 (Meeker).

25. Noyes, *American Socialisms,* 352.

26. Ibid., 378; *Harbinger,* July 19, 1845.

27. *Harbinger,* August 16, 1845.

28. Noyes, *American Socialisms,* 405–7.

29. Guarneri, *Utopian Alternative,* 355–56; Philip Gleason, "From Free Love to Catholicism: Dr. and Mrs. Thomas L. Nichols at Yellow Springs," *Ohio Historical Quarterly* 70, no. 4 (October 1961): 283–307; Rokicky, *Perfect World,* 137.

30. Rokicky, *Perfect World,* 139.

31. *Phalanx,* February 5, 1844; Noyes, *American Socialisms,* 398.

32. *Harbinger,* July 4, 1846.

33. Ibid., February 5, 1844; Noyes, *American Socialisms*, 398, 402–3.

34. Noyes, *American Socialisms*, 392.

35. Ibid.

36. Ibid., 393, 395.

37. *Harbinger*, January 17, 1856.

38. *Phalanx*, October 5, 1843; H. Roger Grant, "Utopias That Failed: The Antebellum Years," *Western Illinois Regional Studies* 2 (Spring 1979), 42.

39. Grant, "Utopias That Failed," 43–44.

40. Noyes, *American Socialisms*, 385–86.

41. Ibid., 409; Grant, "Utopias That Failed," 43 (Spaulding). See also Philip D. Jordan, "The Iowa Pioneer Phalanx," *Palimpsest* 16 (July 1953), 214–15.

42. George Schultz-Behrend, "Communia, Iowa, a Nineteenth-Century German-American Utopia," *Iowa Journal of History and Politics* 48 (January 1950), 41; Carl Wittke, *The Utopian Communist: A Biography of Wilhem Weitling, Nineteenth-Century Reformer* (Baton Rouge: Louisiana State University Press, 1950), 254.

43. Grant, "Utopias That Failed," 47.

44. Ibid., 44; Noyes, *American Socialisms*, 409; Bestor, *Backwoods Utopias*, 258.

45. Jacob A. Swisher, "Hopeville," *Palimpsest* 26 (October 1945), 304; Grant, "Utopias That Failed," 45.

46. Noyes, *American Socialisms*, 407, 408, 409.

47. Joseph Schafer, "The Wisconsin Phalanx," *Wisconsin Magazine of History* 9 (1930): 454–74; Noyes, *Socialisms*, 407–8, 422 (Chase).

48. Noyes, *American Socialisms*, 413; Schafer, "Wisconsin Phalanx," 463 (quote); Hinds, *American Communities*, 281–87.

49. Noyes, *American Socialisms*, 423.

50. Guarneri, *Utopian Alternative*, 199; Noyes, *American Socialisms*, 426–27 (Hine).

51. Sutton, *Secular Communities*, 32; Guarneri, *Utopian Alternative*, 343; Warren Chase, *Life-Line of the Lone One; or Autobiography of the World's Child* (Boston: Bela Marsh, 1858), 129; Noyes, *American Socialisms*, 444, 447.

52. Sutton, *Secular Communities*, 32.

53. Schafer, "Wisconsin Phalanx," 471.

54. *History of the Wisconsin Phalanx* from Noyes, *American Socialisms*, 446–47.

55. Guarneri, *Utopian Alternative*, 274.

56. Berry, *America's Utopian Experiments*, 92; Guarneri, *Utopian Alternative*, 177.

5—Icaria

1. Sutton, *Secular Communities*, 53; Robert Sutton, *Les Icariens: The Utopian Dream in Europe and America* (Urbana and Chicago: University of Illinois Press, 1994), 12, 13.

2. Robert Sutton, trans., *Travels in Icaria, by Étienne Cabet* (Macomb: Western Illinois University Press, 1985), 131.

3. Étienne Cabet, *Ma ligne droite, ou le vrai chemin du salut pour le peuple* (Paris: Prévot, 1841), 17; *Le Populaire*, March 14, 1841. See also Christopher H. Johnson, *Utopian Communism in France: Cabet and the Icarians, 1839–1851* (Ithaca: Cornell University Press, 1974), 66–82, 144–49.

4. Sutton, *Les Icariens*, 44–45.

5. Ibid., 45–47.

6. Ibid., 49–50.

7. Michel Cordillot, ed., *La sociale en Amérique: Dictionnaire biographique du mouvement social francophone aux États-Unis, 1848–1922* (Paris: Les Éditions de l'Atelier, 2002), 217–19; Sutton, *Secular Utopias*, 56; Sutton, *Les Icariens*, 58–59; Jules Prudhommeaux, *Icarie et son fondateur Étienne Cabet* (Paris: Édouard Cornély et Cie,

Éditeurs, 1907; reprint, Porcupine Press, 1972), 240 (Bourg).

8. Sutton, *Secular Communities,* 57; Sutton, *Les Icariens,* 61; Prudhommeaux, *Icarie,* 242.

9. Étienne Cabet, Lettre de M. Cabet, Nauvoo, March 25, 1849, no. 17, folder 8, Cabet Collection, Southern Illinois University, Edwardsville; *Le Populaire,* May 20, 1849.

10. Sutton, *Les Icariens,* 63–64 (63). See also Sutton, "Étienne Cabet and the Nauvoo Icarians: The Mormon Interface," in *John Whitmer Historical Association 2002 Nauvoo Conference Special Edition,* ed. Joni Wilson (Kansas City, Mo.: John Whitmer Historical Association, 2002), 47.

11. Sutton, *Les Icariens,* 66.

12. Ibid., 67. See also Sutton, *Secular Communities,* 59; Fernand Rude, ed., *Voyage en Icarie: Deux ouvriers viennois aux États-Unis en 1855* (Paris: Presses Universitaires de France, 1952), 150–51.

13. Sutton, *Les Icariens,* 77.

14. Ibid., 79; *Le Populaire,* December 2, 1849.

15. Étienne Cabet, *Colonie icarienne aux Etats-Unis d'Amérique. Sa constitution, ses lois, sa situation matérielle et morale après le premier semestre 1855* (Paris: 3 rue Baillet, 1856), 159–60; Émile Vallet, *Communism: History of the Experiment at Nauvoo of the Icarian Settlement* (Nauvoo, Ill.: N.p., 1917), 19.

16. Sutton, *Travels in Icaria,* 73–74, 94–95; Sutton, *Les Icariens,* 80; Vallet, *Communism,* 18–19.

17. Diana M. Garno, "Cabet's Recruitment of Women for the Icarian Emigration to America and Women's Sense of Betrayal," *Communal Societies* 23 (2003): 63–73.

18. Prudhommeaux, *Icarie,* 264; Sutton, *Secular Communities,* 61; *Le Populaire,* February 21, 1853. See also Garno, "Cabot's Recruitment of Women," 68.

19. Sutton, *Les Icariens,* 83; Sutton, *Secular Communities,* 61.

20. *New York Tribune,* July 2, 1853.

21. Sutton, *Les Icariens,* 84.

22. Ibid., 85.

23. Ibid., 87.

24. Ibid., 85–88.

25. Ibid., 89.

26. Ibid., 93–94.

27. Ibid., 95.

28. Sutton, *Secular Communities,* 64.

29. Sutton, *Les Icariens,* 96.

30. Étienne Cabet, *Départ de Nauvoo du fondateur d'Icarie avec les vrais Icariens* (Paris: privately published, 1856), 6–9.

31. Ibid., 20–21.

32. Sutton, *Les Icariens,* 97.

33. Ibid., 98.

34. Benjamin Mercadier, *Compte-rendu de la Gérance à la communauté icarienne à Saint Louis, sur la situation morale et matérielle de la communauté pendant les mois de novembre et décembre 1856 et les mois de janvier et février 1857* (Paris; 3 rue Baillet, 1857), 7.

35. Sutton, *Les Icariens,* 104.

36. Sutton, *Secular Communities,* 65.

37. Ibid., 65–66.

38. Benjamin Mercadier, *Notre situation à Saint Louis* (Paris: 3 rue Baillet, 1857), 5, 10.

39. Benjamin Mercadier, *Inauguration du cours icarien* (Paris: 3 rue Baillet, 1858), 13.

40. Ibid.; Sutton, *Les Icariens,* 112.

41. Jean Pierre Beluze, *Lettre circulaire sur la situation de la colonie de Cheltenham* (Paris: Malteste, 1859); Sutton, *Les Icariens,* 112; Prudhommeaux, *Icarie,* 447–54.

42. Sutton, *Les Icariens,* 113.

43. Ibid., 108; Prudhommeaux, *Icarie,* 443–46; Sutton, *Secular Communities,* 67 (Salarnier).

44. Sutton, *Les Icariens,* 109.

45. Prudhommeaux, *Icarie,* 446; Sutton, *Les Icariens,* 113.

46. Sutton, *Les Icariens,* 113.

47. Prudhommeaux, *Icarie,* 472; Sutton, *Les Icariens,* 116–17.

48. Ibid., 117; Prudhommeaux, *Icarie,* 480–81; Paul S. Gauthier, *Quest for Utopia: The Icarians of Adams County* (Corning, Iowa: Gauthier, 1992), 45–47. While living at Nauvoo in 1853, Cabet planned to move Icaria from Illinois to newly opened federal land in southwest Iowa. The primary reason for relocation was economic. His vision of Icaria projected a community of at least three thousand people, and such a large utopia needed a vast amount of farmland that was either unavailable in Illinois or was being sold at about $3 an acre. In Iowa he arranged for the eventual purchase in his name of thirty-one hundred acres at the federal land office price of $1.25 an acre.

49. Sutton, *Secular Communities,* 68; Sutton, *Les Icariens,* 119.

50. Marie Marchand Ross, *Child of Icaria* (New York: City Printing, 1938).

51. Albert Shaw, *Icaria: A Chapter in the History of Communism* (New York: G. P. Putnam, 1884; reprint, New York: AMS Press, 1973), 158; Sauva from Sutton, *Les Icariens,* 119.

52. Sutton, *Les Icariens,* 123.

53. Sutton, *Secular Communities,* 70.

54. Sutton, *Les Icariens,* 131.

55. Ibid., 130.

56. Ibid., 131.

57. Ibid., 131–32.

58. Gauthier, *Quest for Utopia,* 79.

59. Shaw, *Icaria,* 134; Gauthier, *Quest for Utopia,* 92. See also Sutton, *Les Icariens,* 137; Prudhommeaux, *Icarie,* 649–50.

60. Sutton, *Les Icariens,* 71; Gauthier, *Quest for Utopia,* 95–96.

61. Ross, *Child of Icaria,* 105–9, 114, 130–33.

62. Sutton, *Les Icariens,* 143–44. What happened to the Icarians after the dissolving of the community is covered fully in the epilogue of *Les Icariens,* 144, 179n1.

6—Hutterite Bruderhofs

1. Donald B. Kraybill and Carl Desportes Bowman, *On the Backroad to Heaven: Old Order Hutterites, Mennonites, Amish, and Brethren* (Baltimore and London: Johns Hopkins University Press, 2001), 1–2. See also Werner O. Packull, *Peter Riedemann: Shaper of the Hutterite Tradition* (Kitchener, Ont.: Pandora, 2007); Astrid Von Schlachta, *Hutterites between the Tyrol and America: A Journey through the Centuries* (Innsbruck, Austria: University of Innsbruck Press, 2006). For a full listing of the most important sources on the Hutterites up to 2003, see Sutton, *Religious Communities,* 101n1.

2. Werner O. Packull, *Hutterite Beginnings: Communitarian Experiments during the Reformation* (Baltimore and London: Johns Hopkins University Press, 1995), 252–55; Gertrude E. Huntington, "Living in the Ark: Four Centuries of Hutterite Faith and Community," in Pitzer, *America's Communal Utopias,* 322.

3. Oved, *Two Hundred Years,* 342 (see 342–47 for a summary account of their persecutions).

4. Sutton, *Religious Communities,* 88.

5. Oved, *Two Hundred Years,* 348; John A. Hostetler, *Hutterite Society* (Baltimore and London: Johns Hopkins University Press, 1974), 103.

6. Sutton, *Religious Communities,* 89.

7. Oved, *Two Hundred Years,* 348–49; Hostetler, *Hutterite Society,* 112–13.

8. J. M. Hofer, "The Diary of Paul Tschetter, 1873," *Mennonite Quarterly Review* 5 (April 1931): 206, 217; Sutton, *Religious Communities,* 90 (Grant); Hostetler, *Hutterite Society,* 114.

9. Rod Janzen, "The Prairieleut: A Forgotten Hutterite People," *Communal Societies* 14 (1994): 68. Janzen has written a book-length study, *The Prairie People: Forgotten Anabaptists* (Hanover, N.H.: University Press of New England, 1999). See also his articles in the *Mennonite Quarterly Review:* "The Hutterites and the Bruderhof: The Relationship between an Old Order Religious Society and a Twentieth-Century Communal Group" (October 2005) and "Paul Tschetter's 'Chicago Fire' Hymn" (April 2007).

10. Sutton, *Religious Communities,* 90; Hostetler, *Hutterite Society,* 117.

11. Janzen, "The Prairieleut," (68), 73, (74).

12. Hostetler, *Hutterite Society,* 123; John W. Bennett, *Hutterite Brethren: The Agricultural Economy and Social Organization of a Communal People* (Stanford: Stanford University Press, 1967), 37.

13. Oved, *Two Hundred Years,* 352.

14. Hostetler, *Hutterite Society,* 126. Eleven states passed sedition acts to punish antiwar activists, and "state leaders applied these laws with special zeal." Kermit L. Hall, *The Magic Mirror: Law in American History* (New York: Oxford University Press, 1989), 249–50.

15. Hostetler, *Hutterite Society,* 126–28; Sutton, *Religious Communities,* 91.

16. Hostetler, *Hutterite Society,* 129–30; Sutton, *Religious Communities,* 91–92.

17. Hostetler, *Hutterite Society,* 130n26.

18. Paul K. Conkin, *Two Paths to Utopia: The Hutterites and the Llano Colony* (Lincoln: University of Nebraska Press, 1964), 59–64; Hostetler, *Hutterite Society,* 131; Oved, *Two Hundred Years,* 355–57.

19. Sutton, *Religious Communities,* 92; Hostetler, *Hutterite Society,* 133.

20. Hostetler, *Hutterite Society,* (133), 134.

21. Oved, *Two Hundred Years,* 357; Kraybill and Bowman, *Backroad to Heaven,* 31. In Canada there were one in British Columbia, 146 in Alberta, 57 in Saskatchewan, and 105 in Manitoba.

22. Kraybill and Bowman, *Backroad to Heaven,* 33, 285, 34 (quote).

23. Sutton, *Religious Communities,* 93–94 (93); Kraybill and Bowman, *Backroad to Heaven,* 37.

24. Oved, *Two Hundred Years,* 358; Huntington, "Living in the Ark," 338.

25. Sutton, *Religious Communities,* 94; Huntington, "Living in the Ark," 338–39 (quote).

26. Conkin, *Two Paths to Utopia,* 89–90 (89); Hostetler, *Hutterite Society,* 149; Sutton, *Religious Communities,* 94.

27. Hostetler, *Hutterite Society,* 156–59; Sutton, *Religious Communities,* 94; Conkin, *Two Paths to Utopia,* 88.

28. Sutton, *Religious Communities,* 95; Hostetler, *Hutterite Society,* 353–54.

29. Sutton, *Religious Communities,* 95–96.

30. Ibid.; Hostetler, *Hutterite Society,* 159–62.

31. Hostetler, *Hutterite Society,* 170.

32. Ibid., 173.

33. Conkin, *Two Paths to Utopia,* 91.

34. Kraybill and Bowman, *Backroad to Heaven,* 44; Hostetler, *Hutterite Society,* 236.

35. Hostetler, *Hutterite Society,* 33–34; Sutton, *Religious Communities,* 96.

36. The colony officers were four stewards: the *Haushalter,* or general manager; the *Einkäufer,* or purchaser; the *Furgestelle,* or foreman of various shops and trades; and the *Meier,* or overseer of farming operations. Other than the stewards, there were the *Weinzierl,* or assistant to the Haushalter; the *Kellner,* or manager of the vineyards; and

the *Kastner* or caretaker of storage buildings.

37. Hostetler, *Hutterite Society,* 182–84; Sutton, *Religious Communities,* 97.

38. Sutton, *Religious Communities,* 97; Hostetler, *Hutterite Society,* 190–94.

39. Sutton, *Religious Communities,* 97–98.

40. Hostetler, *Hutterite Society,* 223.

41. Kraybill and Bowman, *Backroad to Heaven,* 45.

42. Hostetler, *Hutterite Society,* 239–40.

43. Sutton, *Religious Communities,* 99.

44. Hostetler, *Hutterite Society,* 32–34, 162–65, (248).

45. Conkin, *Two Paths to Utopia,* 95; Hostetler, *Hutterite Society,* 258.

46. Hostetler, *Hutterite Society,* 279–80. See also Sutton, *Religious Communities,* 100.

47. Hostetler, *Hutterite Society,* 281.

48. Ibid.

49. Kraybill and Bowman, *Backroad to Heaven,* 284.

50. Ibid. See the recent account of life in the Church Communities International found in Justin Peters, "New Meadow Run: A Christian Witness for the Twenty-first Century," in Bill Metcalf, ed., *Shared Visions, Shared Lives: Communal Living around the Globe* (Findhorn, Scotland: Findhorn Press, 1996), 177–96.

7—*Chicago Area Utopias*

1. Philip L. Cook, *Zion City, Illinois: Twentieth-Century Utopia* (Syracuse, N.Y.: Syracuse University Press, 1996), 3, 28. Although Dowie founded his church four years before Pentecostalism was started by Charles Fox Parham near Topeka, Kansas, with its focus on faith healing, speaking in tongues, and holy living, it is considered to be within the larger movement. Today the Christian Catholic Apostolic Church's headquarters is located at 2318 Elisha Avenue in Zion, Illinois.

2. Rolvix Harlan, *John Alexander Dowie and the Christian Catholic Apostolic Church in Zion* (Evansville, WI: Robert M. Antes, 1906), 29.

3. Cook, *Zion City,* 9–10.

4. Edna Sheldrake, *The Personal Letters of John Alexander Dowie* (Zion City, Ill.: Wilbur Glenn Voliva, 1912), 257–65.

5. Cook, *Zion City,* 12–15.

6. *Leaves of Healing,* September 30, 1899; Cook, *Zion City,* 20.

7. Cook, *Zion City,* 21–22.

8. John Alexander Dowie, *Zion's Holy War against the Hosts of Hell in Chicago* (Chicago: Zion, 1900), 31.

9. Sheldrake, *Personal Letters,* 322–25; Paul Gale Chappell, "The Divine Healing Movement in America" (Ph.D. diss., Drew University, 1983), 1; Cook, *Zion City,* 23.

10. Cook, *Zion City,* 32.

11. Ibid., 33.

12. Ibid., 35.

13. Sutton, *Religious Communities,* 146–47.

14. Cook, *Zion City,* 108.

15. Ibid.

16. Sutton, *Religious Communities,* 146–47.

17. Ibid., 147–48.

18. Ibid.

19. Cook, *Zion City,* 123, 124–25.

20. Sutton, *Religious Communities,* 148.

21. Ibid.

22. Sutton, *Religious Communities,* 148–49. See also Cook, *Zion City,* 113.

23. Cook, *Zion City,* 154.

24. Sutton, *Religious Communities*, 149.

25. Cook, *Zion City*, 159–60.

26. Ibid., 163.

27. Ibid., 161. See also Sutton, *Religious Communities*, 149.

28. Cook, *Zion City*, 165.

29. Ibid., 168–70.

30. Ibid., 186–87.

31. Sutton, *Religious Communities*, 149; Cook, *Zion City*, 188.

32. Cook, *Zion City*, 196–97.

33. Ibid., 198. Voliva was referring to an alleged sexual relationship between Dowie and a young deaconess, Ruth Hofer from Zurich, Switzerland, between the spring of 1904 and her return to Europe in January 1905. See Cook, *Zion City*, 200–201.

34. Sutton, *Religious Communities*, 150.

35. Miller, *Quest for Utopia*, 69; Sutton, *Religious Communities*, 150.

36. Miller, *Quest for Utopia*, 69; Cook, *Zion City*, 216.

37. H. Roger Grant, *Spirit Fruit: A Gentle Utopia* (DeKalb: Northern Illinois University Press, 1988), 11; Robert S. Fogarty and H. Roger Grant, "Free Love in Ohio: Jacob Beilhart and the Spirit Fruit Colony," *Ohio History* 89 (Winter 1980): 206.

38. Jacob Beilhart, *Fruit of the Spirit* (Ingleside, Ill.: privately printed, 1908), 3; Grant, *Spirit Fruit*, 12; Beilhart, *Fruit of the Spirit*, 3.

39. Grant, *Spirit Fruit*, 45; Beilhart, *Fruit of the Spirit*, 4.

40. Beilhart, *Fruit of the Spirit*, 5; Fogarty, *All Things New*, 191.

41. Grant, *Spirit Fruit*, 24–27, 32–38, 41–42.

42. Ibid., 39, 70.

43. *Spirit Fruit (Lisbon, Ohio)*, June 1899.

44. See James L. Murphy, *The Reluctant Radicals: Jacob L. Beilhart and the Spirit Fruit Society* (Lanham, Md.: University Press of America, 1989), 62–63, for an account of how Beilhart paid this obligation.

45. Grant, *Spirit Fruit*, 66.

46. Hinds, *American Communities*, 559; Rokicky, *Perfect World*, 141.

47. Grant, *Spirit Fruit*, 70. See also Rokicky, *Perfect World*, 144; Grant, *Spirit Fruit*, 51, 70–71.

48. Fogarty, *All Things New*, 193–94.

49. Grant, *Spirit Fruit*, 71–73.

50. Fogarty, *All Things New*, 194; *Buckeye State*, June 9, 16, 1904.

51. *Buckeye State*, June 23, 1904; Grant, *Spirit Fruit*, 80.

52. *Buckeye State*, Nov. 3, 1904; Fogarty, *All Things New*, 195.

53. Hinds, *American Communities*, 558–59.

54. Grant, *Spirit Fruit*, 87.

55. Ibid., 94–95.

56. Ibid., 98–99.

57. Kanter, *Commitment and Community*; Grant, *Spirit Fruit*, 103; *Cleveland Leader*, June 20, 1905.

58. *Waukegan Daily Sun*, May 26, 1905.

59. Murphy, *Reluctant Radicals*, 137. See also Grant, *Spirit Fruit*, 122.

60. Grant, *Spirit Fruit*, 117; *Philistine* (Feb. 1905): 86–88.

61. Murphy, *Reluctant Radicals*, 166–67.

62. Grant, *Spirit Fruit*, 124–25.

63. Ibid., 126.

64. Ibid., 130.

65. Murphy, *Reluctant Radicals*, 187–91; Grant, *Spirit Fruit*, 136–39; Miller, *Quest for Utopia*, 29.

66. Miller, *Quest for Utopia*, 79; James K. Hopkins, *A Woman to Deliver Her People*

(Austin: University of Texas Press, 1982); G. R. Balleine, *Past Finding Out: The Tragic Story of Joanna Southcott and Her Successors* (New York: Macmillan, 1956).
    67. Robert S. Fogarty, *The Righteous Remnant: The House of David* (Kent, Ohio: Kent State University Press, 1981), 46.
    68. Ibid., 52.
    69. Ibid., 70–71.
    70. Ibid., 76.
    71. Fogarty, *Righteous Remnant,* 80.
    72. Ibid., 81–82, 84.
    73. Ibid., 179n97; Clare Adkin, *Brother Benjamin: A History of the Israelite House of David* (Berrien Springs, Mich.: Andrews University Press, 1990), 155.
    74. Fogarty, *Righteous Remnant,* 95–96.
    75. Ibid., 103–4.
    76. Ibid., 105.
    77. Ibid., 107.
    78. Ibid., 112.
    79. Adkin, *Brother Benjamin,* 147.
    80. Ibid., 191.
    81. Ibid., 210; R. James Taylor, *Mary's City of David* (Benton Harbor, Mich.: Mary's City of David, 1996), 64–65, 89–120.

8—*Contemporary Heartland Utopias*

    1. Dave Jackson and Neta Jackson, *Glimpses of Glory, Thirty Years of Community: The Story of Reba Place Fellowship* (Elgin, Ill.: Brethren Press, 1987), 33, 36n12.
    2. Miller, *Quest for Utopia,* 182–83.
    3. Jackson and Jackson, *Glimpses of Glory,* 40.
    4. Ibid., 41; Miller, *Quest for Utopia,* 183.
    5. Marguerite Guzman Bouvard, *The Intentional Community Movement: Building a New Moral World* (Fort Washington, N.Y.: Kennikat Press, 1975), 73–74.
    6. Jackson and Jackson, *Glimpses of Glory,* 66, 69–70.
    7. Ibid., 125.
    8. [http://plowcreed.org]; David Janzen, "Plow Creek," in David Janzen, *Fire, Salt, and Peace: Intentional Christian Communities Alive in North America* (Evanston, Ill.: Shalom Mission Communities, 1996), 122–25.
    9. Jackson and Jackson, *Glimpses of Glory,* 179, 178.
    10. Ibid., 146–50, 270.
    11. Miller, *Quest for Utopia,* 184; Jackson and Jackson, *Glimpses of Glory,* 270–75.
    12. Foss from Janzen, *Fire, Salt, and Peace,* 128; Robert Sutton, *Modern American Communes: A Dictionary* (Westport, Conn., and London: Greenwood Press, 2005), 140–41; [http://rebaplacefellowship.org].
    13. *Padanaram Settlement* (Williams, Ind.: Padanaram Press, 1998), 2; *Communities Directory* (2000), 310; *Padanaram Settlement,* 2. Initially, Daniel Wright and his wife, Lois, purchased the farm. Later they bought other farms as these became available. Finally, in 1979, they donated this land to Padanaram. By 2007 the community owned three thousand acres. Seven elected elders hold the property in trust for the community.
    14. Jon Wagner, ed., *Sex Roles in Contemporary American Communes* (Bloomington: Indiana University Press, 1982), 211. Wright wrote a single-spaced sixty-three-page letter dated April 18, 1988, on what he considered Wagner's distorted account of Padanaram. A copy of this statement, addressed to "The National Historic Communal Societies Association," is in the archives of the Center for Communal Studies, Southern Indiana University, Evansville.
    15. Daniel Wright, Communes Project interview, July 22, 1997, in Timothy Miller,

"The 60s Communes Project" (Archives, University of Kansas). This project, funded by the National Endowment for the Humanities, is a collection of over five hundred taped and partially transcribed interviews with members of various intentional communities. Miller and Deborah Altus of the University of Kansas faculty collected this material by visiting communities all across the United States, and currently (2009) it is housed in the archives of the Department of Religious Studies, University of Kansas. For a discussion of this project, see Timothy Miller, *The 60s Communes: Hippies and Beyond* (Syracuse, N.Y.: Syracuse University, 1999), xv.

16. Rachel E. Wright-Summerton, "Survey of Letters to Padanaram Settlement, 1967–1991/92," *Communal Societies* 15 (1995): 121.

17. Jon Wagner, "Haran: Charisma and Ideology in a Contemporary American Commune" (Ph.D. diss., Indiana University, 1975); Sutton, *Religious Communities,* 167.

18. Daniel Wright interview, in Miller, "60s Communes Project"; Wagner, *Sex Roles,* 212; Rachel E. Wright-Summerton, "Padanaram: The Valley of the Gods," in Metcalf, *Shared Visions, Shared Lives,* 23. See also Wagner, "Haran," 19–69.

19. Rachel E. Wright-Summerton, interview, July 22, 1997; Wright interview; Steven Fuson, interview, July 22, 1997, all in Miller, "60s Communes Project."

20. Wright-Summerton, Fuson, Wright interviews, ibid.

21. Wagner, *Sex Roles,* 212–15, 218, 221.

22. Rachel Wright-Summerton, "Padanaram Today (2007)," email to Sutton dated March 29, 2007 (in author's possession); Fuson, Wright-Summerton interviews, in Miller, "60s Communes Project."

23. Sutton, *Religious Communities,* 165.

24. Wagner, *Sex Roles,* 218–19, 230.

25. Sutton, *Religious Communities,* 166.

26. Ibid.

27. *Padanaram Settlement,* 6; Wright, Fuson interviews, in Miller, "60s Communes Project"; Wright-Summerton from *Communities Directory* (2000), 310.

28. Rachel Wright-Summerton, telephone interview with Sutton, September 15, 2006 (notes in author's possession); Warrior LaMar, email to Sutton, September 12, 2006; Gloria Lewis, Intentional Communities Database, March 11, 2005 [icdb.org].

29. *Bloomington Hoosier Times,* June 11, 2006.

30. Wright-Summerton, "Padanaram Today (2007)."

31. Corinne McLaughlin and Gordon Davidson, *Builders of the Dawn: Community Lifestyles in a Changing World* (Walpole, N.H.: Stillpoint Publishing, 1985), 244; Cris Popenoe and Oliver Popenoe, *Seeds of Tomorrow: New Age Communities That Work* (San Francisco: Harper & Row, 1984), 31; [http://www.stellecommunity.com].

32. Popenoe and Popenoe, *Seeds of Tomorrow,* 35–36 (36).

33. Susan Fisher, Communes Project interview with Deborah Altus, April 17, 1996, in Miller, "60s Communes Project"; Popenoe and Popenoe, *Seeds of Tomorrow,* 37.

34. Fisher interview, in Miller, "60s Communes Project"; also Popenoe and Popenoe, *Seeds of Tomorrow,* 37.

35. Popenoe and Popenoe, *Seeds of Tomorrow,* 37.

36. [http://en.wikipedia.org/wiki/Stelle,_Illinois]; Miller, *60s Communes,* 183; Sutton, *Secular Communities,* 149.

37. Fisher interview, in Miller, "Communes Project."

38. Popenoe and Popenoe, *Seeds of Tomorrow,* 40–41; Sutton, *Secular Communities,* 150.

39. Sutton, *Secular Communities,* 150.

40. Ibid., 150–51.

41. Fisher interview, in Miller, "60s Communes Project"; [http://en.wikipedia.org/wiki/Stelle,_Illinois].

42. Debra Levy Larson, "Living Sustainably in Stelle," *Agro-Ecology* 14, no. 3 (fall 2005), 2; Mark W. Wilkerson, "The Solar Capital of the Midwest," *Home Power* 77 (June/July 2000): 20–26; Larson, "Living Sustainably," 2; [http://www.stellecommunity.com]; ["goodrebill," icdb.org].

Notes to Pages 171-84

203

43. [www.obmission.org/ceo_msg.php].

44. William Lawrence Smith, "Urban Communitarianism in the 1980s: Seven Religious Communes in Chicago" (Ph.D. diss., Notre Dame University, 1984), 127.

45. Ibid., 129–30.

46. Ibid., 131, 221.

47. Ibid., 132, 134, 139.

48. [www.obmission.org/ceo_msg.php].

49. Miller, *Quest for Utopia*, 15.

50. David Di Sabatino, *The Jesus People Movement: An Annotated Bibliography* (Westport, Conn.: Greenwood Press, 1999), 4; Miller, *60s Communes*, 99; John M. Bozeman, "Jesus People USA: An Examination of an Urban Communitarian Religious Group" (master's thesis, Florida State University, 1990), 27.

51. Lindsay Prorock, Religious Movements Homepage: Jesus People USA, 2, at [http://religiousmovements.lib.virginia.edu/nrms/jpusa.html].

52. Bozeman, "Jesus People USA," 40; Jon Tott, "Life's Lessons: A History of Jesus People USA," ch. 1, 4, at [http://www.jpusa.org]; *Cornerstone* 2, no. 9 (1973): 6–7.

53. Smith, "Urban Communitarianism," 142.

54. Trott, "Life's Lessons," ch. 2, 1.

55. Bozeman, "Jesus People USA," 46, 47 (Tucker).

56. Trott, "Life's Lessons," ch. 2, 4.

57. *Meet Our Family* at [http://www.jpusa.org]; Bozeman, "Jesus People USA," 67–68.

58. Ibid., 73–83.

59. Smith, "Urban Communitarianism," 149, 152–53.

60. [www.jpusa.org/ministries.html].

61. Ibid.

62. Bozeman, "Jesus People USA," 106–7; Snyder Harrar, March 20, 1990, ibid., 107–8.

63. Ibid., 110.

64. J. Gordon Melton, *Encyclopedic Handbook of Cults in America* (New York: Garland, 1986), 102–3.

65. Bozeman, "Jesus People USA," 136; *Communities Directory* (2000), 271; Prorock, Religious Movements Homepage; Tim Bock, *Unless the Lord Builds the House: The Story of Jesus People USA's Mission-Business* (Chicago, Ill.: Cornerstone Press, 2006), 5.

Conclusion

1. Sutton, *Communal Utopias*, both volumes. Although not a part of the Heartland, Shelby County, Missouri, is included in this study because it contained a significant satellite Harmonist community at Bethel. See the maps in Tyler, *Freedom's Ferment*, 113; and Berry, *America's America's Utopian Experiments*, 7.

2. Tyler, *Freedom's Ferment*, 5.

3. Ibid., 34.

4. Kanter, *Commitment and Community*, viii.

5. Ibid., 71–72.

6. Ibid., 73.

7. Ibid., 75.

8. Berry, *America's Utopian Experiments*, xv; Michael Barkun, "Communal Societies as Cyclical Phenomena," *Communal Societies* (1984): 35–48.

9. Berry, *America's Utopian Experiments*, 7.

10. Pitzer, *America's Communal Utopias*, xviii.

Selected Bibliography

The following list includes some of the more important books and articles used in this study. For other useful works consult the citations in the Notes.

Adkin, Clare. *Brother Benjamin: A History of the Israelite House of David.* Berrien Springs, Mich.: Andrews University Press, 1990.

Andelson, Jonathan G. "The Community of True Inspiration from Germany to the Amana Colonies." In Pitzer, *America's Communal Utopias,* 185–203.

Andrews, Edward Deming. *The People Called Shakers: A Search for the Perfect Society.* New York: Oxford University Press, 1953.

Arndt, Karl J. R. *A Documentary History of the Indiana Decade of the Harmony Society, 1814–1824,* 2 vols. Indianapolis: Indiana Historical Society, 1975, 1978.

——. "George Rapp's Harmony Society." In Pitzer, *Communal Utopias,* 57–88.

——. *George Rapp's Harmony Society, 1785–1847.* Rutherford, N.J.: Farleigh Dickinson University Press, 1972.

Bartel, Diane L. *Amana: From Pietist Sect to American Community.* Lincoln: University of Nebraska Press, 1984.

Barton, H. Arnold. "The Eric-Janssonists and the Shifting Contours of Community." *Western Illinois Regional Studies* 12 (Fall 1989): 17–35.

Beecher, Jonathan F. *Charles Fourier: The Visionary and His World.* Berkeley; University of California Press, 1986.

Beilhart, Jacob. *Fruit of the Spirit.* Ingleside, Ill.: privately printed, 1908.

Berry, Brian J. L. *America's Utopian Experiments: Communal Havens from Long-Wave Crises* Hanover, N.H.: University Press of New England, 1992.

Bestor, Arthur, Jr. *Backwoods Utopias: The Sectarian Origins and Owenite Phase of Communitarian Socialism in America, 1663–1829.* Philadelphia: University of Pennsylvania Press, 1970.

Bestor, Arthur, Jr., ed. *Education and Reform at New Harmony: Correspondence of William Maclure and Marie Duclos Fretageot, 1820–1833.* Clifton, N.J.: A. M. Kelley, 1973.

Botscharow-Kamau, Lucy Jayne. "Disharmony in Utopia: Social Categories in Robert Owen's New Harmony." *Communal Societies* 9 (1989): 76–90.

——."Neighbors: Harmony and Conflict on the Indiana Frontier." *Journal of the Early Republic* 11 (Winter 1991): 507–29

Bouvard, Marguerite Guzman. *The Intentional Community Movement: Building a New Moral World.* Fort Washington, N.Y.: Kennikat Press, 1975.

Bozeman, John M. "Jesus People USA: An Examination of an Urban Communitarian Religious Group." M.A. thesis, Florida State University, 1990.

Brewer, Priscilla J. *Shaker Communities, Shaker Lives.* Hanover, N.H.: University Press of New England, 1986.

——. "The Shakers of Mother Ann Lee." In Pitzer, *America's Communal Utopias,* 37–56.

——. "'Tho' of the Weaker Sex': A Reassessment of Gender Equality among the Shakers." In *Women in Spiritual and Communitarian Societies in the United States,* ed. Wendy E. Chmielewski, Louis J. Kern, and Marylyn Klee-Hartzell, 133–49. Syracuse, N.Y.: Syracuse University Press, 1993.

Brown, Paul. *Twelve Months in New Harmony.* Cincinnati, 1827; reprint, Philadelphia: Porcupine Press, 1972.

Carman, Gary D. "The Amana Colonies: Change from Communalism to Capitalism in 1932." *Social Science Journal* 24 (1987): 157–67.

Communities Directory: A Guide to Intentional Communities and Cooperative Living. Rutledge, Mo.: Fellowship for Intentional Community, 2000.

Communities Directory: A Comprehensive Guide to Intentional Communities and Cooperative Living., 4th ed. Rutledge, Mo.: The Fellowship for Intentional Community, 2005.

Conkin, Paul K. Two Paths to Utopia: The Hutterites and the Llano Colony. Lincoln: University of Nebraska Press, 1964.

Cook, Philip L. Zion City, Illinois: Twentieth-Century Utopia. Syracuse, N.Y.: Syracuse University Press, 1996.

Cordillot, Michel, ed. La sociale en Amérique: Dictionnaire biographique du movement social Francophone aux États-Unis 1848–1922. Paris: Les Éditions de l"Atelier, 2002.

Dawson, Elise Schebler. "The Folk Genre Paintings of Olof Krans as Historical Documents." Western Illinois Regional Studies 12 (Fall 1989): 82–104.

Elliott, Josephine Mirabella. "Madame Marie Fretageot: Communitarian Educator." Communal Societies 4 (1984): 167–82.

Elmen, Paul. Wheat Flour Messiah: Eric Jansson of Bishop Hill. Carbondale: Southern Illinois University Press, 1976.

Fogarty, Robert S. All Things New: American Communes and Utopian Movements, 1860–1914. Chicago and London: University of Chicago Press, 1990.

——. Dictionary of American Communal and Utopian History. Westport, Conn., and London: Greenwood Press, 1980.

——. The Righteous Remnant: The House of David. Kent, Ohio: Kent State University Press, 1981.

Garno, Diana M. "Cabet's Recruitment of Women for the Icarian Emigration to America and Women's Sense of Betrayal." Communal Societies 23 (2003): 63–73.

Gauthier, Paul S. Quest for Utopia: The Icarians of Adams County. Corning, IA: Gauthier, 1992.

Gleason, Philip. "From Free Love to Catholicism: Dr. and Mrs. Thomas L. Nichols at Yellow Springs." Ohio Historical Quarterly 70, no. 4 (October 1961): 283–307.

Gooden, Rosemary D. "A Preliminary Examination of Shaker Attitudes toward Work." Communal Societies 3 (1983): 1–15.

Grant, H. Roger. "Missouri's Utopian Communities." Missouri Historical Review (1972): 20–48.

——. Spirit Fruit: A Gentle Utopia. DeKalb: Northern Illinois University Press, 1988.

——. "Utopias that Failed: The Antebellum Years." Western Illinois Regional Studies 2 (Spring 1979): 38–51.

Guarneri, Carl J. "Brook Farm and the Fourierist Phalanxes: Immediatism, Gradualism, and American Utopian Socialism." In Pitzer, America's Communal Utopias, 159–80.

——. The Utopian Alternative: Fourierism in Nineteenth-Century America. Ithaca Cornell University Press, 1991.

Harrison, John F. C. Quest for the New Moral World: Robert Owen and the Owenites in Britain and America. New York: Charles Scribner's Sons, 1969.

Harvey, Rowland Hill. Robert Owen: Social Idealist. Berkeley: University of California Press, 1959.

Hinds, William A. American Communities and Co-operative Colonies. 1878; reprint Philadelphia: Porcupine Press, 1975.

Hopkins, James K. A Woman to Deliver Her People. Austin: University of Texas Press, 1982.

Hostetler, John A. Hutterite Society. Baltimore: Johns Hopkins University Press, 1974.

Huntington, Gertrude E. "Living in the Ark: Four Centuries of Hutterite Faith and Community." In Pitzer, America's Communal Utopias, 319–51.

Isaksson, Olov. Bishop Hill: A Utopia on the Prairie. Stockholm: L. T. Publishing House, 1969.

Jackson, Dave, and Neta Jackson. Glimpses of Glory: Thirty Years of Community, the Story of Reba Place Fellowship. Elgin, Ill.: Brethren Press, 1987.

Janzen, David. *Fire, Salt, and Peace: Intentional Christian Communities Alive in North America.* Evanston, Ill.: Shalom Mission Communities, 1996.

Janzen, Rod. "The Prairieleut: A Forgotten Hutterite People." *Communal Societies* 14 (1994): 67–89.

———. *The Prairie People: Forgotten Anabaptists.* Hanover, N.H.: University Press of New England, 1999.

Johnson, Christopher H. *Utopian Communism in France: Cabet and the Icarians, 1839–1851.* Ithaca, N.Y.: Cornell University Press, 1974.

Kanter, Rosabeth Moss. *Commitment and Community: Communes and Utopias in Sociological Perspective.* Cambridge, Mass.: Harvard University Press, 1972.

Knoedler, Christiana F. *The Harmony Society: A Nineteenth-Century American Utopia.* New York: Vantage Press, 1954.

Kraybill, Donald B., and Carl Desportes Bowman. *On the Backroad to Heaven: Old Order Hutterites, Mennonites, Amish, and Brethren* (Baltimore and London: Johns Hopkins University Press, 2001.

Larson, Debra Levy. "Living Sustainably in Stelle," *Agro-Ecology* 14, no. 3 (fall 2005): 1–5.

LeMaster, Grace I. "A Study of the North Union, Ohio, Society of Believers." Master's thesis, University of Akron, 1950.

Lockwood, George B. *The New Harmony Movement.* New York: Appleton, 1905; reprint, New York: AMS Press, 1971.

MacLean, J. P. *Shakers of Ohio: Fugitive Papers Concerning the Shakers of Ohio, with Unpublished Manuscripts.* Philadelphia: Porcupine Press, 1975.

Metcalf, Bill, ed. *Shared Visions, Shared Lives: Communal Living around the Globe.* Findhorn, Scotland: Findhorn Press, 1996.

Miller, Timothy. *The Quest for Utopia in Twentieth-Century America, 1900–1968.* Syracuse, N.Y.: Syracuse University Press, 1998.

———. *The 60s Communes: Hippies and Beyond.* Syracuse, N.Y.: Syracuse University Press, 1999.

———. "The 60s Communes Project." Archives, University of Kansas.

Morhart, Hilda Deschinger. *Zoar: An Ohio Experiment in Communalism.* Columbus: Ohio Historical Society, 1997.

Murphy, James L. *The Reluctant Radicals: Jacob L. Beilhart and the Spirit Fruit Society.* Lanham, Md.: University Press of America, 1989.

Nelson, Ronald E. "The Building of Bishop Hill." *Western Illinois Regional Studies* 12 (Fall 1989): 46–60.

Nixon, Edgar B. "The Society of Separatists of Zoar." Ph.D. diss., Ohio State University, 1933.

Nordhoff, Charles. *The Communistic Societies of the United States: From Personal Visit and Observation.* London: John Murray, Albemarle Street, 1875.

Noyes, John Humphrey. *History of American Socialisms.* New York: Dover, 1966.

Oved, Yaacov. *Two Hundred Years of American Communes.* New Brunswick, N.J., and Oxford, England: Transaction Books, 1988.

Owen, Robert. *The Life of Robert Owen, Written by Himself, with Selections From His Writings and Correspondence.* 2 vols. London: Effingham Wilson, 1857–1858; reprint, New York: Augustus M. Kelley, 1967.

Packull, Werner O. *Hutterite Beginnings: Communitarian Experiments during the Reformation.* Baltimore: Johns Hopkins University Press, 1995.

———. *Peter Riedemann: Shaper of the Hutterite Tradition.* Kitchener, Ont.: Pandora, 2007.

Padanaram Settlement. Williams, Ind.: Padanaram Press, 1998.

Paterwic, Stephen. "From Individual to Community: Becoming a Shaker at New Lebanon." *Communal Societies* 11 (1991): 18–33.

Pears, Thomas Clinton, Jr., ed. *New Harmony, an Adventure in Happiness: Papers of Thomas and Sarah Pears.* Indianapolis: Indiana Historical Society, 1933.

Pitzer, Donald E. "The New Moral World of Robert Owen and New Harmony." In Pitzer, *America's Communal Utopias,* 88–134.

Pitzer, Donald E., ed. *America's Communal Utopias.* Chapel Hill: University of North Carolina Press, 1997.

Pitzer, Donald E., and Josephine M. Elliott. "New Harmony's First Utopians." *Indiana Magazine of History* 75, no. 3 (September 1979): 225–300.

Popenoe, Cris, and Oliver Popenoe. *Seeds of Tomorrow: New Age Communities That Work.* San Francisco: Harper & Row, 1984.

Prescott, James S. "The History of North Union," 2nd ed. Shaker Manuscript Collection, Western Reserve Historical Society, Cleveland, Ohio.

Proctor-Smith, Marjorie. *Women in Shaker Community and Worship: A Feminist Analysis of the Uses of Religious Symbolism.* Lewiston, Maine: Edwin Mellen Press, 1985.

Prorock, Linda. Religious Movements Homepage: Jesus People USA, 2. [http://religiousmovements.lib.virginia.edu/nrms/jpusa.html].

Prudhommeaux, Jules. *Icarie et son fondateur Étienne Cabet.* Paris: Édouard Cornély et Cie, Éditeurs, 1907; reprint, Porcupine Press, Inc., 1972.

Randall, Emilius O. *History of the Zoar Society.* Columbus, Ohio: Press of Fred J. Heer, 1904.

Rathbun, Reuben. *Reasons Offered for Leaving the Shakers.* Pittsfield, Mass.: Chester Smith, 1800.

Rathbun, Valentine. *An Account of the Matter, Form, and Manner of a New and Strange Religion, Taught and Propagated by a Number of Europeans, Living in a Place Called Nisqueunia, in the State of New-York.* Providence, R.I.: Bennett Wheeler, 1781.

Rokicky, Catherine M. *Creating a Perfect World: Religious and Secular Utopias in Nineteenth-Century Ohio.* Athens: Ohio University Press, 2002.

Ross, Marie Marchand. *Child of Icaria.* New York: City Printing, 1938.

Schafer, Joseph. "The Wisconsin Phalanx." *Wisconsin Magazine of History* 9 (1930): 454–74.

Schlachta, Astrid Von. *Hutterites between the Tyrol and America: A Journey through the Centuries.* Innsbruck, Austria: University of Innsbruck Press, 2006.

Schroeder, Adolf E. *Bethel German Colony, 1844–1879: Religious Beliefs and Practices.* N.p.: Missouri Humanities Council, 1990.

———. *The Musical Life of Bethel German Colony.* N.p.: Missouri Humanities Council, 1990.

Setterdahl, Lilly. "Emigrant Letters by Bishop Hill Colonists from Noma Parish." *Western Illinois Regional Studies* 1 (Fall 1978): 121–75.

Shaw, Albert. *Icaria: A Chapter in the History of Communism.* New York: G. P. Putnam, 1884; reprint, New York: AMS Press, 1973.

Sheldrake, Edna. *The Personal Letters of John Alexander Dowie.* Zion City, Ill.: Wilbur Glenn Voliva, 1912.

Smith, William Lawrence. "Urban Communitarianism in the 1980s: Seven Religious Communes in Chicago." Ph.D. diss., Notre Dame University, 1984.

Snyder, Eugene Edmund. *Aurora, Their Last Utopia: Oregon's Christian Commune, 1845–1883.* Portland, Ore.: Binford & Mort, 1993.

Stein, Stephen J. *The Shaker Experience in America: A History of the United Society of Believers.* New Haven, Conn.: Yale University Press, 1992.

Sutton, Robert P. "An American Elysium: The Icarian Communities." In Pitzer, *America's Communal Utopias,* 279–96.

———. *Communal Utopias and the American Experience: Religious Communities, 1732–2000.* Westport, Conn., and London: Praeger, 2003.

———. *Communal Utopias and the American Experience: Secular Communities, 1824–2004.* Westport, Conn., and London: Praeger, 2004.

———. "Étienne Cabet and the Nauvoo Icarians: The Mormon Interface." In *John Whitmer Historical Association 2002 Nauvoo Conference Special Edition,* ed. Joni

Wilson, 43–51. Kansas City, Mo.: John Whitmer Historical Association, 2002.

———. *Les Icariens: The Utopian Dream in Europe and America.* Urbana and Chicago: University of Illinois Press, 1994.

———. *Modern American Communes: A Dictionary.* Westport, Conn. and London: Greenwood Press, 2005.

Sutton, Robert P., trans. *Travels in Icaria, by Étienne Cabet.* Macomb: Western Illinois University Press, 1985.

Taylor, R. James. *Mary's City of David.* Benton Harbor, Mich.: Mary's City of David, 1996.

Trott, Jon. "Life's Lessons: A History of Jesus People USA." [http://www.jpusa.org].

Tyler, Alice Felt. *Freedom's Ferment: Phases of American Social History from the Colonial Period to the Outbreak of the Civil War.* New York: Harper & Row, 1944.

Vallet, Émile. *Communism: History of the Experiment at Nauvoo of the Icarian Settlement.* Nauvoo, Ill.: N.p., 1917.

Wagner, Jon. "Eric Jansson and the Bishop Hill Colony." In Pitzer, *America's Communal Utopias,* 297–313.

———. "Haran: Charisma and Ideology in a Contemporary American Commune." Ph.D. diss., Indiana University, 1975.

———. "Living in Community: Daily Life in the Bishop Hill Colony." *Western Illinois Regional Studies* 12 (Spring 1989): 61–81.

Wagner, Jon, ed. *Sex Roles in Contemporary American Communes.* Bloomington: Indiana University Press, 1982.

Wheeler, Wayne. "Eric Janssonism: Community and Freedom in Nineteenth-Century Sweden and America." *Western Illinois Regional Studies* 12 (Fall 1989): 7–15.

Wright, Daniel. Communes Project interview, July 22, 1997. Timothy Miller, "The 60s Communes Project," Archives, University of Kansas.

Wright-Summerton, Rachel E. "Padanaram: The Valley of the Gods." In *Shared Visions, Shared Lives: Communal Living around the Globe,* ed. Bill Metcalf, 17–28. Findhorn, Scotland: Findhorn Press, 1996.

———. "Padanaram Today (2007)." Email to Sutton, March 29, 2007, in author's possession.

Index

Association, 85; Trumbull Phalanx,
75–78; Wisconsin Phalanx, 85–87;
Yellow Springs (Memnonia), 79
Fourierist Socialist utopias, 69
Franklin Institute, 39, 41
"Free" church sects, 112
Freedom's Ferment (Tyler), 181
French sedition law, 90
Fretageot, Marie, 46
Fundamentalist Christianity, 162
Funk, John, 114
Fuson, Steven, 164, 165–66
Future (Brisbane), 71

Galfa, Norway, 64
Galva, 68
Garden Grove, 84
Gathering Order revival of 1820s, 27
Gelassenheit (complete submission to
God), 112
Gemein, 124
Gérance, 96
Gérants, 93
Gérard, Jean Paul, 97, 98, 99, 100, 105
German Methodist Church
(Stewardstown), 52
German Separatists, 6, 68
Gesangbuchlein (hymnbook), 122–23
Gibb, Donald, 129
Gibbleut, 129–30
Giesy, Andrew, Jr., 54
Giles, Mildred, 154
God's Valley, 166
Golden Rule, 52
Good Earth Compost Company, 166
Gorham, Maine, 15
Goshen College, 159
"Gospel of Work, the Business and
Relation of Man," 150
Gospel Orders (Meacham), 16
Gouhenant, Adolphe, 91
Gould, Luther, 22
Graham, Sylvester, 28
Grand Ecore, 52
Grand Rapids, Michigan, 152
Granger, Alexander, 140–41
Grant, Elijah P., 72–73
Grant, H. Roger, 142–43, 144, 147,
150–51
Grant, Ulysses S., 114
Grayslake Times (newspaper), 149–50
Great Depression, 8, 64, 118;
communalism and, 6
Grebel, Conrad, 112

Greeley, Horace, 4, 71, 74
Greenlee, Dora, 148
Gregg, David L., 93
Gregory, D. D., 108–9
Griscom, John, 39
Grise, Charles L., 146
Groshen College, Indiana, 158
*Grounds for which the Minority Demands
the Dissolution of the Icarian
Community*, 99
Group of seven, 158
Guarneri, Carl J., 70, 71, 75, 79, 87, 88
Gunn, Alexander, 59
Gutergemeinschaft (community of goods),
112

Hagerstown, Maryland, 40
Half-way house, 40
Hall, Katie, 172
Hälsingland, 64
Hamilton, Illinois, Representative, 105
Hancock Village, 17
Hannaford, William, 155
Hannibal, Missouri, 7, 52; industry in, 53
Hannibal & St. Joseph Railroad, 54
Hansel, John, 156
The Harbinger (semi-monthly magazine),
72, 78, 80, 81, 82
Harmonie Fest, 32
Harmonist Community House, 46
Harmonists, 6, 7, 18
Harmony, 71
Harmony Gazette, 41–42
Harmony Society, 32
*Harmony Songbook Written by Early and
Modern Authors* (hymn book), 34
Harrar, Synder, 178–79
Harris, William, 39
Hart, Charlotte, 27
Hately, John C., 141–42
Haymarket Riot, 148
Hazard's Pavilion, 139
Healdsburg, California, 143
Healdsburg College, 151
Healing, Dowie doctrine of, 136
Hearst, William Randolph, 146
Heartland: as center of utopian building,
4; defined, 3; history of, 3; persistence
of community in, 5
Heggi, Théophile, 99
Heinemann, Barbara, 7, 60
Henrici, Jacob, 116
Herbeson, Katherine, 146–47
Herrin, John, 175–76

www.ingramcontent.com/pod-product-compliance
Lightning Source LLC
Chambersburg PA
CBHW030304100426
42812CB00002B/561